The Kurdish Nationalist Movement
in the 1990s

THE KURDISH NATIONALIST MOVEMENT IN THE 1990s

ITS IMPACT ON TURKEY AND THE MIDDLE EAST

Robert Olson
Editor

THE UNIVERSITY PRESS OF KENTUCKY

Scholarly publisher for the Commonwealth,
serving Bellarmine College, Berea College, Centre
College of Kentucky, Eastern Kentucky University,
The Filson Club, Georgetown College, Kentucky
Historical Society, Kentucky State University,
Morehead State University, Murray State University,
Northern Kentucky University, Transylvania University,
University of Kentucky, University of Louisville,
and Western Kentucky University.

Editorial and Sales Offices: The University Press of Kentucky
663 South Limestone Street, Lexington, Kentucky 40508-4008

00 99 98 97 96 5 4 3 2 1

Library of Congress Cataloging-in-Publication Data

The Kurdish nationalist movement in the 1990s : its impact on Turkey
  and the Middle East / Robert Olson, editor.
      p.   cm.
    Includes bibliographical references (p.   ) and index.
    ISBN 0-8131-1999-5 (cloth : alk. paper).—ISBN 0-8131-0896-9
  (pbk. : alk. paper)
      1. Turkey—Politics and government—1980-   2. Kurds—Turkey—
  Politics and government.   3. Partiya Karkere Kürdistan.   4. Turkey—
  Foreign relations—1980-   5. Nationalism—Turkey.   I. Olson,
  Robert W.
  DR603.K87   1996
  956.103—dc20   96-21501

This book is printed on acid-free recycled paper meeting
the requirements of the American National Standard
for Permanence of Paper for Printed Library Materials.

Manufactured in the United States of America

Contents

ACKNOWLEDGMENTS

An edited book is only as good as all of its contributors. As editor of this book, I was fortunate to have a constellation of internationally recognized scholars who believed in the project and agreed to write chapters, for which I am deeply appreciative. They have made an exciting book that illustrates for the first time the most pressing problem in the Middle East in all of its significance. I also want to acknowledge our computers, which have, through electronic mail, made such internationally collaborative projects possible and easier.

The University Press of Kentucky receives accolades for agreeing to publish this book in a handsome format. The University Press staff responded with alacrity and grace to all of the queries and hurried demands of an anxious author. My friend and colleague, Art Wrobel, agreed to my pleas that he proofread chapters on short notice, and he did so without too much complaint. Gyula Powers, another friend, who also happens to be one of the world's best cartographers, insisted that the book have "two good handmade maps." Lynn Hiler did much to facilitate the word processing as well as to help me with the necessary commands to do mine. Without her good humor and help, I would not have been able to meet press deadlines.

I am most grateful to Aram Nigogosian, who first brought up the idea of publishing an edited book on this subject and who shared his ideas throughout the collection and editing process. Lastly, I am grateful to the faculty and administration of the University of Kentucky, who awarded me with a University Research Professorship for 1995-96 that relieved me of teaching duties and permitted me to undertake the task of editing this work.

NOTE ON SPELLING AND NAMES

In editing this volume, I have followed, for the most part, modern Turkish spelling, as it renders correctly the pronunciation of Turkish and Kurdish names, thus making the proper names and place names more understandable not only to the Turkish speaker but also to the English speaker and reader. In modern Turkish, the letters *ö* and *ü* are similar to the German letters. The letter *i* is pronounced as it is in *sit* in English. There is also an undotted *ı* in Turkish, which sounds like the *u* in *stadium.* The letters *ç* and *ş* are similar to the *ch* in *church* and the *sh* in *should.* The *c* is pronounced like the *j* in *John.* Turkish also has a letter *ğ,* which has the effect of lengthening the preceding vowel and sometimes obviates the need to pronounce the following consonants, as in *ağa* (large landowner). The one exception to this scheme is in chapter 3, which deals with Iraqi Kurdistan where Kurdish names and places have an Arabic transliteration.

English Translations of Political Parties and Organizations in Turkey

Translations	English	Turkish
Committee of Union and Progress	CUP	ITC
Democracy Party	DP	DEP
Democratic Party	DP	DP
Democratic Left Party	DLP	DSP
Federation of Revolutionary Youth in Turkey	FRYT	DEV-GENÇ
Justice Party	JP	AP
Kurdistan Workers' Party	KWP	PKK
Motherland Party	MP	ANAP
Nationalist Action Party	NAP	MHP
National Liberation Front of Kurdistan	NLFK	ERNK
National Salvation Party	NSP	MSP
New Democratic Movement	NDM	YDH
New Democratic Party	NDP	YDP
New Party	NP	YP
Party of New Turkey	PNT	YTP
Peoples Democracy Party	PDP	HADEP
Peoples Labor Party	PLP	HEP
Peoples Liberation Army of Kurdistan	PLAK	ARGK
Republican Peoples' Party	RPP	CHP
Social Democratic Party	SDP	SHP
Social Democratic Populist Party	SDPP	SHP
Socialist Party of Turkey-Kurdistan	SPK-T	TKSP
Kurdistan Socialist Party	KSP	KSP
True Path Party	TPP	DYP
Turkish Workers' Party	TWP	TIP
Welfare Party	WP	RP
Union Party of Turkey	UPT	TBP

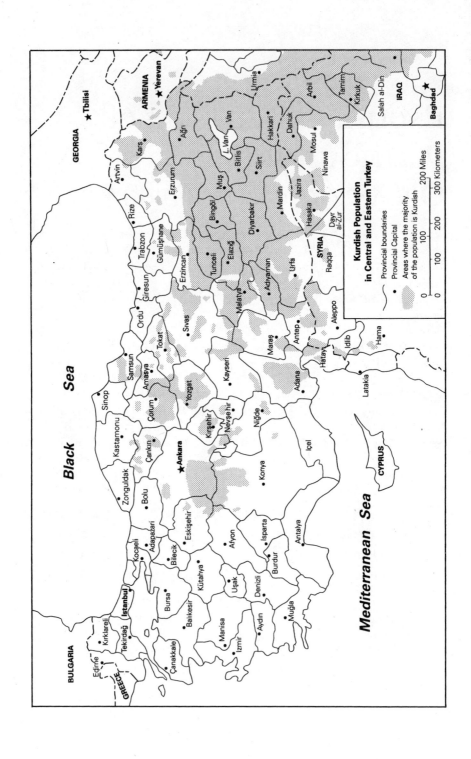

Kurdish Population
in Central and Eastern Turkey

⌒ Provincial boundaries
• Provincial Capital
░ Areas where the majority
   of the population is Kurdish

0   100   200 Miles
0   100   200   300 Kilometers

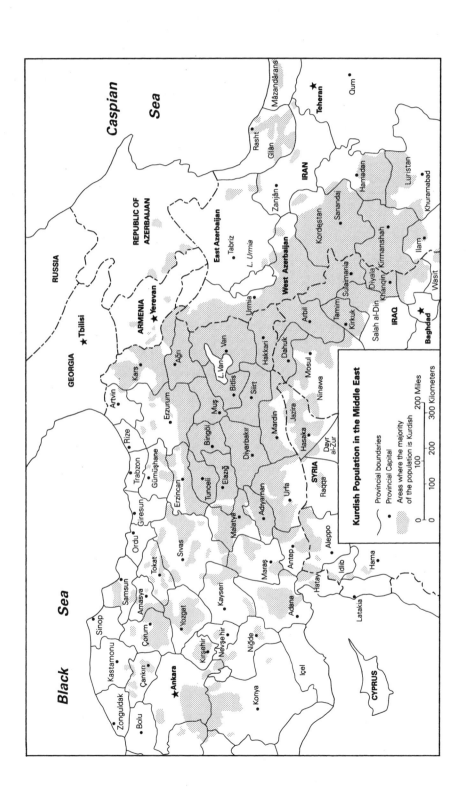

Kurdish Population in the Middle East

—— Provincial boundaries

• Provincial Capital

⬚ Areas where the majority
of the population is Kurdish

0   100   200   300 Kilometers

0   100   200 Miles

INTRODUCTION

This is the first book of which I am aware, in any language, to deal exclusively with the impact of the Kurdish nationalist movement on Turkey and the Middle East during the 1990s. As the contributors to this volume make clear, this is a period when the Kurdish nationalist movement has mounted its biggest challenge to the Turkish state in the twentieth century. In the aftermath of the Gulf war, the challenge escalated to new dimensions. Other than Michael Gunter's *The Kurds in Turkey: A Political Dilemma* (1990), no full-length scholarly monographs or books have been devoted exclusively to the Kurdish nationalist movement in Turkey during the 1990s. David McDowall, in his recent *A History of the Kurds* (1996), devotes two chapters to the Kurds in Turkey, but they are embedded in the larger history. The volume presented here is the first treatment to attempt to cover comprehensively the domestic, foreign, economic, political and judicial challenges facing Turkey from the growth and spread of the Kurdish nationalist movement. The Gulf war in 1991 gave substantial impetus to the Kurdish nationalist movement throughout the Middle East, as the contributors make clear. But this volume focuses on Turkey. Because of its pro-West orientation since it joined NATO in 1952 and its geopolitic and geostrategic alliance with the West since then, less attention has been paid in the West, especially in the United States, to the history and politics of Turkey. It seems that government and academic circles think it best not to draw attention to some of Turkey's unpleasant politics and policies. Chief among these are Turkey's policies to control, constrain and eliminate the Kurdish nationalist movement wherever it rears its head. Turkey has pursued this policy since the Sheikh Said rebellion in 1925.

If the Kurdish nationalist movement was the sore thumb of the Turkish republic after its creation in 1923, it became the Achilles heel of the Turkish state in the 1980s and 1990s. Led by the Kurdistan Workers' Party, known under its Kurdish acronym, PKK, the Kurdish nationalist movement challenges the very structure of the state and its legitimizing Kemalist ideology. The nature of this multifaceted challenge is the topic of this volume.

Gülistan Gürbey starts off the discussion by analyzing the challenge posed to the Turkish state by the growth of the Kurdish nationalist movement in the 1980s and 1990s and the array of political, judicial, constitutional and ideological constructs and the military and police power with which the Turkish state sought to control, constrain and eliminate Kurdish nationalism. She notes that by the

1990s the Kurdish challenge had become so great that even established political parties, most of which included Kurdish members, began to officially proffer "solutions" to the "Kurdish problem," as Kurdish nationalism is euphemistically called in Turkey. Although, as other contributors note, Turkey's president Turgut Özal (who died on 17 April 1993) may well have had unstated motives for encouraging political parties to "recognize" the Kurdish movement in Turkey. Özal, and certain government circles, may have wanted to take advantage of the Gulf war and may have thought that the U.S.-led allied forces would encourage Turkey to invade northern Iraq and thus legitimize Turkey's occupation of part of northern Iraq. Official recognition of the Kurdish minority in Turkey would provide Ankara with the moral cover it needed to incorporate portions of northern Iraq under Turkish political jurisdiction. Gürbey draws our attention to the conjuncture between Turkey's response to the Kurdish challenge within Turkey itself and its wider geopolitic and geostrategic concerns in the Middle East, the Balkans, the Caucasus and Central Asia in the post-Soviet period. She contends that a potential breakthrough between the state and the PKK could occur if genuine representatives of the Kurdish nationalists and political parties were allowed to exit. But as Hamit Bozarslan points out, such a dialogue has not yet been allowed to be established. The Democracy Party or DEP, a political party representing Kurdish interests in the 1990s, became the main target of the army, the political establishment and the media because none of them could tolerate an independent Kurdish representation. Given the Turkish state's lack of response to Kurdish demands for genuine political representation, Gürbey hopes that an earnest dialogue can be established with the mediation of a array of international organizations.

Aram Nigogosian takes Gürbey's arguments further by focusing on the PKK itself, the most militant Kurdish response to the Turkish state and the most effective in internationalizing the nationalist cause of the Kurds. He notes the great number of armed, security, police and intelligence forces deployed against the PKK and the scorched earth and ethnic cleansing policies that Turkey has pursued in its attempts to eradicate the PKK presence in eastern and southeastern Turkey. Nigogosian is pessimistic about a peaceful resolution, but he sees the possibility for increased dialogue, as there are circles in Turkey, especially wealthy businessmen, who think that a political resolution of the conflict is the only way to negotiate differences.

The miscalculations of the late president Özal are ably demonstrated by Michael Gunter. Rather than Turkey receiving international legitimacy for its occupation of portions of northern Iraq as part of the allied war effort, Ankara has been compelled to make several large incursions into northern Iraq since the end of the Gulf war in order to root out PKK bases. The greater irony, at least for Ankara, was that in August 1995 the PKK decided that it was in its best interest to attack the forces of the Kurdistan Democratic Party (KDP), one of the two leading Kurdish nationalist organizations in Iraqi Kurdistan, which had developed increasingly closer relations with Turkey since the end of the Gulf war. The PKK attack on the KDP threw a monkey wrench into the policies Turkey had pursued to contain the Kurdish nationalist movement in the aftermath of the war. The PKK attempt to become an accepted player in the Kurdish politics of Iraqi Kurdistan was squarely contrary to the Turkish government's attempts to contain the challenge of the PKK within Turkey. The PKK decision to attack the KDP is one of the most unexpected developments of the Gulf war.

Indeed, as Henri Barkey demonstrates convincingly, the consequences of the Gulf war and the subsequent escalation of the activities of the Kurdish nationalist movement both in Iraq and in Europe, have put Turkish domestic and foreign policies literally "under the gun." Barkey depicts lucidly the debilitating political, economic—but primarily diplomatic and foreign—policy effects on the demands of Turkey to constrain Kurdish nationalism. In spite of continued U.S. and European support for Turkey against the PKK, the relationship is troubled by the different positions of Ankara and Washington toward northern Iraq. Ankara thinks, "the entity in northern Iraq is acquiring attributes that can potentially influence Kurds living in Turkey." U.S. policy contributes, especially through the activities of Operation Provide Comfort (OPC), to the Kurdish nationalist movement in northern Iraq, aiding its attempts to acquire those very attributes. That is the rub. Ironically, Syria and Iran, both with large Kurdish populations of their own, cooperate with Turkey to prevent the development of an independent state in northern Iraq. The differing positions of the U.S. and Turkey toward northern Iraq represent a classic clash between the interests of a middle-level power and its major patron. Barkey concludes that, as another unexpected consequence of the Gulf war, Ankara has transformed the Kurdish issue into its greatest vulnerability and has been "imprisoned in a cage of its own making."

Robert Olson, in his contribution, emphasizes some of the points made by Barkey and dwells particularly on the Kurdish question and its role in Turkey's foreign policy with Syria, Iraq, Iran and Russia. Since other contributors discuss specific aspects of Turkey's relations with Iraq and Syria, it is interesting to note that the Kurdish question is also one of the factors, perhaps the major one, that compels cooperative relations between Ankara and Tehran. As Olson makes clear, the main reason for this steady cooperation is fear of the geopolitic and geostrategic consequences if the entity in northern Iraq acquires more attributes of an independent state. The relations between Turkey and its southern neighbors demonstrate that Turkey is fortunate that all three of its southern neighbors—Syria, Iraq and Iran—have large Kurdish populations. If they did not, they would undoubtedly use the "Kurdish card" more effectively against Turkey, which is exactly what Russia has done to prevent greater Turkish support for the Chechens in their war against Russia. Moscow, Olson shows, has made it clear that any substantial Turkish support for the Chechens would led to more substantive Russian support for the Kurdish nationalist movement, especially the Kurdistan parliament in exile (KPE).

Philip Robins offers a nuanced explanation of the degree to which the Kurdish issue affects European-Turkish relations. He suggests that despite the loud denunciations of some European countries and political organizations, especially the European Parliament, of Turkish human rights violations against the Kurds, the Kurdish issue as a factor in Euro-Turkish relations is "more apparent than real." He divides the Europeans into small players and big players. The small players, who generally have fewer economic relations with Turkey, emphasize human rights violations while the big players—United Kingdom, France, Germany, Italy—tend not to let human rights or the Kurdish issue in its wider application interfere with increasing economic ties between them and Turkey. This policy was confirmed by the European Union's overwhelming vote—343 for, 149 against and 36 abstentions—on 13 December 1995 to accept Turkey as a full member into the European Customs Union.

In a brilliant contribution, Hamit Bozarslan provides an assessment of the contradictions of the mechanisms, instruments and ideologies the Turkish state has utilized to eliminate, constrain and channel the challenge of Kurdish nationalism movement to the Kemalist state or, as Bozarslan has it, the Gökalpian state. He traces the ideological origins of these contradictions while indicating the flexibility within the contradictions. Among other actors, including political Islam and Alevism, Bozarslan states that Kurdish nationalism has contributed to the fragmentation of the Gökalpian construct and notes that Kurds have been important political players in Turkey's political space since the 1920s and have asserted themselves, with the exceptions of the coup d'etat periods. He stresses, however, that the impact of increased Kurdish nationalism from the 1970s onward changed the patterns of negotiations between the state, the political parties (whether they were conservative or social-democratic) and the Kurds. The lack of success of these negotiations led to a further weakening of the political parties with the exception of the islamist Welfare Party (WP).

Bozarslan draws attention to the relative success of the WP to attract Kurdish votes as compared to other parties. This became clearer as the WP emerged as Turkey's largest political force in the Parliamentary elections held on 24 December 1995, in which it won 21.3 percent of the vote. Its leading rival, the Motherland Party (MP), received 19.6 percent and the incumbent party, the True Path Party (TPP), got 19.1 percent. Bozarslan suggests several reasons for the WP's success: (1) it has no historical legacy in the Kurdish areas; (2) of all the political parties it is most in disfavor with the army; (3) it profited from the banishment of the Kurdish oriented Peoples Labor Party (PLP or HEP) and the Democracy Party (DP or DEP) in the 1990s; (4) its islamist discourse stresses Muslim solidarity between Kurds and Turks; (5) it supports the supra-ethnic Muslim Brotherhoods (*tarikats*), which played an important role in the Kurdish nationalist movements in the 1920s and 1930s; (5) locally the WP is Kurdified; (6) the WP is the only political party using an anti-Kemalist discourse; and (7) the WP is perceived by some Kurds as being more autonomous from the state than other political parties. As a result of the suppression of other genuine Kurdish representation, the WP continues to gather support from the Kurdish people. Bozarslan also notes that the appeal of HEP and DEP was limited by the competition of the PKK in the 1990s. In conclusion, he argues that only a victory by the WP and a continuation of its sustained challenge to Kemalist discourse "seems to be able to change the situation." The Turkish state can assure its durability, but one of the conditions for doing so is to enlarge the Kurdish electoral base. Bozarslan makes it clear that it is the Kurdish constituency of the WP as much as its islamist center and anti-Kemalist discourse that makes it open to attack by the media, the army and right wing parties such as the TTP, ANAP and NAP.

In a co-authored piece, Robert Olson and Yücel Bozdağlıoğlu take the political fragmentation so ably described by Hamit Bozarslan and demonstrate that the challenge of Kurdish nationalism has been one of the major factors in the creation of a new political party in Turkey, the New Democracy Movement (NDM). They argue that the main appeal of the NDM is its open, official and public acknowledgement of the "Kurdish problem." The NDM was the first Turkish-dominated political party to place the Kurdish problem on the top of its agenda. But as Olson and Bozdağlıoğlu stress, the NDM in no way advocates political autonomy or exclusive political rights for the Kurds. Their Kurdish program boils down to offering cultural and linguistic rights to the Kurds. It is not even clear to what extent they support language rights, for example, the right of the Kurds to create a university in which the Kurdish language would be the medium of instruction.

The NDM planned to carry out its Kurdish agenda while pursuing a neoliberal capitalistic economic program: a program that necessarily would have adversely impacted the Kurds. The NDP hopes that the Kurds perceive the decentralization aspects of its program to be in their ethnic interest. The two authors are pessimistic as to the potential appeal of the NDM to a Kurdish constituency. This pessimism seems to be vindicated by the poor showing of the NDM in the 24 December 1995 parliamentary elections, in which the NDM received only 135,000 votes—less than 1 percent of the total vote. In the heavily populated Kurdish provinces, the NDM received more than 2 percent of the vote in only the provinces of Şırnak (4.41) and Van (2.67). It received more than 1 percent of the vote in Bitlis (1.83); Bingöl (1.06); Ağrı (1.05); Diyarbakır (1.59); Muş (1.12) and Siirt (1.30).

In the concluding chapter Mark Muller provides a useful detailed description of how the Turkish state utilized the instruments of the law—constitutional, criminal, civil—based exclusively on a defined concept of Turkish nationalism, to eliminate Kurdish political activism and participation during the 1990s. In the end, the suppression of Kurdish nationalism had to meet the twin lethality of the armed forces and the coercive power of the legal system of the state. Muller draws parallels between the militarization of the conflict with the Kurds and the militarization of the Turkish legal structure, especially the introduction of comprehensive and broadly defined anti-terror laws, such as the notorious Article 8 introduced in 1991. He states that the Turkish anti-Kurdish legal structure contradicts the European Convention governing the establishment of fair trials and notes that much of the harassment of the Kurdish nationalists was outside of the official legal structure: dismissal from employment, stalking and even assassination, and in the case of political parties, banishment. Muller concludes that not only have the repressive legal measures led to the unlikelihood of meaningful political negotiations between the state, its representatives and the Kurds, but also have contributed to a static state political structure more and more immune to change. He ends by calling for an abolition of the legal measures that led to the elimination of Kurdish representation in the civil society of Turkey. He notes carefully that Turkey's entry into the European Customs Union will not, by itself, create the political will to stop the violations of Kurdish human and political rights. He insists political reform must accompany legal reform.

Together, the essays presented here draw a complex portrait of the the Kurdish nationalist movement in Turkey and the Middle East during the 1990s.

Part I

The Development of the Kurdish Nationalist Movement in Turkey since the 1980s

1

THE KURDISH NATIONALIST MOVEMENT IN TURKEY SINCE THE 1980s

Gülistan Gürbey

For more than ten years, the "secret" war between the Turkish military and the militant Kurdistan Workers' Party (PKK) has affected the civilian population in the Kurdish regions in southeastern Turkey, subjecting them to severe violations of human rights. Long-term prison sentences for Kurdish parliamentarians have put the Kurdish issue into the limelight. When the conflict began to expand not only to other parts of Turkey but to Europe as well, in particular to Germany, reaching the Kurds and Turks living there, it finally became apparent that this conflict is characterized by a dimension that crosses borders and endangers peace. This chapter deals with the internal and external factors and the causes and effects of the Kurdish issue in Turkey. The main focus is on the specific characteristics of the conflict, the various interests of the conflicting parties, the causes of the conflict, and possible solutions. The following issues are analyzed in detail: Turkish interests, aims and the measures and effects of Turkish policy toward the Kurds—in particular, the question of whether the domestic situation with its prevailing interests allows for a peaceful and mutual resolution of the Kurdish issue; Kurdish interests and forms of advocacy, as well as possibilities and limits of a legal representation of the Kurds; complications of the various options for conflict resolution, as proposed by the conflicting parties themselves, and means to end the conflict through external influence by international organizations to which Turkey belongs.

POLITICAL AND LEGAL FRAMEWORK OF THE TURKISH POLICY

The treatment of the Kurdish issue in Turkey warrants a discussion of the position of ethnic minorities in the Turkish legal and constitutional system, as one important characteristic lies in the inextricable link between the minority issue in Turkey and the ideological structure of the Turkish legal and constitutional system. Thus, one can maintain that the causes of the Kurdish issue must be sought in the political and legal system of Turkey itself. The rigid political and legal system, particularly in its current form, has important inadequacies when examined in the context of Turkey's obligations, especially within the framework of the Organization for Security and Cooperation in Europe (OSCE) and the Council of Europe.[1] The restrictive constitutional rules and regulations attempt to prescribe the means for political and social life in as much detail as possible, thus hindering pluralization and democratization of society and politics. A strict Turkish centralism and a strict concept of a nation-state in combination with extreme nationalism are the essential characteristics of Turkish state ideology, referred to as "Kemalism" after the state's founder, Mustafa Kemal Atatürk. However, the population structure of Turkey displays a high degree of ethnic, linguistic, and religious diversity. At least forty-seven distinct population groups can be differentiated.[2] Among them, the Kurds are the largest linguistic and ethnic group.

The Kemalist Concept of Nation Versus Ethnic Minorities

The primary internal cause of conflict is the strict application of the Kemalist concept of nation[3] in Turkey, which defines the Turkish nation as a sum of citizens without consideration of ethnic identity and negates in its legal interpretation the existence and protection of ethnic minorities. Underlying this concept of nation is the attempt to create, after the fall of the Ottoman Empire, a nationally and culturally homogenous, unified state on the territory of the Turkish Republic with the help of a new integrating ideology of Turkish nationalism. Thus, any type of articulation of cultural difference was and is perceived as a threat to cultural and national unity and is strictly prohibited. On the basis of the Kemalist definition of the Turkish nation and the resulting principle of equality, any expression of Kurdish identity is forbidden and persecuted. As members of the Turkish nation, the Kurds have equal rights in all aspects; however, the right to care for and develop their ethnicity, culture and language is not included in the understanding of equality. This policy of assimilation and homogeneity has influenced and continues to influence the forms of Kurdish resistance and is a cause of the open use of violence. On the whole, the emergence of the militant Kurdistan Workers' Party, known under its Kurdish acronym, PKK, must be viewed in this framework.

Moreover, one must consider a second component, which is very important in the pluralization of society and the process of democratization in Turkey: The Kemalist concept of nation cannot be viewed as separate from the principle of the "indivisible unity of a state's people and its territory" and the concept of "national culture" (Article 3, Turkish constitution 1982).

The principle of the indivisible unity of a state's people and its territory plays a central role in connection with the issue of protection of minorities. One wonders whether this principle is already violated when minorities are granted cultural autonomy or rights to self-administration. Basic rights and liberties can be restricted to protect this principle, as is consistently reflected within the legal system in numerous regulations: Article 125 of the criminal code prescribes capital punishment for those who attempt, with or without violence, to separate portions of the state's territory from the state union or attempt to pull away from the control of the central government. Propaganda against the indivisible unity of the state's people and its territory is subject to penalty under Article 8 of the Anti-Terror Law (ATL).[4]

The ATL is an example of the legal-political dilemma of Turkey—for example, on one hand, it desires to relax its criminal code and move closer to the requirements of a European standard on human rights; on the other hand, it wants to secure the claim to power of a centralist state and its ideology. This dilemma has led to an infringement of fundamental civil rights.

Article 8 of the ATL allows for the identification of separatist tendencies in their nascent stage. Written and oral propaganda as well as meetings and demonstrations that aim to destroy the indivisible unity of the state's people and its territory, by whatever ideas, goals or means, are prohibited. The numerous regulations of the ATL contradict the requirements of a democratic society and of human rights and prevent discussion of the Kurdish issue, as any discussion per se is in danger of being persecuted as propaganda against the indivisible unity of the state's people and its territory. Legally operating organizations, the media and persons committed to the Kurdish issue but also the civilian population in the crisis regions in southeastern Turkey are subjected to violations of human rights and political persecution. In fact, trials against dissident opinions refer almost exclusively to pro-Kurdish commitment. At the present time, more than one hundred persons are imprisoned, predominantly intellectuals, journalists, writers and scientists.

The changes to Article 8 of ATL (27 October 1995)—as a result of strong European pressure and negotiations leading to the initiation of a Customs Union between Turkey and the European Union—only apply to a reduction of prison sentences. The maximum penalty was lowered from five to three years, some prison sentences were converted to fines and some sentences were replaced with probation. "Separatist propaganda" still remains punishable under the law.

The concept of minority, as understood by state and international law, is referred to by Turkish law only in connection with the clause on minorities of the Lausanne Peace Treaty of 1923 (Article 37-42).[5] It refers only to the non-Muslim minorities (Greeks, Armenians and Jews). The internationally accepted rights of minorities, applicable to religious but also ethnic and linguistic minorities in particular, have not been accepted by Turkey on the grounds of its strict concept of a nation-state.

The concept of minority exists on a legal level in connection with the prohibition of "creating minority groups" (as, for example, in Article 81 of the Law on Political Parties). Political parties and associations may not claim the existence on Turkey's territory of minorities that are distinguished by differences in their national or religious culture, confession, ethnicity or language. They may not pursue the goal of "creating minority groups" on Turkish territory, to avoid disrupting the "integrity of the nation" through the caring for, developing and propagating of languages and cultures other than Turkish.

The change of constitutional regulations in July 1995 led neither to a relaxation of the central elements of state ideology anchored in the constitution nor to an adjustment of the concept of minority in line with the European standard. The changes merely allow for a greater political participation of groups, as, for example, clubs, professional associations and cooperatives, trade unions, university lecturers and students.

The Role of Civilian and Military Authorities as Decision-Makers

The military assumes a special position in the political system in Turkey, which can be attributed to several factors. In the Ottoman Empire, a strong army was the central instrument of state politics. The founder of the republic, Atatürk himself, was a member of the military. The link between the military and politics today is characterized in particular by the central role of the military as a "political force of order." In its role as "keeper and protector" of Kemalist principles, the military has become an extremely important agent in Turkish politics.[6]

The sphere of influence of the military in politics is strengthened by means of constitutional-legal mechanisms. In the so-called "National Security Council," the military is given a constitutionally secured position. After the first military intervention of 27 May 1960, this body was incorporated into the constitution of 1961 (Article 11). Thus, the until-then "hidden participation" of the military in the implementation of political power became legally fortified.[7]

The constitution determines two important tasks of the National Security Council (Article 118, Turkish constitution 1982): on one hand, the protection and defense of "national security" against internal and external dangers and, on the other hand, the "definition, determination, and application of a national security policy," based on the principle of the indivisible unity of a state's people and its territory according to the Kemalist state doctrine.[8] It is essential to note that the tasks of the National Security Council are very extensive and its limits are not clearly defined. Within the scope of its tasks are not only national security and defence but regulation of aspects of the entire life of the society. Thus, the concept of national security has been extended with the help of the formula that protects "the welfare and security of the community."

The legal expert on constitutional law and former Turkish foreign minister Mümtaz Soysal draws the following conclusion regarding the function of the National Security Council:

> Because the National Security Council is a body which is in a better position to express opinions concerning issues of national security due to its proximity

to detailed information, it is only natural that the Council of Ministers "gives preference" to these opinions. The real danger here lies in the fact that the concept of "national security" is being used in a very broad and all-encompassing manner—and includes almost all issues which fall under the responsibility of the government—and because of this broad interpretation, a new mixed decision-making body is created which is nearly parallel to the Council of Ministers, but does not carry political responsibility.[9]

Apart from this, the decisions of the National Security Council, which are to be "given preference" by the Council of Ministers, have been given a certain political and moral binding power. The National Security Council, as a "planning and controlling body," plays an active and determining role in the definition and application of policy aims and measures and is in no way responsible to Parliament.[10] Therefore, the political system of Turkey has two centers of decision-making: the civilian authority (in the form of the Council of Ministers and Parliament) and the military authority (in the form of the National Security Council). The decision-making process demonstrates an interrelationship of forces that results in an imbalance of power at the expense of the civilian authority. The existence of the military authority in the political system impedes and hinders the pluralization, democratization and development of a civilized society and politics. As the Kurdish issue in the self-definition of Turkish politics and the military is a national problem—a potential source of danger for the "indivisible unity of the state's people and its territory"—and Kurdish claims for increased self-realization are viewed a priori as a "separatist" threat, it is evident that the National Security Council is the primary decision-maker in the Kurdish issue.

Constants, Fluctuations and Effects of Turkish Policy

The basis for the military option for the treatment of the Kurdish issue had already been laid in Turkey's founding years. The Kemalist policy of the national state and attempts to consolidate all ethnic minorities in Turkey into one homogenous nation led to several Kurdish insurrections. Between 1925 and 1940 there were over twenty Kurdish uprisings[11] in the Kurdish regions in southeastern Turkey, which were violently suppressed by the Turkish military. At least from that time on, the use of military power combined with a concurrent suppression and assimilation policy has been the core of the Turkish policy toward the Kurds. For decades, the Kurds have been officially declared to be *mountain Turks,* and the use of the expressions *Kurds, Kurdish,* and *Kurdistan,* as well as the Kurdish language, were prohibited. For decades, the Kurdish regions have been subjected to emergency decree, a regionally specific legal system, state military control and, at the same time, economic neglect.[12]

The first change in Turkish policy toward the Kurds occurred during the era of Turgut Özal (1983-93). This era was generally characterized by a policy of structural change with economic and political modernization and a gradual forcing out of the traditionally dominant and established elite from the bureaucracy and military in favor of the functional elite, predominantly from business circles. It is only at a later phase during the era of Turgut Özal that the Kurdish policy practiced thus far began to change. Although the military-state repression and control continued, this era saw the introduction of a liberalization in the cultural sphere, economic development of the predominantly Kurdish-settled regions, and the attempt to engage the PKK politically. Özal tried to implement the liberalization of the policy toward the Kurds despite severe criticism by the Turkish elite in politics, the military and government bureaucracy, as well as by a large portion of the Turkish press and media. Because of changes in world politics and internal and external pressures on Turkey regarding the Kurdish issue, Turgut Özal took the initiative during the Gulf crisis in 1991 and successfully initiated a new policy toward the Kurds. While his liberal-conservative party, ANAP (Motherland Party), wavered between the former Kemalist position and a more liberal Kurdish policy, his was a policy aimed primarily at dialogue. Özal viewed the Gulf crisis[13] as an opportunity to strengthen the political position of Turkey with its NATO allies in the Middle East, and for this reason he joined the anti-Iraq policy of the United States, despite the protest of high-ranking army officers and parliamentary opposition forces.

In a meeting of the National Security Council on 25 January 1991,[14] Özal pointed out the necessity of reform on the Kurdish issue, stressing that after the Gulf war, Turkey must be prepared for new developments in the region, and thus, on the Kurdish issue as well. Özal initiated dialogue with the Iraqi Kurds to gain insight on the position of parties affected by the Gulf war and on the situation in Iraq and the Middle East. Again and again, he stressed the position of Turkey, which desires to prevent the formation of an independent Kurdish state, but did not intervene against the autonomy of Iraqi Kurdistan. At the same time, he demanded that the Iraqi Kurds not support the PKK.[15]

The legalization of the Kurdish language through the repeal of the law prohibiting other languages (1983) on 12 April 1991 was a further important step toward a new orientation in the Kurdish issue. So far, this had been the most far-reaching gesture toward the Kurds living in Turkey. While Kurdish was spoken freely for the first time, a many-voiced debate began on the new orientation in the Kurdish issue.[16] Özal used this opportunity to democratically engage the Kurds in their own country and encouraged discussion on new reforms regarding the Kurdish issue by introducing new proposals, thus incurring criticism from different sectors of society: political, military and the media. For example, he suggested that the Kurdish language be introduced into the educational system and into TV and radio broadcasts. On the whole, Özal gave priority to the political resolution of the Kurdish issue. He viewed the parliamentarians of the pro-Kurdish Peoples' Democracy Party (HEP), and later the Democracy Party (DEP), as partners in dialogue and described such dialogue as an opportunity to end the war with the

PKK. To this aim, he asked the HEP and later the DEP representatives to influence the PKK to take steps toward ending the strife. For this purpose, several representatives held talks with the PKK leader, Abdullah Öcalan; these negotiations in particular later played a role in the stripping of their parliamentary immunity and sentencing. Özal was convinced that peace could be achieved only through negotiations with the PKK and that a cease-fire was essential for the introduction of specific steps in the peace process. In contrast to the coalition government and the military, he welcomed the unilateral cease-fire declaration of the PKK in March 1993. He saw it as an opportunity to engage the PKK politically and to pave the way for a political solution through specific measures, such as, for example, the granting of amnesty.[17] But his sudden death on 17 April 1993 brought the first liberal attempts to change the Kurdish policy to an abrupt halt.

On 21 November 1991, the coalition government of the Social-Democratic People's Party (SHP) and the conservative True Path Party (DTP) came to power by making promising declarations of their intent. This government has refused to recognize the Kurds as an ethnic minority even though they have recognized the "Kurdish reality." With regard to the issue of protection of minorities, they refer to the provisions of the constitution and to the fact that all Turkish citizens have equal rights and responsibilities under the law. Only those groups referred to as minorities by the Lausanne Peace Treaty are recognized as such; however, the Kurds are not mentioned in the treaty. Regional or cultural autonomy is not viewed as a solution. Moreover, institutionalization of the rights of minorities would lead to a division of the Turkish Republic. The coalition government makes intensive use of the military option, whereby it strongly leans on the military for support. There is essentially no change in the coalition government's legal view of the Kurdish issue as a minority issue, even though the government program explicitly mentions its aim to adjust the Kurdish minority status to the European standards, as well as to find a peaceful solution.[18]

The military and police measures that were already in place and practiced during the era of Turgut Özal are now being used to their fullest extent by the coalition government. For example, the enforcement of an emergency decree in ten Kurdish provinces in southeastern Turkey was intensified.[19] Further measures in the year 1990 led to massive infringements of freedom of the press and on the guarantee of due legal process. Since that time, less reliable information has appeared in the press concerning developments in the crisis regions. In August 1990, basic rights in the crisis regions in the southeast were suspended, which was justified because of threats to national security. The emergency decree was further intensified by the so-called Censorship and Banishment Decree, which grants further authority to the special governor of the Kurdish provinces. In the region bordering Iraq, where more severe fighting between the military and the PKK had taken place, several districts were closed to journalists and civil servants. Only a few left-wing newspapers—namely, the pro-Kurdish *Özgür Gündem* (Free Agenda), published under the name *Özgür Politika* (Free Politics)—still dare to criticize and condemn the illegal actions of the security forces, suffering numerous confiscations of property and threats of disproportionately high penalties for their actions.

The implementation of the security measures in southeastern Turkey is carried out by the paramilitary gendarmerie, predominantly in the rural areas; under the jurisdiction of the minister of the interior; by the police, predominantly in the urban areas; by the military, who has at its disposal special commando units experienced in winter combat with the capability for cross-border operations and air reconnaissance by plane and helicopters, called "Rambos" by the population; and by village guards. Since July 1987, the new post of multiregional governor, known as "Super Governor," was institutionalized and granted comprehensive powers similar to a commander of martial law who is authorized to suspend basic civil rights and liberties. The governor's seat is in Diyarbakır.[20]

The so-called "village guards," which by early 1996 were estimated to number sixty-seven thousand, are recruited from Kurdish tribal groups opposed to the PKK and are armed and lucratively paid by the state. A new cycle of violence has been introduced by these village guards, as they not only lead the fight against the PKK but also incite tribal strife and feuds between families. The PKK has declared these village guards to be "enemies of the people" and has brought its acts of violence on themselves and their families.[21]

Not only large-scale military operations but also expansive forced resettlements and food embargoes are fundamental elements of the security measures in the Kurdish crisis regions in southeastern Turkey. The depopulation of the rural areas in which the PKK operates is carried out by forced evacuations, deportations and bombardments of villages and settlements, accompanied by the destruction of nature. Underlying this forced expulsion of the Kurds from their regions were plans to create a fifteen- to forty-kilometer-wide security corridor along the Turkish border with Syria, Iraq and Iran. These plans have been implemented in particular in the Botan region (Hakkari, Mardin, Siirt), the center of the PKK's activities. The policy of deportation and the establishment of restricted military zones in strategically important areas, where the PKK fighting develops, occurs concurrently with the attempt to drain the PKK of logistic support by the establishment of so-called "strategic villages" and to keep the Kurdish population under state and military control. The displaced flee to the nearby cities and towns and live there in slums and temporary dwellings.

The cross-border actions of the Turkish military are based on security treaties with Iraq, which allow for such operations up to forty kilometers into each other's territories. Turkey presents its military interventions in Iraqi Kurdistan as part of its security measures against "terrorism." It has carried out several such military operations, partly in cooperation with Iraqi-Kurdish parties, as, for example, in October 1992 and for several months in the spring of 1995. By these actions, Turkey attempts to undermine support for the PKK fighters among the Iraqi Kurds and to prevent the flight of the PKK into Iraqi-Kurdish territory. At the same time, it tries to counteract the formation of a Kurdish nationalist state in Iraq and the entire region with the help of trilateral agreements and treaties between Ankara, Damascus and Tehran, initiated by Ankara and met with interest by the neighboring states. A further aim of the Turkish regional and Middle Eastern policy is to exploit the contradictions between the various Kurdish movements in meeting its objectives.

The "secret war" in southeastern Turkey between the Turkish security forces (the army, the gendarmerie, the militia, the political police, the secret service, the anti-terror units and the village guards) and the militant PKK has meanwhile led to a growing politicization of the population, a polarization of the conflicting parties and a militarization of politics, accompanied by massive violations of human rights, both at the hands of the state security forces and the PKK.[22] The escalation of violence has had serious consequences: The closing down of shops has become a part of everyday life in the Kurdish provinces while the burials of the victims of state violence regularly develop into larger demonstrations, which are, in turn, met with deadly shots into the crowd by security forces. In addition, there have been numerous murders of both critical and Kurdish journalists;[23] prominent lawyers and representatives of political parties, especially of the prohibited pro-Kurdish HEP and DEP parties; and Kurdish businessmen.[24] The security forces make no special effort to solve these murders. Rumors in the press speak of activities of an anti-guerrilla unit (*Kontrgerilla*), similar to the death squads operating in Latin America, which executes or allows the disappearance of legally employed pro-Kurdish persons as well as critics of the state military policy, with the secret approval of state bodies. Many circumstances point to the existence of certain mechanisms that are no longer under the control of the government. Furthermore, the steadily growing support of the PKK by the Kurdish population is not only an expression of their despair at the everyday suffering inflicted by Turkish security forces but also an expression of Kurdish emancipation as a result of a growing national consciousness of the Kurds.

On the whole, the discrimination and the attacks against the Kurds have increased in western Turkey. The situation of the Kurdish refugees in western Turkish cities has become more difficult. They are the first to be arrested during police raids and searches, as often they are suspected on grounds of Kurdish origin alone. Since many Turks feel helpless in reacting to PKK attacks, they play out their frustration by carrying out general attacks against the Kurds. Provocations and attacks occur in particular during mourning ceremonies for PKK victims. Each mourning ceremony becomes transformed into a demonstrative show of power aimed at the Kurds. In several towns of the Aegean and Mediterranean regions, attacks on Kurds and their facilities, lasting several days, have taken place (for example, in Izmir, Mersin, Manisa, Aydın, Nazilli, Turgutlu, Fethiye, Urla, Alanya, Denizli, Antalya, Konya, and Adana). They range from physical violence, destruction of Kurdish shops and attacks on predominantly Kurdish districts of cities to various methods of discrimination, such as refusing apartments to Kurds and boycotting of shops run by Kurds.[25] As a rule, this repressive policy against the Kurds, which is accompanied by arbitrary police searches in predominantly Kurdish districts and systematic provocations by right extremist nationalist forces, activists of the ultra-right Nationalist Action Party (MHP), is tolerated by the city administration. Many Kurds have left the cities after such incidents.

The growing process of alienation between the Kurds and the state, as well as between Kurds and Turks, the basis of which had already been laid with the foundation of the republic, leads to a strengthening of nationalist sentiments among the majority of the Turkish population, resulting in hostility and vengeful sentiments, which in turn have effects on the development of Kurdish nationalism and Kurdish resistance.[26] Anti-Kurdish propaganda and press coverage in the Turkish media contribute to an escalation of the situation. In today's situation, a majority of the Turkish public is skeptical toward a consistent and neutral human rights policy and increasingly calls for uncompromising statements against the PKK.[27]

The efforts of state power to build up Islamic and right-wing radical nationalist groups, in particular the MHP, as a counterweight to the PKK have led to a further cycle of violence. A considerable portion of the special units and security forces are preferentially recruited from the ranks of MHP activists. Press reports speak of efforts of state power and the *Kontrgerilla,* with the help of NAP activists, to build up so-called defense organizations directly on location, which are used in the fight against the PKK and their sympathizers and to win over the population for the MHP. Apart from the *Kontrgerilla,* the Turkish variant of *Hizbullah,* allegedly not only supported by but founded by the *Kontrgerilla* organization, is held responsible for numerous unsolved murder cases and disappearances.[28]

Another consequence of the escalation of violence is the flight of the Kurds into the cities of the Kurdish regions in southeastern and western Turkey and northern Iraq. Concurrent with forced deportations, so far more than twenty-three hundred villages have been cleared, destroyed or bombarded; crops, trees and meadows, as well as about 10 million hectares (about 2.5 billion acres) of forest, have been burned in southeast Turkey. More than 2 million Kurds have been driven out of their home villages. On the outskirts of the cities, illegal Kurdish settlements have been established and have the potential for becoming targets of repression. However, politicization continues there as well, which enables the PKK to organize in the cities. The policy of deportation has, on the whole, broadened the conflict by carrying it, and with it the PKK, into the urban areas.[29]

According to reports of the Turkish Association for Human Rights,[30] twelve thousand Kurds have meanwhile fled to northern Iraq (Kurdistan Regional Government-Iraq) and live in camps there. Most have fled because of their fear of the arbitrary behavior of local administration and Turkish security forces, which have set villages on fire or bombarded them because of the citizens' refusal to fight as village guards against the PKK. However, the Turkish Foreign Ministry claims that the PKK has forced the inhabitants into northern Iraq to support their claims that the Kurds flee alleged Turkish repression.[31]

Another consequence of this "secret war" is the enormous economic burden. The costs of military actions in southeast Turkey are rising daily. The fight against the PKK places an additional strain of approximately 13 million deutsche mark annually on the Turkish budget. The conflict intensifies the imbalance between the western and eastern parts of the country and prevents economic upswing. The economic crisis increasingly endangers social peace. Meanwhile, even the largest Turkish association of employers and entrepreneurs, TÜSIAD, has warned of an impending "social explosion" in its recent report.[32] Various groups that profit from the resulting wartime economy are fundamentally interested in the continuation of the conflict. The object of the secret war that the population has financed for more than ten years comes increasingly under question. In January 1994, the government extended military service by three months.

Positions of Turkish Parties

With regard to an assessment of the Kurdish issue, the parties share the view that the Kurdish problem in Turkey does not exist in the sense of an ethnic minority issue (with the exception of the HEP and DEP). It is reduced instead to a "problem of terrorism" or a "socio-economic problem" or both. This stereotypical assertion, as well as the ideology of the national state and the centralist unitary state, is strictly adhered to. The Social-Democratic People's Party (SHP)—today the Republican People's Party (CHP) following the fusion of CHP and SHP in early 1995—issued a report in July 1990 that calls for a halt to the military measures practiced thus far, a limited decentralization of state administration, and a strengthening of democracy, accompanied by programs of economic and socio-cultural development but does not include a far-reaching political resolution of Kurdish autonomy. Only a few CHP parliamentarians demand that Kurds be granted cultural rights and that the provisions of the OSCE, which Turkey has signed as a member state, be applied. As partner in the government coalition, the CHP is responsible for a policy based on a military option that represents repression, oppression, and violence.

Although the "Kurdish reality" is recognized by the CHP, the True Path Party (DYP), and the Motherland Party (ANAP), it is not linked to the granting of rights to Kurds; the right-wing radical Nationalist Action Party (MHP) negates this reality and denies the existence of the Kurdish people and language. The NAP is convinced that there is no Kurdish issue but a "PKK issue" and that a special organization should be established to fight it.[33] It also consistently speaks against a dialogue-oriented policy toward the Kurds, which the ANAP and the Democratic Left Party (DSP) look upon with reservation.

A solution may lie in the unrestricted application of the legal principle of equality and the liberal guarantees to civil rights in the constitution. A far-reaching political resolution of cultural and political autonomy is not even discussed by any of the major political parties. The parties share the common view that an actual cultural and political autonomy would lead to a fragmentation of the Turkish state. This perceived threat of a division of the Turkish national state by the Kurdish issue is shared and politically exploited by all political parties (except HEP and DEP). The expression *terrorism* is turned into a verdict that the parties (except HEP and DEP) attribute to any Kurdish attempt at self-realization and thus provides a theoretical justification for its suppression.[34]

On the whole, the parties are characterized by an amorphous conceptualization of the Kurdish issue. Neither is the majority of the parties ready to initiate a political dialogue with the Kurds. This is demonstrated by the fact that the exclusion of DEP from Parliament has been consistently supported by the opposition parties.

An exception is the New Democracy Movement (NDM) of young businessman Cem Boyner, founded in January 1995, which has been supported by many Turkish intellectuals, scientists, journalists, businessmen and former generals. It views itself as an essential political alternative to all parties and pursues economic and political liberalism. It aims for the formation of a civil society in the sense of a civic society and questions the strict application of the Kemalist state doctrine and the Turkish policy practiced thus far toward the Kurds. The movement views the following as specific steps in a resolution of the Kurdish issue: the pluralization and democratization of society; the granting of cultural rights and freedom for representing Kurdish interests without endangering the unitary structure of the state; and the implementation of a dialogue-oriented policy toward the Kurds. The National Security Council, as a constitutional-legal body, is to be dissolved so as to pave the way for a truly civilized political development.[35] Whether the New Democracy Movement will attain broad support from the society at large remains to be seen, although, on the basis of its pluralistic and liberal understanding of politics, it should be able to work toward a political and democratic resolution of the Kurdish issue.

On a societal level, meanwhile, the Kurdish issue is partly discussed in connection with basic societal and political reforms and a renunciation of Kemalist state ideology. Ideas range from a democratization of the country, a decentralization of the state, a change of the Turkish constitution, a removal of the military authority from politics and the granting of cultural and political autonomy to the Kurds to the establishment of federalist structures. This discussion is conducted primarily within circles of intellectuals, a few journalists, businessmen, writers, artists and scientists, and within some interest groups and new liberal movements. The concept of "civil society" (from sociologist Murat Belge), the "Islamic reformist" concept (from authors Ali Bulaç and Abdurrahman Dilipak), and the "neo-Ottoman" and "second republican" concepts (from economist and columnist Mehmet Altan) represent the various political currents in this multifaceted debate.[36]

The few civil organizations[37] that exist in the form of interest groups, foundations and associations attempt to seek alternatives to state politics. They are subject, however, to the numerous restrictive legal regulations and the authoritarian concept of basic civil rights and the state. Thus, the scope of their activities and impact is very limited. In particular, associations and organizations that concern themselves with Kurdish politics and culture are affected by political repression in law and in practice. The escalation of violence by the state and the PKK, as well as the growing influence of the military authority in the political system, endanger the existence of the few civil organizations attempting to survive as forms of expression in a society that is only beginning to develop a civil character.

KURDS STRIVING FOR AUTONOMY

Atatürk's promise to the Kurds to create a common state for the Turks and Kurds was not kept after the formation of the Turkish Republic. Instead, all Kurdish organizations, publications and schools were prohibited. Thus, the attempt to "build a nation" laid the basis for a policy of forced assimilation and a destruction of Kurdish culture.[38] The status of autonomy that the Kurds enjoyed during the Ottoman Empire was dissolved in favor of an overall centralization of the state and a homogenization of society. The Treaty of Sèvres of 10 August 1920, which foresaw the creation of a Kurdish and an Armenian state but was replaced by the Lausanne Peace Treaty (1923) after the successful Turkish War of Independence, had an enormous impact on Kurdish nationalism,[39] which reached its peak with the formation of the short-lived Kurdish Republic of Mahabad in the Kurdish regions of Iran (22 January through 15 December 1946). Even today, both of these historic moments are effective symbols, as they were the first manifestations of Kurdish nationalism (in the formation of a state).

The Resurgence of Kurdish Nationalism

Although the repression, deportations and suppressions drained the Kurdish population of their energy for a renewed insurrection, numerous uprisings in the early era of the Turkish Republic introduced a new phase of Kurdish nationalism and Kurdish resistance, which continued by other means in the following decades. While the sixties were characterized by an emergence of numerous Kurdish organizations and magazines concerning themselves with Kurdish language, culture, history and literature, a radicalization of Kurdish demands was observed in subsequent years.[40]

Since the mid-1980s, Kurdish nationalism in Turkey has seen another resurgence. External factors have included the end of the East-West conflict and the establishment of new states on the territory of the former Soviet Union, demonstrating that peoples' yearnings, long-cherished, can be fulfilled. The Arab-Israeli peace process in the Middle East also gave hope to the Kurds for a similar resolution and has confirmed for them the effectiveness of political struggle in achieving their aims. In addition, the massacre of several thousand civilians by use of toxic gases in March 1988 in Halabja in Iraqi Kurdistan, carried out by Baghdad, combined with the refugee drama of Iraqi Kurds at the end of the second Gulf war not only brought the Kurds and their various organizations closer together but also led to an internationalization of the Kurdish issue, which thus far had been viewed primarily as an internal affairs issue of the countries in question. Moreover, the proclamation of the Kurdistan Regional Government-Iraq in October 1992 had a catalyzing effect on the Kurds. In the event of its survival, it will tremendously increase the hope for a peaceful resolution of the Kurdish issue in the remaining regions in the near future.

The inappropriate Turkish policy, which attempts to carry out forced assimilation of the Kurds through military violence and which excludes a dialogue with the Kurds, represents the internal factor responsible for the strengthening of Kurdish nationalism. The "secret war" in the Kurdish region in southeast Turkey has contributed to a development of national consciousness among the Kurdish population. Kurds, Kurdish intellectuals, and refugees in exile and diaspora have always played and still continue to play an important role in the process of the creation of a nation. Media is particularly important in this process in the age of satellite transmission, as can be observed with the Kurdish channel MED-TV, licensed in Great Britain, which has been transmitting a daily satellite program in Europe and Kurdistan since 24 December 1994. Through audiovisualization of the Kurdish culture and issue and its cross-border transmission, the channel has the potential to sensitize large portions of the population to the Kurdish issue in the diaspora and in all parts of Kurdistan and to speed up the process of the creation of a nation.

Kurdish Underground Resistance

The Kurdish organizations in Turkey—the Kurdistan Workers' Party (PKK) and the Socialist Party of Kurdistan (PSK)—stem from three political movements: the nationalist movement, which in its development has essentially been influenced by the KDP-Iraq (Democratic Party of Kurdistan-Iraq); a movement that developed from the Workers' Party of Turkey (TIP), of which the Socialist Party of Kurdistan (PSK), founded in 1974, belongs; and a movement that developed from the Turkish Federation of Revolutionary Youth of Turkey (DEV-GENÇ), to which the founding members of the PKK belong.[41]

Currently the PKK is the leading organization setting the tone of the underground resistance, while, at the same time, it is the most controversial. PKK and PSK share the view that the Kurdish region is a colony of the Turkish state and that federalism within the Turkish Republic represents a realistic resolution. The parties, however, disagree on the issue of the use of violence—not only against a foreign central power but also in the internal fight against political opponents—as a political device.

The PKK, founded on 27 November 1978 and reactivated in 1982 after the 1980 military coup in Turkey, no longer strives toward the aim of an independent Kurdish state. No longer does it claim to be the sole representative of all parts of Kurdistan. Its primary aim today is the resolution of the Kurdish issue through the establishment of federalism within the Turkish borders. The PKK differs from the other Kurdish organizations on the issue of violence. The armed fight that the PKK has led since August 1984 is based on "revolutionary violence" as a means of achieving mobilization and liberation. Violence is not only used against the Turkish government but also in the struggle against its political opponents (dissidents from its own ranks, other Kurdish and Turkish organizations, tribal leaders, village guards and civilians).[42]

At their third congress (25-30 October 1986), the PKK resolved to intensify political activity in the cities, to extend military operations in the urban areas, to intensify the relationship with other political organizations, both national and international, and to establish the Peoples' Liberation Army of Kurdistan (ARGK); the National Liberation Front of Kurdistan (ERNK) was founded in 1985. The cycle of violence continues, carried out by various means: attacks on state facilities and tourist centers in Turkey; the kidnapping of tourists and the hostage-taking of civilians in Turkey and abroad; the murder of village guards and teachers;[43] attacks on Turkish facilities in western Europe; and the use of violence against other Kurdish and Turkish organizations and PKK dissidents.

The broad political structure of the organization became apparent in spring 1990, or in 1992 at the latest, when mass demonstrations took place in the cities of Cizre and Nusaybin, considered by the PKK as *serhildan*(s) or uprisings, a Kurdish *intifada*.[44] The guerrilla strategy of the PKK and the anti-guerrilla strategy of the Turkish government still determine the scope of violence: The PKK, which declared a one-sided cease-fire in March 1993, opened a new round of violence and counterviolence when PKK units broke the cease-fire in May 1993. The sudden death of Turgut Özal during the period of cease-fire had an effect on the PKK; a political vacuum emerged after his death and the PKK considered that its loss of an approachable partner meant the end of the chance for dialogue. Subsequently, the PKK carried out elections for a Kurdish national parliament amongst the Kurds living in Europe. In October 1993 it demanded, under threat of violence, that the Turkish parties and media close their offices in southeast Turkey because of their one-sided representation of the interests of the Turkish state at the expense of the Kurdish people; PKK's actions disregarded freedoms of the press and speech in southeast Turkey in order to prevent local elections in March 1994.

The PKK intended to issue two signals by the one-sided declaration of cease-fire (17 March through 24 May 1993): on the one hand, its readiness for negotiations, and on the other, the turning back from its ultimate aim of creating a Kurdish state. The PKK no longer insists on this demand but instead strives toward the aim of finding a federalist resolution within Turkey, which could take various forms. Basically, the PKK views a mutual cease-fire as a necessary prerequisite for talks and the paving of the way for a political resolution.[45] In this regard, the leader of the PKK, Abdullah Öcalan, on the occasion of the International Northwest Kurdistan Conference in Brussels in March 1994, as well as at the Summit Meeting of the OSCE Member States in Budapest in December 1994, requested in writing that the leaders of Germany, Great Britain, France, and the United States mediate between Turkey and the PKK. As the latest effort in this regard, Öcalan repeated this appeal in a written memorandum to the U.S. president on 13 October 1995. All these requests, however, propose that the mutual cease-fire be conducted under international control and involve negotiations. The PKK has declared its readiness to sign the Geneva War Convention. The Turkish government, however, considers this a ploy by the PKK and vehemently refuses dialogue with the "terrorists."[46]

In contrast to the Kurdish uprisings in Turkey thus far, the PKK is characterized by a broad organizational structure and a force capable of extraordinary mobilization. It possesses a broad network not only in the Kurdish parts of Turkey and other countries in the region but also in western Europe. Meanwhile, it recruits guerrillas in both the Kurdish regions of crisis and among the Kurds living in western Europe. Among the recruits is a strikingly large proportion of very young people, including girls and young women. On the whole, one can maintain that the PKK enjoys enormous support among the Kurdish population, not only in the crisis regions and their cities but also in western Europe.[47] Former Turkish General Chief of Staff Doğan Güreş admitted publicly in July 1993 that roughly one-tenth of the Kurdish population in the Kurdish regions, or approximately four hundred thousand persons, must be regarded as active sympathizers of the PKK. Official German reports speak of approximately sixty-nine hundred PKK members in Germany.[48] At mass rallies, the PKK succeeds in mobilizing a much higher number of sympathizers than is reported by official sources; for example, the Second Kurdistan Festival, initiated by the PKK on 4 September 1993 in the Frankfurter Waldstadion (Frankfurt Forest Stadium), was attended by forty-five thousand persons according to police sources, versus PKK reports of up to one hundred thousand attendees from the whole of Germany and neighboring countries.

A significant characteristic of the PKK is that, on the one hand, it leads the guerrilla war in the Kurdish regions of southeast Anatolia as a militant organization while, on the other hand, it has the political flexibility to adapt to international and regional conditions. It performs widespread, intensive activity abroad in public relations and has attempted to form a political wing in order to be able to act as a partner in dialogue. It has turned back from its ultimate aim of establishing an independent Kurdish state in favor of a new goal of a federalist resolution within the boundaries of the Turkish state. At the same time, it has declared its readiness to dialogue. To this end, the PKK has declared one-sided cease-fires. The attempt to create a Kurdish parliament in exile, including the DEP representatives in exile, is a further essential step on the way to the creation of a political wing. On 23 January 1995, the PKK handed a declaration to the International Red Cross and the Foreign Ministry of Switzerland, in which it stated that the International Red Cross is granted entry into the war regions to be able to monitor that the Geneva treaty and its supplemental protocols are being adhered to by the PKK. With this diplomatic step, the PKK intends to be internationally recognized as a warring party and demands that Turkey abide by the Geneva Convention. Thus, it attempts to pave the way for dialogue and to state that it does not insist on a violent military resolution. The PKK has passed resolutions toward a political dialogue during its Fifth Party Congress (8-27 January 1995). The party authorized Abdullah Öcalan to make offers for a political dialogue and the opening of political negotiations.[49]

The founding of the Kurdish parliament in exile on 12 April 1995 in The Hague must be evaluated as a turning point in the progression of the conflict and its development. On one hand, the parliament in exile functions as a partner in dialogue and, on the other hand, it proves that the prohibition of the DEP has brought the PKK and the DEP parliamentarians in exile closer together. The obviously common activities of the two parties have resulted in the fact that a process of dialogue and peace that disregards the PKK would be difficult to realize. The parliament in exile represents this cooperation.[50]

The source for the broad support of the PKK, called "guerrilla"[51] by the population in the crisis region, can be found not in its Marxist-Leninist ideology but primarily in its growing Kurdish nationalism.

The Socialist Party of Kurdistan (PSK), founded in 1974,[52] which is led by the former leading member of the TIP, Kemal Burkay, is another important Kurdish organization working underground. The PSK supports the right of the Kurdish people to self-determination but does not define this right as a one-sided claim to establish an independent Kurdish state. Priority is given to federalism, maintaining the territorial integrity of Turkey. In this regard, this does not differ from the aims of the PKK. Burkay proposes a "Turkish-Kurdish Federation" and cites Belgium as an example. In contrast to the PKK, the use of violence as a political means is rejected on principle. The Kurdish issue in Turkey stems from the repression of the Kurdish people, whom the Turkish government has denied all legal possibility for representing their interests. The problem can be solved only by negotiations, with the prerequisite that Turkey accept the Kurds as an equal partner in dialogue. A process of dialogue should include all Kurdish organizations, including the PKK. It is not so much the PKK but rather the Turkish government itself that has stood in the way of a peaceful solution. The PSK has welcomed the one-sided declarations of cease-fire and the readiness of the PKK to participate in a dialogue while giving up their ultimate aims. Together with the PKK, on the day of its proclamation of one-sided cease-fire (19 March 1993) the TKSP signed a protocol that determines the cooperation between the Kurdish organizations.

This step introduced the founding of a "National Front of Kurdistan," comprised of twelve Kurdish organizations in Turkey. The program states two possibilities for a resolution: the formation of an independent republic or a federation with equal rights within Turkey. Moreover, it demands an immediate halt of the state of emergency and of military measures, a cease-fire, a general amnesty, and the granting of cultural rights.[53]

Possibilities and Limits of Parliamentary Representation of Interests

The seven SHP representatives who took part in the conference on the Kurdish issue in Paris in October 1989 and who were ousted from their party because of their statements on the Kurdish issue in Turkey, founded the pro-Kurdish People's Labor Party (HEP) on 7 June 1990. Through an agreement that included HEP candidates on the party roster of Social-Democratic People's Party (SHP), the HEP was voted into Parliament during parliamentary elections in October 1991. The first turbulences came during the swearing in of the Parliament, when two HEP parliamentarians added a few remarks in Kurdish at the end of their oath. The reaction to this was extremely strong; images, which could be seen for the first time in the history of the Parliament, were transmitted for several days in the Turkish media. Both HEP parliamentarians were accused of "separatist propaganda." The HEP criticized the policy practiced thus far against the Kurds, stating that the Kurdish issue cannot be reduced to a "terrorism problem," and insisted that a political solution is urgently needed. It condemned the military option and stressed that the PKK is not a "terrorist movement." It maintained that the government should begin a process of dialogue that includes the PKK. To this aim, they would take upon themselves the role of mediator, so that the cycle of violence can be broken. The HEP provided a written list of conditions to then-head of SHP, Erdal Inönü, in which it demanded a halt to the state of emergency and military measures; the granting of cultural rights (school education in the Kurdish language, Kurdish TV and radio programs), as well as opportunities to form organizations. The HEP's lifespan was brief, as it was banned by the Constitutional Court because of "separatist activities."[54]

In May 1993, the former HEP parliamentarians founded the Democracy Party (DEP). DEP has also concentrated its criticism on government policies that employ only a military resolution of the Kurdish issue, denying the real problem that has existed in Turkey for decades. Political steps must follow the recognition of the "Kurdish reality" by the coalition government. In contrast to other Turkish parties, the DEP views the PKK as a political organization, with which negotiations must take place for a peaceful and democratic solution. It is of the opinion that a political solution must include the PKK; otherwise it is unrealistic and will not yield results. The DEP also stresses that the state itself uses violence against its own population. A first step toward a political resolution would be the end of the special regulations for the Kurdish regions in southeast Turkey, a mutual rejection of the use of violence and a cease-fire. The Kurds represent an ethnic minority with a claim to minority rights, which the Turkish government committed to in the OSCE provisions. The granting of minority status would not lead to a division of Turkey; the Kurds would still desire to live together with the Turks in Turkey.[55]

Both the government and a significant portion of the press and media call the DEP an "extended arm of the PKK." The DEP faces a systematic campaign of intimidation by forces of state order and fundamentalist underground organizations.[56] Prior to the local elections on 27 March 1994, the situation culminated in a massive campaign against several DEP mayoral candidates in the southeast provinces.[57] A bomb attack on the party offices in Ankara on 18 February 1994 killed one person and injured twenty-two. In March 1994, the Turkish Parliament repealed the parliamentary immunity of six DEP parliamentarians who were accused of "separatist activities," an offense that carries the penalty of capital punishment in Turkey. On 25 February 1994, the DEP withdrew from the local elections, explaining that, out of fear because of increasing intimidation and the murder of several DEP politicians, it decided by majority vote not to participate in the elections.

The repeal of the DEP parliamentarians' immunity, which critics have also called "the civilian coup of 2 March 1994" goes along with the government campaign under Tansu Çiller to "remove the PKK from Parliament." Through the DEP's withdrawal from local elections, the government reached its aim of domestic policy, namely, to prevent the Kurdish electorate from casting their votes for the DEP.

On 16 June 1994, the DEP was banned by the Constitutional Court; the DEP parliamentarians' mandates were repealed. Shortly before the ban, six DEP representatives fled abroad, while the remaining two, Sedat Yurtdaş and Selim Sadak, were arrested and imprisoned a short time later. The Constitutional Court justified the party ban with the claim that the DEP developed "separatist activities and propaganda against the indivisible unity of the state's people and its territory." Initially, proceedings were instituted against the imprisoned members of Parliament on the grounds of Article 125 of the Turkish criminal code, which carries the death penalty. However, in early December 1994, because of fear of consequences that would affect the international reputation of Turkey, the eight members of Parliament (one independent and seven DEP representatives), were sentenced to imprisonment: Two representatives were to serve three and a half years, one received seven and a half years, and the remaining five were sentenced to fifteen years, on the grounds of Articles 168 and 169 of the criminal code, referring to support of and membership in the forbidden PKK. The two members of Parliament sentenced to three and a half years were released shortly afterward.[58] The DEP parliamentarians in exile have meanwhile founded the parliament in exile together with the PKK, which must be recognized as a partner in dialogue, not only by the Turkish government but on the international level as well. The

DEP representatives justify their participation in the parliament in exile by the fact that the Turkish government has rejected all peaceful means for the representation of Kurdish interests on both parliamentary and legal levels. The parliament in exile is both a result of and a reaction to this policy.

The exclusion of the DEP from Parliament and the sentencing of its parliamentarians clearly demonstrates the possibilities and limits of a representation of Kurdish interests within a political parliamentary framework. It becomes clear that politicians and Parliament are not ready to begin dialogue with the legitimate Kurdish representatives of the DEP; in fact, their insistence on excluding Kurdish representation of interests gains strength. The prime minister has celebrated as a personal success the ban of the DEP, the party that could have initiated a dialogue. At the same time, the exclusion of the Kurdish representatives from politics and Parliament has had a symbolic effect on their supporters: They feel shut out of political and social life. At the least, the "undecided masses" who are under the pressure of both the PKK and the Turkish security forces could now give preference to a decision in favor of the PKK. Thus, the PKK would be able to assert that Turkey does not accept the political representation of Kurdish interests, so that only armed conflict remains viable.

At this point, one must consider that the DEP ban and the sentencing of its parliamentarians occurred because of the free expression of opinion and not because of acts of violence by the DEP representatives. Moreover, they have been accused of maintaining contact with the PKK. This justification is essentially in contradiction to the freedom of speech and opinion, which, in the case of the people's legitimate representatives, is additionally protected by political immunity. Thus, parliamentary immunity loses its essential function.

The basic political line of counteracting representation of Kurdish interests in politics and Parliament is also displayed toward the pro-Kurdish Democracy Party of the People (HADEP), a successor to the DEP, founded in May 1994. Claims by the Turkish press that even the First Party Congress (26 June 1994) had degenerated into a PKK congress left a mark on the HADEP, the impact of which should not be underestimated.[59] At the congress, the leader of the party, Murat Bozlak, stressed the necessity to change the Constitution and the Anti-Terror Law, to revoke the state of emergency and military measures, and to grant a general amnesty. Meanwhile, Kurdish circles increasingly strive for the establishment of new parties. The aim is to find a legal platform for Kurdish politics and to strive for a peaceful resolution of the Kurdish issue. The spectrum of newly founded parties ranges from conservative-liberal (Serafettin Elçi) to supporters of the political line of the Socialist Party of Kurdistan (PSK) (Ibrahim Aksoy). The attempt to establish new parties coincides with, on the one hand, the intensive fight between the Turkish military and the PKK and, on the other hand, the coming together of the DEP and the PKK and the formation of the parliament in exile.

POSSIBILITIES FOR CONFLICT RESOLUTION AND EXTERNAL INFLUENCE

The Kurdish organizations demand the right to self-determination for the Kurdish people in their respective countries in accordance with the UN Charter (Articles 1 and 2). They define this right as a free decision for membership to a state and for the forms of such membership. In general, they demand primarily the granting of an autonomy status within the boundaries of the Turkish Republic, the forms of which could be various. Though the right to self-determination must be considered as *ius cogens*, its content and scope are completely controversial. It is still primarily viewed in connection with the process of decolonization that has occurred since World War II. The states where the Kurds live oppose this granting of the right to self-determination to the Kurds. On an international level, self-determination in the form of an independent Kurdish national state has not been accepted. This would disrupt the regional balance of political power in the Near and Middle East and endanger peace in the region.

The Kurdish organizations in Turkey understand the right to self-determination as autonomy (cultural and political). The PKK also insists on a right to self-determination, which it desires to be realized as federalism within the boundaries of Turkey. As the foundation of a national state in the region is considered to be unrealistic because of the various political interests and established balance of power, the Kurdish organizations concentrate their demands on the realization of autonomy (cultural and political) in the respective states without endangering the territorial integrity of these states.

Thus the understanding of Kurdish autonomy in Turkey comprises several forms: cultural autonomy, local self-administration, and federalism. As examples of the latter, the Kurds cite in particular Switzerland, the Federal Republic of Germany, Belgium, Spain, and the internationally unrecognized Kurdistan Regional Government-Iraq, with Cyprus being mentioned as well, where, in principle, the foundation of a bizonal and binational federation is foreseen although not yet realized. They strive for the formation of an autonomous region in the Kurdish districts in southeast Turkey, which has the largest population of Kurds. They maintain that regional parliament and government must possess decision-making authority over important aspects of state sovereignty. This particular solution stems from the conviction that the Kurdish issue is neither a problem of human rights nor an ethnic minority issue but rather a national issue. The key to a solution to the national Kurdish issue is a constitutional recognition of the existence of the Kurdish people within Turkey, with their own language and culture. Therefore, those concepts for a resolution based on federalist structures, which at the same time make co-existence possible within the same state, namely the Turkish state, are to be given preference.[60] Opponents of federalist options for a resolution justify their criticism by maintaining that Turkey has never had federalism in its tradition as a state. Neither the economic process of integration nor the process of formation of a nation have been completed, so that a federation at this stage of development would lead to a segregation of society. After all, one cannot maintain that a unitary state model is by necessity always authoritarian. Moreover, the war in the former Yugoslavia has shown that federalism does not always work. They assert that a federalist resolution is also complicated by the fact that the Kurdish population lives in wide distribution throughout Turkey.

Cultural autonomy and local self-administration are other forms of an autonomy status for the Kurds in Turkey, a view represented by the pro-Kurdish DEP. The DEP is also supported by some Turkish intellectuals, journalists, scientists, businessmen, and politicians of the SHP, ANAP, and the New Democracy Movement. This view is based primarily on human rights and the rights of minorities as laid down in international treaties that have been signed by Turkey. So far, the Turkish government has refused cultural autonomy and local self-administration for the Kurds; however, it supports the autonomy status of the Iraqi Kurds, since it desires not only to weaken Saddam Hussein but also to play a vanguard role in the region through influence on the Iraqi Kurds.

First steps toward a lasting resolution would be a combined policy toward the Kurds that includes (1) a demilitarization of the region (a repeal of the state of emergency, the withdrawal of the special military units, a stop to the deportation activities, and the provision of means for the resettlement of former residents); (2) a comprehensive and unhindered cultural autonomy (opportunity for free expression through the introduction of the Kurdish language in media and education, the right to establish Kurdish cultural associations, and the formation of departments of Kurdish studies at universities); (3) a comprehensive guarantee of democratic human and civil rights; and (4) a policy for regional development. These measures would affect neither the state integrity nor the national unity of Turkey. They would only legalize the Kurdish culture existing in parallel and would support its development without threatening the dominance of the Turkish culture in the public sphere. At the same time, these measures would not provide increased political autonomy for the Kurds—that is, no special political position in their areas of settlement.

It is only when the termination of the armed conflict, democratization, recognition of cultural plurality, and the granting of human and cultural rights is achieved by a process of dialogue between the Turkish government and the Kurds (including the PKK) that, in the second stage, alternatives to a unitary centralist state model could be discussed and a societal consensus on regional reorganization could be reached.

Possibilities for Influence within the Framework of International Organizations

The external possibilities for influence stemming from the framework of the provisions of various treaties and documents—which Turkey is subject to as a member state—gain additional importance because the internal situation in Turkey at this moment does not allow for a political resolution of the Kurdish issue. Therefore, the concerted action of international organizations becomes a significant option for influencing Turkey toward a more flexible stance in its policy toward the Kurds.

The system of protection of minorities within the United Nations, the OSCE, and the Council of Europe plays a role in the resolution of the Kurdish issue, since Turkey, as a member of these organizations, has committed itself to the realization and protection of a common system of values and actions. Turkey is considering the ratification of the UN Treaty on civil and political rights (19 December 1966, in effect since 1976), two provisions of which refer to rights that could be granted to a collective: Article 1 of the Treaty, which speaks of the right of peoples to self-determination; and Article 27, which contains a clause on the right of members of minority groups to religious, cultural, and linguistic freedoms.[61] Disagreement continues regarding the interpretation of Article 27, specifically, whether rights are granted to minority groups as a collective, or rather, to separate members of the minority groups individually. Turkey's reservations on the minority issue represent the classic Turkish view that legally there are no minorities outside the provisions of the Lausanne Treaty and that Article 27 of the UN Treaty is interpreted in this sense.

While the OSCE, as an instrument for the building of trust across blocs, had concerned itself primarily with issues of human rights and disarmament in Europe during the time of the cold war, today its role and composition has changed. Currently, it mainly serves the purpose of crisis resolution, maintenance of peace and conflict prevention, although the development of permanent OSCE institutions and structures is not yet completed. The principles of human rights in the Helsinki Human Rights Accord (1975) have been gradually expanded, as the human dimension—the strengthening and expansion of the system for the protection of minorities—was discussed at meetings of the Conference for Security and Cooperation in Europe (1989 in Paris, 1990 in Copenhagen, and 1991 in Moscow). The Copenhagen Resolution on the human dimension calls for the protection of minority rights and provides guarantees for members of minority groups against discrimination. The Paris Charter for a New Europe includes the right of national minorities to freely express and further develop their identity without discrimination.

In its program, the Turkish government refers explicitly to these rulings, on the basis of which it desires to handle the issues. Its statements and actions thus far, however, point to the fact that it has to a large extent succeeded in freeing itself from the binding power of these rulings. An important problem in this regard is that the OSCE resolutions are themselves ambivalent: on the one hand, they contain the political declaration to protect and support minorities in their existence and their interests while, on the other hand, they stress the limits for an external influence on matters of a sovereign state as understood by the principle of sovereignty and the right of every state to protect itself effectively against attacks on its integrity and sovereignty. Both factors are not easily compatible and in an extreme case can become contradictory to each other. Moreover, the effect of the various OSCE resolutions regarding minorities is significantly reduced by the fact that there is no internationally codified collective right for minorities, in contrast to the democratic and civil human rights relating to the individual. When Turkey is confronted with reproaches in this regard, it always justifies itself by pointing to the rights of states included in the very same document and accuses its critics of supporting anti-Turkey terrorist actions.

The Council of Europe, of which Turkey is a member, has a differentiated protection and monitoring mechanism in the area of human rights. The European Convention on Human Rights has been supplemented by the Convention on the Prevention of Torture, the additional sixth protocol on the abolition of the death penalty, and the agreement on an individual's right to privacy of information. The parliamentary meeting of the Council of Europe has taken the initiative to pay particular attention to the rights of minorities within the council's framework of the protection of human rights.

Within the OSCE, the Council of Europe, the UN and the European Union are the beginnings of a constructive influence in the direction of a clear yet cautious reorientation of the Turkish policy toward the Kurds. This could comprise two aspects: the application of consistent and permanent pressure with regard to the agreed-upon standards while, at the same time, condemning PKK's acts of violence. All measures should be used to support the pressure by practical and political means. Here one can point to the fact that Turkey, as party to the treaty, consistently offends the mutually agreed-upon political principles by its treatment of the Kurdish issue and human rights. One measure would be an intensive dispatch of fact-finding missions. Based on a combined policy that would consistently include monitoring mechanisms for the treaties' provisions, Turkey should be assisted in conforming its understanding of minorities to the European standards, both politically and legally; creating the conditions for an open discussion for a resolution of the Kurdish issue; granting the Kurds the possibility of legal and political representation of interests; and, in particular, not only recognizing the legitimate DEP representatives as partners in dialogue but also opening a political dialogue with the PKK. Here, one must explicitly state that a declaration of nonaggression and cease-fire is the prerequisite for a mutual military de-escalation. In this regard, the Kurdish parliament in exile could be considered as a partner in the negotiation process. Concurrently, the appropriate international bodies should be prepared to mediate between the parties in conflict. An intensification of this relationship on a transnational level, in particular with civilian organizations, individuals and those groups in Turkey that have a critical view of Turkish policies, is necessary so that the mediating function could secure societal backing.

NOTES

1. For a more detailed analysis see Christian Rumpf, "Minderheiten in der Türkei und die Frage nach ihrem rechtlichen Schutz," in *Zeitschrift für Türkeistudien*, Jg. 6., Heft 2 (1993), 173-209; Christian Rumpf, "Die Kurdenfrage in der Türkei, Bemerkungen zu neueren Entwicklungen mit einem Exkurs zur Kurdenfrage im internationalen Recht," in *Zeitschrift für Türkeistudien*, Jg. 5, Heft 2 (1992), 205-20.

2. See Peter A. Andrews, ed., *Ethnic Groups in Turkey* (Wiesbaden: 1989).

3. The preamble, Articles 2 and 66, of the Turkish constitution of 1982, see Christian Rumpf, "Die Verfassung der Republik Türkei," in *Beiträge zur Konfliktforschung* (Köln: 1983), 105-74.

4. See Bülent Tanör, "Gedanken zum türkischen Gesetz Nr. 3713 zur Bekämpfung des Terrors ("Antiterrorgesetz-ATG")," in *Zeitschrift für Türkeistudien*, Jg. 4, Heft 2 (1991), 153-74; Insan Hakları Derneği-Menschenrechtsverein, ed., *Terörle Mücadele Yasası ve Insan Hakları* (Istanbul: 1991), 7.

5. S.L. Meray, *Lozan Barış Konferansı, Tutanak ve Belgeler* (Ankara: 1973), ser. 1, vol. 1, 154.

6. For more information on the relationship between the military, politics and democracy in Turkey, see Metin Heper, "The State, the Military, and Democracy in Turkey," in *The Jerusalem Journal of International Relations*, vol. 9, no. 3 (1987), 52-64; Hikmet Özdemir, *Devlet Krizi, T.C. Cumhurbaskanlığı Seçimleri* (Istanbul: 1989), 55-77; Hikmet Özdemir: *Rejim ve Asker* (Istanbul: 1989), 70-90; Ümit Bozdağ, *Ordu-Siyaset Ilişkisi, Atatürk ve İnönü dönemleri* (Ankara: 1991), 175.

7. See Hikmet Özdemir, *Rejim ve Asker*, 107.

8. The constitional law regarding the internal service of the armed forces, which gives the army the task to "protect the Republic and to provide for its security," has thus far been used as a legitimization for all military interventions (1960, 1971, 1980).

9. As quoted in Mümtaz Soysal, *Anayasanın Anlamı* (Istanbul: 1986), 346.

10. See Hikmet Özdemir, *Rejim ve Asker*, 317-20; Ümit Bozdağ, *Ordu-Siyaset Ilişkisi*, 178.

11. For more information on the Kurdish uprisings during the years between 1925 and 1938, see *Genelkurmay belgelerinde Kürt isyanları* (Istanbul: 1992), vols. 2 and 3.

12. Even during the period of the formation of the state, Atatürk still spoke of the "nation of Turkey." Within the framework of a unitary state, he even foresaw an autonomy for the Kurdish region. In particular, see Uğur Mumcu, *Kürtlere Özerklik*, in *Milliyet*, 2 March 1992; *Ikibine Doğru*, no. 20 (26 Sept. 1987). 20-22; Mehmet Bayrak, *Kürtler ve Ulusal-Demokratik Mücadeleleri, Gizli Belgeler-Araştırmalar-Notlar* (Ankara: 1993); Mehmet Bayrak, *Açık-Gizli/Resmi-Gayriresmi Belgeleri* (Ankara: 1994).

13. For a detailed analysis of Turkish interests during the Gulf war (1991), see Gülistan Gürbey, "Die Türkei und der Nahe Osten-Die politische Interessenkonstellation der Türkei im Golfkrieg," in *Südosteuropa-Mitteilungen*, Jg. 31, Heft 3 (1991), 209-24; Heinz Kramer, *Die Türkei und der Golfkrieg* (Ebenhausen: 1991).

14. See Mehmet Ali Birand, *APO ve PKK* (Istanbul: 1992), 8th ed., 263. APO is the acronym for Abdullah Öcalan (the leader of the PKK) and means in the Kurdish language "the uncle on the father's side."

15. See Ferhad Ibrahim, "Die Kurdenpolitik der Türkei nach dem iranisch-irakischen Kreig," in Berliner Institut für Vergleichende Sozialforschung, ed., *Kurden im Exil: Ein Handbuch kurdischer Kultur, Politik und Wissenschaft* (Berlin: 1991), vol. 1; Michael M.

Gunter: "A *de facto* Kurdish state in nortern Iraq," *Orient*, vol. 34, no. 3 (1993), 387; Presse- und Informationsamt, ed., *Newspot* (Ankara: 4 Oct. 1990); Henri J. Barkey: "Turkey's Kurdish Dilemma," *Survival* (winter 1993-94), 51-70.

16. A discussion took place in the Turkish media regarding examples such as Spain and the ETA, as well as England and the IRA, and options for the Turkish Republic. See *Milliyet*, 13, 15 and 30 October 1993.

17. See Yavuz Gökmen, *Özal yaşasaydı* (Ankara: 1994), 106-9, 287-92; *Hürriyet*, 19 Dec. 1994; *Milliyet*, 19 Dec. 1994; *Özgür Ülke*, 24 Dec. 1994.

18. See the interview with former minister of the interior Ismet Sezgin, *Nokta*, 23 Feb. 1995, 10-11; interview with former foreign minister Mümtaz Soysal, *Focus*, 31 Oct. 1994, 350-52; Fikret Bila, "Demirel: 'Bölünme korkumuz var,'" *Milliyet* 17 July 1994; interview with Süleyman Demirel, *Sabah*, 17 Dec. 1993.

19. The provinces that have been under emergency decree since 1987 are Bingöl, Diyarbakır, Hakkari, Mardin, Siirt, Tunceli, Şırnak, Van, Bitlis, Batman.

20. *Turkish Probe*, 1 April 1994, 14-15; for more detail on the powers of the super governor, see Michael Gunter, *The Kurds in Turkey: A Political Dilemma* (Boulder: 1990), 83.

21. In November 1993, twelve Kurdish tribal leaders with enormous influence on approximately 1 million people in the region were invited to Ankara. Talks were conducted with them on the highest state level to substantiate their cooperation in fighting the PKK; the government demanded that during the upcoming local elections of March 1994 they either support the candidates of the large parties or nominate their own candidates. The tribal leaders once again confirmed their loyalty to the state and agreed to support in fighting the PKK. The 67,000 figure is the estimate of Amnesty International.

22. See, in particular, Amnesty International, *Turkey, A Policy of Denial* (London: 1995).

23. Meanwhile, more than thirty journalists, the majority from the pro-Kurdish daily *Özgür Gündem* (today *Özgür Politika*) were murdered. So far these murders have not been solved. In the beginning of December 1994, there was a bomb attack on the publishing offices of *Özgür Ülke* in Istanbul and Ankara, during which one person died and more than twenty were injured; see *Helsinki Watch Report on Human Rights in Turkey* (Feb. 1994).

24. Turkish prime minister Tansu Çiller stated on 4 November 1993 in the Holiday Inn Hotel in Istanbul: "Turkey has come face-to-face with an expanding terrorism which has turned into a militia movement. We know the names of the businessmen and artists from whom money is being extorted by the PKK. We will make them pay." (As quoted in *Turkish Probe*, 24 June 1994, 5.) Two months later, several Kurdish businessmen (seven at last count) were murdered or declared to have "disappeared." The corpses of the murdered, showing traces of severe torture, were found later in various sites. See *Aktüel*, no. 16, 22 June 1994.

25. See *Turkish Probe*, 1 April (1994), 13-14; *Özgür Gündem*, 19 Aug. 1992; 22 Nov. 1992; 3 Oct. 1992; 5 Oct. 1992; 1 Nov. 1992; 2 Nov. 1992; 12 Jan. 1993; *Cumhuriyet*, 4 May 1992; Mehmet Ali Birand, *APO ve PKK*, 280-82; *Aktüel*, Feb. 1992.

26. See Yalçın Doğan: "Kürt rönesancı," *Milliyet*, 27 Feb. 1992; interview with Prof. Doğu Ergil, *Milliyet*, 17 Feb. 1995. Both Ergil and Yalçın stress that a majority of the Kurdish population is against a fragmentation of the country, while it supports autonomy. This is also confirmed by the now-publicized results of a study on "The Southeast Problem," which Doğu Ergil carried out for the Turkish Union of Professional Associations and Stock Exchanges (TOBB). This so-called TOBB Report triggered a controversial discussion, especially in the media, the press and political and scientific circles. It is interesting that 75 percent of those surveyed (altogether 1,267 people in the cities of Diyarbakır, Batman,

Mardin, Adana, Mersin, and Antalya) spoke in favor of the granting of cultural and political rights and the rights to self-administration. This percentage is distributed in the following way: 42.5 percent support a federation, 13 percent an autonomy, and 19.4 percent other forms (the extension of cultural and political rights). A second important result is that 34.8 percent of those surveyed have relatives in the PKK. See *Milliyet*, 17 Aug. 1995.

27. At demonstrations occurring during burials of PKK victims, nationalistic and Islamist slogans predominate, directed against human rights and democratization but also against HEP and DEP. See *Milliyet*, 24 March 1992; *Hürriyet*, 24 March 1992; *Nokta*, 16 Feb. 1992.

28. See *Nokta*, 16 Feb. 1992; 23 Feb. 1992; 7 July 1993; *Aktüel*, no. 11, 17 Nov. 1993; *Özgür Ülke*, 24 Nov. 1994; 25 Nov. 1994; *Ikibin'e Doğru*, 7 Feb. 1993.

29. See *Hürriyet*, 5 Feb. 1995; *Milliyet*, 16 Dec. 1994.

30. For a more detailed study of the Turkish Association for Human Rights, see Heidi Wedel,"Vom Motor der Demokratisierung zum Opfer der eskalierenden Gewalt? Der Menschenrechtsverein in der Türkei," in Jörg Späth, ed., ". . . alles ändert sich die ganze Zeit." *Soziale Bewegung(en) in Nahen Osten* (Freiburg: 1994), 128-34.

31. See *Turkish Probe*, 1 April (1994), 14-15; 13 May (1994), 18; *Frankfurter Allgemeine Zeitung*, 1 July 1994; *IHD Şube ve Temsilciliklerinin Olağanüstü Hal Bölge Raporu*, 17-83.

32. See *Junge Welt*, 9 Feb. 1995.

33. For information on the views of MHP chairman Alparslan Türkeş, see *Aktüel*, no.15, 21 July 1993, 50-53; *Milliyet*, 12 Jan. 1995.

34. See Hidir Göktaş/Ruşen Çakır, *Vatan Millet Pragmatizm, Türk Sağında Ideoloji ve Politika* (Istanbul: 1991), 25-32; *Türkiye Sosyal Ekonomik Siyasal Araştırmalar Vakfı: Sosyal demokrasi açısından Kürt sorunu* (Istanbul: 1992); Mehmet Bedri Gültekin: *Ikibinlerin eşiğinde Kürt sorunu* (Istanbul: 1993); *Nokta*, 3 and 10 June 1990.

35. See *Milliyet*, 19 and 20 Jan. 1995; speech of Cem Boyner in Washington, D.C., 6 Nov. 1994.

36. See, in particular, Metin Sever/Cem Dizdar; *Cumhuriyet Tartışmaları* (Ankara: 1993); Murat Belge, "The Kurdish Question in Turkey Today. A Personal Assessment," in *Zeitschrift für Türkeistudien*, 5. Jg., Heft 2 (1992), 259-66.

37. For a study of the new social movements, see Heidi Wedel, "Ansätze einer Zivilgesellschaft in der Türkischen Republik—Träger der Demokratisierung oder neue Eliteorganisation?" in Ferhad Ibrahim/Heidi Wedel, eds., *Probleme der Zivilgesellschaft im Vorderen Orient* (Opladen: 1995), 113-14; Gülistan Gürbey, "Politische und rechtliche Hindernisse auf dem Wege der Herausbildung einer Zivilgesellschaft in der Türkei," ibid., 95-111.

38. See Karl W. Deutsch and W.J. Foltz, eds., *Nation-building* (New York: 1963).

39. For an analysis of the concepts of nationalism, nation, and ethnicity, see in particular Georg Elwert, *Nationalismus und Ethnizität* (Berlin: 1989).

40. See Martin van Bruinessen, "The Ethnic Identity of the Kurds," in Peter A. Andrews, *Ethnic Groups in Turkey*, 613-21; Martin van Bruinessen, "Ursprung und Entwicklung des Kurdischen Nationalismus in der Türkei," Berliner Institut für Vergleichende sozial furschung, eds.; *Kurden im Exil*, vol. 3 (1993), 18-22; Martin van Bruinessen, *Agha, Scheich und Staat, Politik und Gesellschaft Kurdistans* (Berlin: 1989), 51-3; Günter Behrendt, *Nationalismus in Kurdistan Vorgeschichte, Entstehungsbedingungen und erste Manifestationen bis 1925* (Hamburg: 1993).

41. See Lothar A. Heinrich, *Die kurdische Nationalbewegung in der Türkei* (Hamburg: 1989), 9-41; Ferhad Ibrahim, "Ethnischer Konflikt, soziale Marginalisierung und

Gewalt: Zum Befreiungskonzept der "Partiya Karkeren Kurdistan," in Thomas Scheffler, ed., *Ethnizität und Gewalt* (Hamburg: 1991), 81-87.

42. See *PKK: Der Weg der Revolution Kurdistans (Manifesto)* (Koln: 1978/86; *PKK, Programm* (Koln: 1978/84); Ismet G. Imset, *A Report on Separatist Violence in Turkey* (Ankara: 1992).

43. Abdullah Öcalan stated that the PKK does not murder civilians or members of civilian organizations but those that fight it under "civilian" guise. Furthermore, he claimed that it does not murder teachers; the murdered teachers were not true teachers but members of NAP/MHP units. See *Özgür Ülke*, 6 Nov. 1994.

44. See Mehmet Ali Birand, *APO ve PKK*, 276; Ömer Erzeren,"Von der Guerilla zur Intifada? Die türkische Arbeiterpartei Kurdistans PKK," in Bahmand Niruman, ed., *Die kurdische Arbeiterpartei Kurdistans, PKK* (Hamburg: 1992), 163-64; interview with former member of the Turkish secret service Prof. Mahir Kaynak, *Nokta*, 5 April 1992.

45. For information on the views of PKK leader Adullah Öcalan, see in particular Rafet Balli, *Kürt Dosyası* (Istanbul: 1992), 202-308; Nezih Tavlas, Semih Idiz, Aziz Utkan, Sema Emiroğlu, *APO'yla yüzyüze* (Ankara: 1992), 11-14, 21-5, 64, 71-73, 79-80; Doğu Perincek, *Abdullah Öcalan ile Görüşme* (Istanbul: 1990), 63-5; *Hürriyet*, 6 Dec. 1994; *Nokta*, 23 Feb. (1992): 12-13; *Nokta*, 4 Oct. (1993), 12-13 (interview with Kani Yılmaz, the ERNK European representative); *Milliyet*, 26-7 March 1992; (article by Yalcın Doğan on his interview with Öcalan); *Özgür Ülke*, 4 June 1994; (interview with Öcalan); *Özgür Ülke*, 30 Sept. 1994.

46. See Nezih Tavlas et al., 61-62; *Özgür Ülke*, 27 Nov. 1994; 4 Dec. 1994; *Hürriyet*, 29 Nov. 1994; *Özgür Politika*, 22 Oct. 1995.

47. Turkish columnist Yalcın Doğan declared after an interview with Öcalan and a visit to the southeast that the majority of the Kurdish population supports the PKK. He stated that the PKK has obviously made progress and has become a political organization there. The Kurdish movement has become so strong that it will continue to exist even without the PKK. An economic integration of the crisis regions through the giant South Anatolia Project (GAP) would not solve the problem; cultural rights have to be granted in parallel to it. See *Nokta*, 5 April (1992), 10-11.

48. See *Landesamt für Ausländerextremismus in Berlin*, vol. 1, no. 4 (1994), 16.

49. See *Kurdistan Report* (Bonn), no. 74, May-June 1995, 23.

50. See *Özgür Ülke*, 18, 21, 22, 24, 26, 27 Jan. 1995; *Millieyt*, 11 Jan. 1995; *Hürriyet*, 13 Jan. 1995; *Frankfurter Allgemeine*, 13 April 1995; *Frankfurter Rundschau*, 13 April 1995. The Kurdistan parliament in exile (KPE) has sixty-five members. The political wing of the PKK, the National Liberation Front of Kurdistan (ERNK), with twelve seats, is the strongest force. Second in strength is the banned DEP, with six parliamentarians. The parliament in exile expressly views itself as an approachable partner in the negotiation process. In its thirty-five-point program, it has determined its goals for the future, including, among others to get the Kurdish issue on the agenda of international bodies, to obtain observer status in these organizations, to intensify diplomatic and political relations, to convene a national congress and a national parliament on the soil of a free Kurdistan, and to fight for the recognition of an international status of Kurdistan. See *Kurdistan Parliament in Exile*, 12-16 April 1995 (The Hague, The Netherlands), 23-25.

51. See *Milliyet*, 24 Feb. 1992; Sahın Alpay: "PKK meselesi," *Milliyet*, 26 Jan. 1995; interview with Doğu Ergil, *Aktüel*, 28 Oct. 1993; 3 Nov. (1993), 65, 70.

52. For a detailed analysis see Kemal Burkay, "Türk Hukuk Sistemi ve Kürtler," in *Paris Kürt Enstitüsü: Uluslararası Paris Kürt Konferansı 14-15. Ekim 1989* (Istanbul:

1992), 142-47; Rafet Balli, *Kürt Dosyası*, 376f; *Hürriyet*, 2 Oct. 1994; *Milliyet*, 20 Feb. 1995; *Nokta*, 5 April (1992), 21.

53. See *Aktüel*, 26 Aug. 1993, 25-28.

54. See Sengül Kılıç, *Biz ve Onlar*, 11-113; *Milliyet*, 27 Feb. 1992; 14 April 1992; 14 Dec. 1993; *Nokta*, 2 Feb. 1992, 11; *Hürriyet*, 15 July 1993.

55. For information on the positions of the DEP, see interviews of the author with the deputy party chairman of the DEP, Remzi Kartal (Van) and the DEP-parliamentarian Sedat Yurtdaş (Diyarbakır) on 5 May 1994 in Ankara; letter by Leyla Zana in *Süddeutsche Zeitung*, 9 Dec. 1994; Interview with DEP chairman Hatip Dicle in *Milliyet*, 14 Feb. 1993; *Özgür Ülke*, 26 July 1994; *Milliyet*, 11 Dec. 1994; *Nokta*, 24 March 1991, 14; 1 March 1992, 18; *Sabah*, 14 Dec. 1993.

56. In September 1993, DEP parliamentarian Mehmet Sincar was murdered in the open streets of Batman while investigating "mysterious murders" there.

57. More than seventy DEP activists have been murdered. The murders have not yet been solved. In early February 1994, general secretary of the DEP Murat Bozlak was attacked and wounded in Ankara. Meanwhile, the wave of violence has spread to include lawyers who defend the DEP and its parliamentarians.

58. Sedat Yurtdaş and Ahmet Türk were released in October 1995.

59. See *Hürriyet*, 27 June 1994; *Milliyet*, 27 June 1994.

60. See *Kürt Halkının Hakları Bildirgesi*, in *Stockholm Kürt Konferansı*, 171-75; Ismet Cheriff Vanly, *Kurden im Exil*, vol. 1, part 3, 14-15.

61. See Heiner Bielefeldt, Volkmar Deile, Bernd Thomsen, eds., *Amnesty International: Menschenrechte vor der Jahrtausendwende* (Frankfurt: 1993), 85-87; Christian Rumpf, *Die Kurdenfrage in der Türkei*, 218-19; Stefan Oeter, "Minderheitenschutz in internationalen Abkommen," in Forschungsinstitut der Friedrich-Ebert-Stiftung, ed., *Minderheitenund Antidiskriminierungspolitik: Alternativen zur Integration?* (Bonn: 1994), 27-42.

2

TURKEY'S KURDISH PROBLEM: RECENT TRENDS

Aram Nigogosian

Turkey's Kurdish problem seemed isolated and under control for decades, but the ramifications of this bitter struggle in the post–cold war era have made it Turkey's most salient internal as well as external crisis. In this chapter I concentrate mainly on the internal dimension and analyze the evolving process of polarization resulting from this fierce struggle between forces of suppression and those of resistance and the clash of two antagonistic nationalisms. Critical policy choices made by both sides will be examined. Relevant areas of concern include economic, cultural and coercive factors, but the primary focus will be on the political arena. Significant goals enunciated by leaders on both sides will be evaluated to see what they have actually accomplished.

While for the moment both sides can claim to have scored a degree of success, neither side can claim to have secured its maximum objectives. The Turkish state has not been able to suppress effectively the Kurdish insurgency, in spite of allocations of a great deal of the nation's resources. The Kurdish nationalist movement has not merely sustained its resistance but has grown in strength. It has, however, been unable to establish a separate state or even to secure exclusive control over areas where it is active.

Specific factors shape the evolutionary path of this conflict in Turkey. Given recent trends, the resulting synthesis can only insure increasing suppression, resistance, polarization, alienation and violence. I examine significant obstacles to resolving Turkey's Kurdish problem but, given this deadly dynamic, also consider factors that can help reverse this process. I conclude by analyzing when and under what conditions such opportunities could be generated and under what conditions they may be exploited.

DYNAMICS OF THE CONFLICT

Since the Gulf war, the conflict between forces of the state attempting to suppress a widespread insurrection by a national liberation movement of Turkey's Kurds and the movement's attempt to resist and to force the state to recognize cultural and more troublesome ethnic-based political demands has turned more vicious. Not only has the intensity and scale of the violence on both sides increased, but, given the transnational nature of the problem, the struggle has been projected on to the international arena.

The Turkish state has been attempting to eradicate Kurdish uprisings since the establishment of the republic. It has often used a combination of policies, including military repression, forced assimilation and cooptation. Confining the conflict primarily to the southeast has been a mixed blessing. It has enabled the state to use its coercive capabilities more fully, but it has also enabled the countervailing forces of Kurdish nationalists to find sanctuary in these remote and rugged areas. Given the inaccessible nature of some of the terrain, even today's Turkish armed forces have difficulties locating and eradicating the insurgents.

This isolation began to break down with the establishment of multiparty politics in the post–World War II era. Competition for votes was the engine of penetration by the state. Communication networks began to link the southeast to the rest of Turkey as well as to the rest of the world. Possibilities of an alternative political order for the Kurdish inhabitants of southeast Turkey, led by the siren call for cultural rights, became the vehicle for group-based political demands. Suppression of such manifestations became increasingly difficult. The possibility of exiting the region and finding success in economic arenas—even in political life or the military—became possible, as long as manifestations of politicized Kurdishness were extinguished. While the effects of the communication revolution and international demonstration of it penetrated the region through TV and radio, providing the attraction of alternative lifestyles, the dislocation of the local economy as the direct result of the Gulf war slammed the door shut on hopes of economic improvements. This occurred at the very time that the Kurds of Turkey were witnessing the establishment of a quasi-state of Kurds in Iraq. Surely, Turkey's Kurds could also take a chance. It was in this pregnant moment that the Kurdistan Workers' Party (PKK) called for the Kurds of the region to gather under its banner and found a receptive audience. The mass demonstrations of resistance, the uprisings (*serhildans*) and the large-scale attacks on military posts at first surprised the state. But deployments of security forces numbering some four hundred thousand along with the introduction of air power seemed to curb the PKK's military capabilities. As is normal in counterinsurgency operations, the Turkish armed forces' inability to sort out those directly responsible for attacks against its forces, the over-utilization of brute force and the neglect of positive sanctions played right into the PKK's hands. For lack of alternatives, the PKK became the defender of Turkey's Kurds who were under massive assaults by Turkey's security forces. Its supporters and followers numbered in the millions and its militia grew from ragtag bands into battle-hardened units totaling thirty thousand. And if PKK leader Abdullah Öcalan's plans are fulfilled, the Popular Army for the

Liberation of Kurdistan (ARGK) will reach fifty to sixty thousand, as called for in the PKK's 5th Congress in 1995.[1]

How have these forces fared thus far? Their activities seem to have been checked in many areas in which they dominated a few years ago. Prudent and often innovative, the organization has limited its exposure by confining its military operations near places that offer sanctuary. Seizing the initiative, they can mount ambushes and retreat. But the large-scale destruction of Kurdish settlements accompanied by the evacuation of the population who provided the guerrilla units with intelligence, food and shelter have made their survival more difficult. Therefore operations are launched in the outer perimeters of traditional Kurdistan and even beyond, to places like Sıvas and Hatay, to thin Turkish deployments and lessen the pressure on their strongholds.[2]

As the number of military operations is reduced, the work of political organizations in the metropolitan regions of Turkey, with millions of displaced or migrant Kurds, progresses. More advances are being made in the international arena; the Kurdistan parliament in exile (KPE) is having meetings and Kurdish organizations are attempting to secure recognition from international agencies and Non-Governmental Organizations (NGOs). These developments are not uncommon for national liberation movements. After having secured a degree of military capability, such movements generally attempt to shift the focus to the negotiating table. Although the PKK's offers to negotiate have, as of yet, been rebuffed by Ankara, the fact that the head of German intelligence met with Öcalan[3] and that Ma`sud Barzani, the leader of the Kurdistan Democratic Party (KDP) in Iraqi Kurdistan, invited Öcalan to a meeting recently[4] has established that this organization, which has survived for seventeen years, cannot be ignored.

OUSTER FROM PARLIAMENT

In addition to the military dimension, the most important political action to capture the degree of alienation between a large portion of Turkey's Kurds and its government is the expulsion of Kurdish representatives from the National Assembly, the banning of the Kurdish-supported Democracy Party (DEP), and the arrest and imprisonment of eight parliamentarians in the spring and fall of 1994. The expulsion of the parliamentarians seems to have been triggered in part by Prime Minister Tansu Çiller's desire to play to the nationalist vote in forthcoming elections.[5] Democracy Party chair Hatip Dicle's characterization of five people, including military cadets, who were killed in an explosion at a train station, as appropriate targets in a war could not have come at a better time for the prime minister. In response, she stated, "The time has come to take care of the case of the PKK sheltering under the Parliament's roof. If behind the shield of immunity those who have the blood of babies in their hands are protected in Parliament this has nothing to do with democracy."[6] Pushed by then-chief of staff Doğan Güreş, the process of lifting the immunities of the most vociferous defenders of Kurdish claims—Selim Sadak, Hatip Dicle, Orhan Doğan, Sırrı Sakık, Leyla Zana, Ahmet Türk, and Mahmut Alınak—took place on 2 and 3 March 1994. On 3 August they were indicted on charges of treason/sedition under Article 125, punishable by death, on flimsy evidence and dubious testimony. They were tried on reduced non-capital charges (Article 168, 169) for belonging to or assisting an illegal armed group (the PKK) and sentenced to three and a half to fifteen years on 7 December. On 16 October 1995, Turkey's appeals court upheld the fifteen-year sentences of the most outspoken of the group and released two for retrial. Chief prosecutor Nusret Demiral was outraged and stated the defendants should have been executed. In June 1994 the Constitutional Court also suspended the mandate of thirteen members of the Democracy Party. Six of these fled to Brussels to meet up with former party chair Yaşar Kaya. Together they went on to establish the Kurdistan parliament in exile (KPE).

The KPE was established to give voice to inhabitants of Kurdistan. Dominated by parliamentarians of Kurdish origin expelled from the Turkish National Assembly, an attempt has been made to incorporate a cross section composed of politicians, writers, members of youth and religious organizations and minority groups, such as the Assyrians, the Yezidis, and the Alevis. The PKK and its adjunct organizations comprise the largest single block of the KPE's sixty-five members. The first meeting of the KPE took place in The Hague in April 1995, in spite of a great deal of pressure from the Turkish and U.S. governments that this body not be permitted to meet. Turkey withdrew its ambassador from The Netherlands in protest and stopped military purchases—temporarily, as it turned out—from the Dutch. In July the KPE's second and more discrete meeting took place in Vienna. But it was the KPE's third meeting in Moscow in November 1995 that raised serious concerns in Ankara as well as in Washington. Since the dissolution of the Soviet Union, Turkey has envisaged an important role for itself in Central Asia given its linguistic affinities and historical connections with that region. Europe and the United States encouraged this vision, hoping to exploit the enhanced presence of Turkey in Central Asia for their own geopolitic and geostrategic interests. Europe and the United States are interested particularly in the large oil and natural gas resources of Central Asia. Turkish aspirations, however, clashed with extensive Russian presence in the region. The fact that Russian government authorities allowed the KPE to meet in Moscow, even though the Yeltsin administration did not officially support the meeting, coupled with Russian claims that Turkish intelligence was actively supporting the Chechens in their war against Russia, seems to indicate that both sides have prepared the ground for carrying on proxy wars in each other's backyards, as Robert Olson argues in a subsequent chapter.

The KPE's success in receiving recognition from several European governments and setting up information centers in several European cities, as well as establishing close connections with a plethora of international organizations and other Non-Governmental Organizations (NGOs), have contributed to keeping

Turkey's Kurdish problem in the international limelight. Following the example of the PLO before it became a respected organization, the KPE attempts to place the plight of the Kurds, particularly the Kurds of Turkey, on the international agenda. Its various committees have been tasked to work on a array of judicial, educational, cultural, ethnic, religious and human rights issues that affect the Kurdish people. The KEP, at least in its public announcements, advocates a negotiated resolution to the Kurdish problem in Turkey. It offers a spectrum of solutions ranging from regional autonomy and binational federation to various schemes of political devolution. The most critical issues in these proffered solutions are the separation and delegation of powers and the equitable distribution of resources.[7]

The disenfranchisement and ouster of elected Kurdish parliamentarians is tantamount to the closure of the political process to a significant portion of Turkey's Kurds who elected them in overwhelming numbers. This sense of being ousted from legitimate political discourse has increased support for the forces of the Kurdish liberation movement in Turkey. It is no wonder that PKK is seen by a large number of Turkey's Kurds as the only effective organization left defending the interests as well as the honor of Turkey's Kurds. Attempts by others, including Kurdish as well as non-Kurdish politicians, to bring grievances of Turkey's Kurds to the National Assembly have secured little in the way of remedies.

Scorched Earth

In conjunction with efforts to curtail the actions of the most outspoken of Kurdish representatives in Parliament, the Turkish military took measures that further alienated Turkey's Kurds. In order to deny aid and shelter to the guerrilla forces of the PKK, large scale destruction and evacuation of villages and settlements began near the Syrian and Iraqi borders. In 1994 these measures were applied in Tunceli and its outlying neighboring provinces of Bingöl and even as far as Sıvas. More than half the villages and hamlets in Tunceli have been destroyed and the population has either fled or been forced out. The Netherlands Kurdish Society and the Human Rights Organization of Turkey have documented these atrocities.[8] The savagery even outraged members of the Turkish government. The minister of state for human rights, Azimet Köylüoğlu, commented that "in Tunceli, it is the state that is evacuating and burning villages. Acts of terrorism in other regions are done by the PKK. In Tunceli it is state terrorism." This was noted on 10 October 1994.[9] Today more than twenty-five hundred villages and settlements have been made uninhabitable and more than 2 million people have been forced out. Kamer Genç, Tunceli MP representative and formerly deputy chairman of the Parliament, claimed 70 to 80 percent of villagers in Tunceli had been driven out of their homes and pastures.[10] Algan Hacaloğlu, Köylüoğlu's replacement, after returning from a visit to Tunceli in August 1995, stated, "Tunceli looks like Bosnia or Palestine—people in their difficulties, in their hunger, are no different."[11] He also complained that the state was not providing assistance to those who needed it.[12]

The PKK has been able to channel into political as well as military arenas the raw anger generated by the state security forces' indiscriminate measures.

PKK's Agenda for the Near Future

Having examined the Turkish state's attempt to control the PKK-led insurgency, which has been transformed into a national liberation struggle, in the action-reaction scenario, can we predict in which direction the PKK will take the fight? Decisions taken by its 5th Congress in January 1995 may provide some answers.[13] There seems to be a strong call for centralized control. As it happens, all organizations that rapidly expand face communication and control problems. As usual for the PKK, there is sharp criticism of those tasked with implementing policies and pointing out serious shortcomings. The formulators of policy, on the other hand, continue to be beyond reproach. In the military arena, a decision to increase the size of ARGK to fifty to sixty thousand,[14] with its command structure being closely monitored by the central committee as well as by political officers down the chain of command, indicates possible inadequacies brought on by rapid expansion of forces. If these plans are implemented, the Turkish security forces will also have to increase their capabilities in order to be able to keep PKK forces in check. But it is in the political arena of the national liberation movement (ERNK) that one can discern changes. The call for respecting the Geneva Conventions on treatment of POWs and of civilian noncombatants is stipulated but often is breached.[15] The base of the organization has been expanded by appealing to all inhabitants of Kurdistan, from all ethnic groups and religious sects.[16] The ability of the PKK to organize groups that have traditionally experienced enmities and insecurities in their relations—which the state has exploited and continues to do so—is a significant accomplishment that has enabled the PKK to broaden its scope of operations, compelling security forces to be thinly stretched.

The establishment of a National Assembly, as well as a Temporary Revolutionary Government, is planned.[17] In addition, Iraqi Kurdistan is targeted for an unfriendly merger, if that is what it will take to unify Kurdistan.[18] This is the true meaning of the 2 August offensive. The decision to utilize a diplomatic offensive to secure recognition, acceptance and eventually legitimacy from NGOs, the United Nations, the European Union and the European Parliament as well as from the European Human Rights Commission for the ERNK, the Popular Liberation Front for Kurdistan, is specified. The PKK in particular would like ERNK recognized as a legitimate political entity. Even political cosmetics have not been neglected: Ever ready to adapt to changing circumstances, the hammer and sickle have been dropped from the flag, acknowledging the passing of the cold war.[19]

In addition to the military and political aspects of their organization, culture and education also get attention. Opening schools and the teaching of Kurdish language and culture will be implemented. MED TV, which is alleged not to be directly linked to the PKK, is broadcasting via satellite from Europe to all Kurds in the Middle East should go a long way to providing some of these functions.

PROSPECTS

At best, Turkey faces a precarious balance of forces, obtained at great human and material cost. More than 200,000 have died since 1985 and Turkey spent an estimated $8 billion fighting the war in 1995. The array of forces rallying around Prime Minister Çiller for the forthcoming elections will most likely press with even more vigor to eradicate the Kurdish nationalist movement led by the PKK. The PKK will in turn attempt to broaden its struggle, perhaps through the mediation of Alevi Kurds and/or by making alliances with the large and increasingly unhappy, both Kurdish and Turkish, Alevi population.[20] The formation of an alliance between disaffected Kurds and Alevis, mediated by Kurdish Alevis (of the estimated 20 million Alevis, an estimated 3 to 4 million are Kurdish), is a nightmare scenario for any government in Turkey. Numbering close to 20 million, Alevis believe in a more tolerant version of Islam than the mainstream Sunni orthodoxy that predominates in Turkey. Alevism is close to Twelver Shi`ism (such as exists in Iran) in much of its belief system, practices, rituals and traditions. The Alevis are known for emphasizing egalitarian treatment of women and condone drinking of alcohol, as well as dancing and music. These very practices have set them at odds with their Sunni neighbors from time to time. The Alevis heterodoxy makes them suspect by some Sunnis. During the early days of the republic, the Alevis were strong supporters of the declared secular state, especially before the multiparty period that commenced in 1950, because the state suppressed and tamed the dominant Sunni religious hierarchy.

In the 1990s, as more provinces, cities, towns and smaller governmental units coming under the administrative sway of the Welfare Party (WP), the Alevis have come under increasing pressures. On occasions their prayer houses (*cemevis*) have been threatened. Alevis of Kurdish origin, as mentioned above, perhaps amounting to 20 to 25 percent of all Alevis in Turkey, face double jeopardy: They are both non-orthodox and Kurdish. Increasing pressures on the Alevi communities exploded in riots in Istanbul, Ankara, Izmir and other cities in March 1995. Particularly fierce were clashes in Istanbul, where twenty Alevis were shot to death by the police and many others were wounded. Property damage was considerable, accompanied by looting and arson. Order was restored only after intervention by the Turkish army. It was no coincidence that some of the rioters were Alevi Kurds displaced after their villages and homes in southeast Turkey had been destroyed by the Turkish armed forces.

In order to counter the possibility of increased dissent among the Alevis, and especially the Kurds among them, the Turkish government has attempted to coopt or, at least, to divide the Alevi community by favoring the more moderate elements within the community. Ankara also purportedly offers financial incentives to those groups demonstrating allegiance to the government. The Alevi problem, like the Kurdish problem, is not confined to any one region. Recent clashes between Turkish armed forces in the provinces of Hatay, which is adjacent to the Syrian border, and a large Alevi population of Arab ethnic origin, as well as in Sıvas, may be harbingers of developments to come.

HOPEFUL SIGNS

In this overwhelmingly bleak landscape there are a few small rays of hope. There are those in Turkey, Kurd and Turk, who, at their own peril, put forth the possibility of a political resolution of Turkey's Kurdish question. Doğu Ergil's *The Southeast Report* (Güney Doğu Sorunu), and a study, *Report on Eastern Anatolia*, just issued by Sakıp Sabancı, one of the leading industrialists in Turkey, are efforts in this direction. The state security court dropped its investigation of Ergil's work as being inflammatory and separatist in December 1995, while Mr. Sabancı prudently edited out part of his report dealing with the political basis of Turkey's eastern problem. Article 8 of the Anti-Terror Law, which has recently been modified but not abolished, will keep a lid on open discussion and advocacy of political solutions such as devolution, more local autonomy, federation and other proposals.

While the Ergil work aroused a lot of controversy and criticism because of the scientific methodology it utilized in carrying out the survey as well as some taboos that it articulated concerning the unity of the state, a selective review of its findings is constructive. From a stratified sample from Diyabakır, Batman, (Kızıltepe and Nüseybin districts of) Mardin, as well as from Adana, Mersin and Antalya where, large numbers of Kurds have settled, 1,267 respondents were interviewed. Results would perhaps be more robust if Tunceli and Istanbul had been included. Ergil's work did, however, come up with some interesting statistics, whatever their provenance. The following are among its findings: 91 percent identified themselves as Kurds; 65 percent said they used Kurdish at home; 63 percent wanted Kurdish as the second state language; 35 percent admitted having someone close in the PKK; 77 percent did not think the Turkish army could suppress the PKK; 47 percent of those who responded—65 percent did not—supported PKK actions; 48 percent were appalled by the PKK's violence and intolerance; and a total of 88 percent called for new political structures for Turkey. Of those surveyed, 13 percent were for independence, 43 percent for federation, 19 percent for local self-government, and 13 percent for autonomy. It is remarkable that 35 percent of the respondents admitted to having someone close in the ranks of the PKK, especially given the fact that the Kurdish regions are under extremely tight security. Relations of known PKK members are routinely harassed, detained and tortured. Some disappear without a trace, while others turn up dead.

One of the most significant findings of Ergil's study, which, it must be remembered, was conducted under the aegis of the government, makes credible the claim that the PKK is not a handful of terrorists but a liberation movement with a wide popular base. Seventy-seven percent of the respondents stated that they did not think the Turkish army would be able to defeat the PKK. Such statements may be bravado and reflect an unrealistic appraisal of the state's military capabilities, but they do demonstrate a high degree of motivation and morale among the Kurds, which will make suppression, especially political suppression, of this movement difficult.

Eighty-eight percent of the respondents' unhappiness with the present status is also significant. While those calling for total independence from Turkey are few (13 percent), the call for new political arrangements is overwhelming. This suggests that to continue to avoid addressing a political formula to defuse Turkey's Kurdish problem will only make it worse. Finally, and not surprisingly, 77 percent of those who had migrated did not expect to be happy in their new situations, and 84 percent did not think they would ever live in peace.

These troublesome findings may change for the better if economic growth improves the average Kurd's life and if changes in government policy enable Turkey's Kurds to preserve and to propagate their culture and identities: To do less will make the resolution of this conflict even more difficult. It is not surprising that influential businessmen who appreciate the great expenses incurred in the state's attempts to crush the Kurdish nationalist movement by military means were the sponsors of Doğu Ergil's study. It may be a trial balloon and merely an attempt to ascertain what the Kurds want or what they would be satisfied with in order to make informed policy decisions. One result of better informed policy decisions could, of course, be continued, or even more, suppression. But even if the strong rebuff from the nationalists and the military dampen discussion of alternatives, this study does create an environment that at least suggests dialogue between the two parties. Whether it will amount to more remains to be seen.

ELECTION OUTCOMES

In the elections of 24 December 1995, the WP came in first with 21.4 percent of the vote and 158 representatives in the parliament. The MP won 19.7 percent of the vote but, because of the electoral system, obtained 132 seats. The TPP won 19.1 percent of the vote and 135 seats. The DLP captured 14.6 percent of the vote and 76 seats, and the RPP ended up with 10.7 percent of the votes and 48 seats.[21]

Seven other parties failed to secure the required national threshold of 10 percent and, thus, were awarded no seats. Of these, the most significant were the National Action Party (NAP), which received 8.2 percent, and the Kurdish-supported Peoples' Democracy Party (PDP), known as HADEP, that secured only 4.2 percent of the vote. HADEP had made significant gains in the heavily Kurdish populated areas of the southeast but failed to obtain the votes of millions of Kurds who had moved to cities in the west of Turkey. In rural areas, particularly in Mardin and Tunceli, security forces may have intimidated voters against voting for HADEP. In the cities, new migrants may not have been registered, but this in itself does not explain fully why HADEP did not do better in the cities in the west of Turkey.

Because HADEP did not receive sufficient votes to pass the national threshold, the WP scored impressive wins in some of the Kurdish-inhabited provinces. It won more than 50 percent of the parliamentary seats in Diyarbakır (50 percent); Bingöl (100 percent); Erzurum (75 percent); Van (50 percent); Ağrı (60 percent); Bitlis (50 percent); Elazığ (60 percent); Siirt (67 percent); Malatya (57 percent); Muş 50 percent); Mardin (50 percent); and Şanlıurfa (50 percent). In a five-way race, the results demonstrate an impressive achievement for the WP. Its strong showing in the 1995 election will provide the WP with an enhanced organizational base in future campaigns.

In contrast, HADEP, which staged the largest rallies and secured the support of 30 to 50 percent of voters in southeast provinces, did not do well with Kurdish voters outside of this region. The new migrants to western urban areas, assisted in their transition to urban life by WP's Tammany Hall-like apparatuses, may not have wanted to risk such support by voting for a party that championed Kurdish rights and defended Kurdish nationalist aspirations. Many urban centers had been under WP administration for a number of years. They had organized their constituents at the grass roots, down to the block level. HADEP decided to run only a few months before the elections were to take place. Nevertheless, it seems that their appeals based on Kurdish nationalism and in defense of Kurdish social and cultural rights could not compete with the WP's concrete assistance programs delivered along with Islamist discourse. Some of the Kurds in the west may also have made the calculation that the present administration, headed by Prime Minister Tansu Çiller, which is hostile to the Kurds, could only be brought down by a WP victory. This voting calculus may also have contributed to HADEP's poor showing.

It seems clear that a True Path Party (TTP)-Motherland Party (MP) coalition with a Democratic Left Party (DLP), a Republican Peoples' Party (RPP), or a TPP-National Action Party (NAP) coalition will result in continuing suppression and political impasse. A MP-WP coalition, if permitted by the military, may attempt a less confrontational approach to dealing with Turkey's Kurdish problem. If the threat to Turkey's secularism, raised by the WP's participation in government, is not sufficient, rapprochement with Turkey's alienated Kurds may precipitate a military intervention. The repeated reminders by chief of the general staff, General Hakkı Karadayı, that "Turkish Armed Forces are the guarantors of a democratic and secular republic,"[22] should not be taken lightly. President Demirel's statement that "Turkey is a unitary state. There is one state, one country, one flag and one language; this cannot be changed,"[23] may not be sufficiently reassuring to keep the military in their garrisons if such a coalition were to come to power.

Given the demographics of this unhappy population, which does not seem to be broken in spirit even under today's harsh conditions in Turkey, it is certainly possible that recruiters for the PKK will not have serious difficulties in making their quotas from this group. But as the scale of violence between state repression and Kurdish resistance escalates and the costs become even more burdensome, other brave souls may come forward. Certainly, weak coalition governments, to which Turkey seems destined in the foreseeable future, cannot realistically undertake the needed steps toward change. Unconditional support of Turkey's current policies by its closest allies also does not encourage the necessary political change. It seems most likely that even the recently announced limited constitutional changes would not have been implemented without external pressure. Both internal and external pressures may be useful, but Professor Ergil's point that "we have to find the means to integrate them [Kurds] in Turkey while there is still time,"[24] is critical.

NOTES

1. *PKK 5. Kongre Kararları,* "Decisions of 5th Congress of the PKK" (Koln: Ağrı Verlag, 1995). See also Eric Rouleau, "The Challenge to Turkey," *Foreign Affairs,* Nov. 1993, 10, where his estimate is sixty thousand PKK fighters.
2. Tammy Arbuckle, "Winter Campaign in Kurdistan," *International Defense Review* 28, no. 2 (1 Feb. 1995), 59.
3. *Reuters,* 25 Nov. 1995.
4. *Reuters,* 2 Dec. 1995.
5. *Reuters,* 22 Feb. 1995. The parliamentary elections were finally held on 24 December 1995. Also see Hamit Bozarslan's chapter in this book for more analysis of the election results insofar as the Kurdish nationalist movement is concerned.
6. *Reuters,* 22 Feb. 1995.
7. *Kurdish Parliament in Exile* (Brussels: 1995); interview with F. Başboğa of the KPE's executive council, 10 Dec. 1995, in Washington, D.C.
8. *Forced Evacuations and Destruction of Villages of Dersim (Tunceli) and Western Part of Bingöl, Turkish Kurdistan, September–November 1994* (Amsterdam: Netherlands Kurdistan Society), 11995; *Yakılan Köylerden Bir Kesit* (A Cross Section of Burned Villages) (Ankara: Human Rights Organization, May 1994); Aliza Marcus, "Turkish army targets Kurdish villages," Reuters World Service, 25 Nov. 1994.
9. *Cumhuriyet,* 10 Oct. 1994.
10. *Cumhuriyet,* 6 Aug. 1995.
11. *Cumhuriyet,* 13 Aug. 1995.
12. *Cumhuriyet,* 13 Aug. 1995.
13. See *PKK 5. Kongre Kararları.*
14. Ibid., 37.
15. Ibid., 78.
16. Ibid., 78-101.
17. Ibid., 133-35.

18. Ibid., 208-10; "Güneyde Devrim" (Revolution in the South), *Serwebun* 165 (Sept. 1995), 6-9.

19. Ferhat Çelik, "PKK Holds 5th Congress," *Kurdistan Report* 21 (May-June 1995), 19-20.

20. *MED TV,* 13 Dec. 1995, in BBC Summary of World Broadcasts, Central Europe, 17 Dec. 1995.

21. *Cumhuriyet,* 4 Jan. 1996.

22. *Cumhuriyet,* 29 Dec. 1995.

23. *Turkish Daily News,* 21 Jan. 1996.

24. InterPress Service, 14 Aug. 1995.

3

KURDISH INFIGHTING:
THE PKK-KDP CONFLICT

Michael Gunter

At first glance it might be expected that, given the oft-quoted maxim "The Kurds have no friends," the various Kurdish groups at least would be natural allies. A brief survey of the numerous and at times bitter divisions in Kurdish society, however, would quickly disabuse one of this notion.[1] Since 1994, for example, the two main Iraqi Kurdish parties, Mas`ud Barzani's Kurdistan Democratic Party (KDP)[2] and Jalal Talanbani's Patriotic Union of Kurdistan (PUK)[3] have been locked in an on-again, off-again struggle that has cost some three thousand lives while bringing chaos and ruin to much of their domain. In addition, of course, the divide-and-rule strategies of the neighboring states containing Kurdish populations have reinforced these differences.

On 26 August 1995, yet another dimension of this Kurdish divide erupted. With the tacit cooperation of Syria, Iran and the PUK, Abullah (Apo) Öcalan's Kurdistan Workers' Party (PKK)[4]—the most violent, radical and successful Kurdish movement to emerge in Turkey in many years—was able to mass up to twenty-five hundred fighters and suddenly attack some twenty KDP bases and offices in its Bahdiani homeland in northern Iraq. Sporadic but bitter fighting led to hundreds of deaths throughout the fall of 1995, until the PKK finally declared a provisional cease-fire early in December 1995. The purpose of this chapter is to analyze the checkered and often obscure relationship between these two Kurdish parties that has led to the present situation. In so doing, light will not only be thrown upon recent events in Iraqi Kurdistan but upon various other aspects of the Kurdish question in the Middle East.

EARLIER ALLIANCES

Ironically, the PKK and KDP were once former allies. In July 1983 the two signed an accord called "Principles of Solidarity" under which they each agreed upon a unified commitment against every kind of imperialism, with American imperialism at the top of the list, and a struggle against the plans and plots of imperialism in the region.[5] The two also committed themselves to "cooperating with other revolutionary forces in the region and the creation of new alliances."

Another provision of their protocol emphasized that the struggle "should depend on the force of the Kurdish people." Article 10 of the agreement states that neither party should interfere in the internal affairs of the other or commit actions that could damage the other. The eleventh and final article declares that if one of them makes a mistake in implementing their alliance and ignores a warning from the other, then the alliance could be terminated.

At first the accord worked well for both parties. PKK militants being trained in Syrian and Lebanese camps were slowly moved to northern Iraq, where new camps were established. PKK leaders apparently traveled mostly through Tehran and then to northern Iraq, while the foot soldiers moved from Syria as armed groups over the Turkish border near Silopi and Cizre. From there they traveled on foot over the Silopi-Şırnak-Uludere path into northern Iraq.

Soon the Lolan camp, located in the triangle of land where Turkey, Iran and Iraq meet, became the PKK's largest base in this newfound sanctuary. This camp also contained the PKK press and publications center, as well as the KDP's headquarters and clandestine radio stations. It was at this time in 1984 that Barzani and Öcalan actually met each other in Damascus for the first and apparently the only time.[6]

Relations between the two began to cool in 1985, however, because of the PKK's violence against women and children and even members of the KDP itself considered by the PKK as collaborators with Turkey. In May 1987, the KDP issued a warning to the PKK, as required under their accord of 1983. In this caveat, the KDP declared that "it is clear they [the PKK] have adopted an aggressive attitude towards the leadership of our party, towards its policies and the friends of our party."[7]

Barzani's KDP denounced what it called "terrorist operations within the country and abroad and their actions to liquidate human beings" and went on to observe that "the mentality behind such actions is against humanity and democracy and is not in line with the national liberation of Kurdistan." Turkish pressures also played a role in ending the PKK-KDP alliance, which was severed completely by the end of 1987.

A little more than a year later, the other major Kurdish party in Iraq, Talabani's PUK, signed a "Protocol of Understanding" with the PKK in Damascus[8] that called for strengthening Kurdish unity and for cooperation and joint action by Kurdish groups. Indeed, Talabani even threatened to give overt support to Öcalan if Turkey repeated its earlier military incursions into northern Iraq in search of PKK guerrillas hiding there.[9] Within a year, however, Öcalan declared the protocol with Talabani "null and void."[10]

TURKEY'S ROLE

In May 1988, shortly after the KDP and PKK formally ended their alliance, the KDP and PUK officially announced the creation of the Iraqi Kurdistan Front (IKF) between their two parties and at one time or another six other, smaller groups in Iraqi Kurdistan. As the results of the Gulf war in 1991 began to bring the Turks and Iraqi Kurds together,[11] the IKF declared on 7 October 1991 its intention to "combat the PKK."[12] Although the Turkish bombing of PKK camps in northern Iraq momentarily caused Barzani to consider rescinding this decision, the logic of the Turkish connection prevailed.

At regular intervals Turkey has renewed the mandate of the U.S.-supported Operation Provide Comfort (OPC), based in southeastern Turkey, to enforce the no-fly zone that protects the Iraqi Kurdish enclave from Saddam Hussein. Although by so doing Turkey was supporting the emergence of an embryonic Iraqi Kurdish state that was anathema to its interests, abandoning the OPC would simply lead it to regroup elsewhere and thus strip Ankara of any influence over the course of events. Begrudgingly, therefore, Turkey continued to play its new role as part-time protector of the Iraqi Kurds.

For their part, the Iraqi Kurds felt dependent on Turkey. Given the catch-22, double economic blockade imposed on them by both the United Nations and Saddam Hussein, the Habur (Ibrahim al-Khalil) border crossing point with Turkey just north of Zakho was the only legal entry point for commerce and customs revenues, which amounted to approximately $150,000 per day. Hoshyar Zebari, a foreign policy spokesman for the KDP, explained: "Turkey is our lifeline to the West and the whole world in our fight against Saddam Hussein. We are able to secure allied air protection and international aid through Turkey's cooperation. If Poised Hammer [OPC] is withdrawn, Saddam's units will again reign in this region and we will lose everything."[13]

For his part, Talabani concluded that "Turkey must be considered a country friendly to the [Iraqi] Kurds."[14] By the time he met with Turkish Prime Minister Süleyman Demirel in June 1992, the Turkish leader was referring to the PUK leader as "my dear brother Talabani,"[15] while Talabani declared that "the people in northern Iraq will never forget the help of the Turkish Government and people in their difficult days." Talabani even went so far as to suggest that the Iraqi Kurds might want to be annexed by Turkey. Given the PKK's longstanding struggle against Turkey, this pro-Turkish position of the Iraqi Kurds began to cause Öcalan increasing difficulties.

Talabani apparently made one last attempt to bring Öcalan around by arguing that the "PKK must respond positively to Turkish President Turgut Özal's statement [on Kurdish rights] by halting its armed activities and by looking for a dialogue with the Turkish government."[16] Late in November 1991, the PUK leader reported that the PKK had agreed to a four-month cease-fire so long as Turkey did not initiate any further hostilities: "Öcalan will not resort to armed activities until Nawroz [Nevroz-21 March]."[17]

The purported offer came after a month of direct contacts between the PKK and the Iraqi Kurds who were acting for the Turks. One of the PKK negotiators was even quoted as declaring: "The PKK no longer pursues a claim of independence and does not want any further bloodshed."[18] Öcalan himself went on to argue: "They say we are separatists and want to separate. This is nonsense! We have nine hundred years of togetherness with Turkey."[19] Calling Öcalan's offer into question, however, PKK representatives in Germany denied that the organization had agreed to a cease-fire and declared that attacks in the southeast of Turkey would continue.[20]

PKK-IRAQI KURDISH POLEMICS

In the middle of December 1991, Öcalan reportedly crossed into northern Iraq from his safehouse in Syria to meet Talabani at his headquarters. Their meeting took place amid reports that Talabani's military forces (*peshmergas*) had arrested seven members of the PKK Central Committee. Although no statement was issued by the two Kurdish leaders, presumably they failed to come to an agreement. Shortly afterward Öcalan sarcastically declared that Talabani had written him from Ankara to "lay down your arms unilaterally, accept a cease-fire, come to Ankara and sit at the table with obscure people, and be thankful and grateful for whatever you are given."[21]

Defiantly, Öcalan declared: "I am allergic to such letters," adding that "if they try to make us collaborate, we will react with more fervor than they could muster to defend that policy." Talabani was told "to forget about the 'new world order,' 'U.S. support,' and 'freedom to the Kurds,' slogans," and instead, "join the militarization and resistance effort" and "not act as a minor broker in dealing with the people." For Barzani, Öcalan had even worse remarks: "Barzani does the same job in a more pompous manner."[22] The KDP leader "had made very bad business dealings in Kurdish blood. His is the policy of a broker."

In February 1992, the IKF issued a warning to the PKK that "if it failed to cease activities against Turkey, it would be purged from the region."[23] Talabani declared that "his party does not approve of activities directed against Turkey by the terrorist organization active in southeastern Anatolia,"[24] while Barzani maintained that "the behavior of the . . . [PKK] has led to the ruin of the reputation of Kurds everywhere."[25] Barzani also denounced the PKK actions during Nawroz [Nevroz] in March 1992 as "savagery" and "terrorist."[26]

Öcalan called Barzani a "collaborator, . . . reactionary, feudal person and a primitive nationalist."[27] He accused both Barzani and Talabani of "trying to stab the PKK in the back by cooperating with Turkey and noted that the two leaders have signed their own death warrants."[28] The PKK leader added that "the first thing we must do is remove these leeches. . . . They espouse the views of the fascist Turks. These two leaders are now our enemies."

Öcalan went on to claim that he would challenge Barzani and Talabani both militarily and politically in northern Iraq and isolate them.[29] Indeed, earlier Öcalan had already questioned the very support Barzani and Talabani had among their followers: "These organizations and leadership, which have little support among the people, are . . . a narrowly based clique."[30] Now the PKK leader claimed that his party had "a sister organization"[31] in northern Iraq, the Kurdistan Liberation Party (PAK), which would be able to challenge Barzani and Talabani on their own grounds.

EARLIER FIGHTING

Finally, in the summer of 1992, these intra-Kurdish diatribes began to break out into actual hostilities following the killing of the Sindi tribal leader Sadik Omer (Sadık Ömer) in Zakho on 29 June.[32] Reportedly, Omer had abandoned the KDP after having supported it for the previous twenty-one years and had become associated with the PAK, the new pro-PKK organization mentioned above. The PKK claimed that the assassination of Omer had been carried out by Sadun Mutni, the local KDP chief in Dohuk. In apparent retaliation, the PKK then killed KDP "Commander Mehmet Shefik" and three of his comrades in a rocket ambush in Dohuk.

In response, the KDP launched large attacks on the Sindi tribe that resulted in civilians being taken hostage and others fleeing to the mountains. The KDP carried out further operations against the PKK's urban network in July, detaining "Tirej," a senior member of the PAK central committee, and blockading the PKK camps along the Turkish border.

On 24 July, the PKK responded by successfully placing an embargo on trade between Turkey and northern Iraq. This PKK-imposed ban threatened to cut the Iraqi Kurds' economic lifeline, as local drivers, in fear of the consequences, stopped taking supplies to northern Iraq. Soon a shortage of foodstuffs and medicine resulted, and prices doubled and tripled. The PKK asserted that it would lift the trade ban only if Barzani would remove his blockade of the PKK camps.

Barzani declared that the PKK was challenging the very sovereignty of the new Kurdistan Regional Government (KRG) that had been established that very summer in 1992. "Öcalan's men acted as if they were the authorities and started to control roads and collect taxes" and "threatened to expel the government and parliament from Irbil [the seat of the KRG]. They said they would hang all those 'who sold out the homeland.' They even threatened to expel us from Dahuk and al-Sulaymaniyah and started to form espionage, terrorism, and sabotage networks inside cities. It has unequivocally been proven that they are conspiring and planning to undermine the existing situation in Kurdistan and its experiment [the KRG]."[33] Talabani supported Barzani by charging that the PKK "intended to establish a revolutionary authority . . . a state to replace the [Iraqi Kurdistan Front."[34]

The KRG added that the PKK "has seized over 30 border villages and has prevented farmers from returning to their homes."[35] Furthermore, by making northern Iraq a base against Turkey, "the villages, from where they [the raids against Turkey] are staged, are bombed on the pretext that PKK forces and bases are located there." The KRG even charged that "the PKK is collaborating with Iraqi officials," adding that "the Iraqi, Iranian, and Syrian governments help the PKK against the Iraqi Kurdish movement . . . because they do not want our parliamentary and governmental experiment to be successful."[36]

To meet the perceived threat and retain Turkey's support, the Iraqi Kurds, on 4 October 1992, launched major assaults against the PKK at its main base in the Khwakurt region where northern Iraq meets Turkey and Iran and further to the west in the Zakho area across the Turkish border at Habur and Silopi. Since this was the very day that the Iraqi Kurds also declared a federated state, a proclamation which the Turks viewed unfavorably, the importance of retaining Turkey's trust was obvious as heavy fighting between the Iraqi Kurds and the PKK ensued. Some twelve days later the Turks entered the battle in force. By 28 October the fighting supposedly had forced the PKK to surrender to the PUK, a situation that gradually helped lead to a detente in their relations, while those between the PKK and KDP remained hostile.

Initially, however, the Turks claimed that "more than 2,000 Turkish PKK separatist guerrillas have been killed."[37] Indeed, several months later the Turkish Chief of Staff General Doğan Güreş still claimed that "Öcalan's legs have been broken" and that the PKK had "lost 4,000 to 5,000 men."[38] It gradually became clear, however, that the actual figure was probably no greater than three hundred.[39] Based on the tremendous escalation of the PKK guerrilla war against Turkey in June 1993, it became obvious that its supposed near destruction the previous October had been greatly exaggerated.

NEW DEVELOPMENTS

Many Turkish commentators began to accuse Talabani of having provided a new base and safehouse for the PKK in the Zaleh camp northeast of Sulaymaniya where some seventeen hundred PKK fighters had been forced into supposed internment after surrendering at the end of October 1992. Accordingly, the Turkish air force destroyed the camp in January 1994, but again it appeared that its occupants had largely melted away before the blow fell.

Further illustrating the emerging PKK-PUK detente, Talabani and Öcalan met in Syria during the second half of February 1993 to discuss a new ceasefire proposal between the PKK and Turkey. A month later, praising Talabani's good offices, Öcalan actually proclaimed one, but the death of Turkish President Turgut Özal on 17 April and the Turkish belief that Öcalan had been defeated the previous November (1992) eventually led to a renewal of the hostilities at the end of May 1993.

The outbreak of civil war between the KDP and PUK in May 1994 and the resulting anarchy created new opportunities for the PKK to establish bases in the Bahinani area of northern Iraq adjacent to the Turkish border. This area, of course, lay within Barzani's territory as Talabani's writ ran further to the south and east. Thus the reestablished PKK base only presented a threat to the KDP and indeed could be seen by the PUK as a second front against the KDP, which was now its enemy.

In March and again in July of 1995, Turkish troops once again crossed into Iraqi Kurdistan in attempts to destroy the PKK units camped there. The March incursion entailed some thirty-five thousand soldiers, the largest foreign expedition in the history of the Turkish republic. Although both the KDP and PUK officially opposed these Turkish actions, the KDP partially cooperated with the Turks since the PKK presence in Barzani's portion of Iraqi Kurdistan is what had called forth the Turkish incursions in the first place. Inevitably, therefore, the Turkish incursions furthered the ill will between the PKK and KDP.

PKK-KDP Hostilities

When the U.S.-brokered Drogheda (Dublin) talks in early August 1995 appeared to be leading to a settlement of the KDP-PUK fighting in Iraqi Kurdistan as well as security guarantees for Turkey in the form of the KDP policing the border, the PKK struck out at the KDP in an attempt to derail the truce that would constrain its freedom to maneuver along the Turkish border in northern Iraq. The PKK also sought to build on its "pilot regions" in Iraqi Kurdistan by establishing some type of government in exile or Kurdish federation. A detailed analysis of these events follows.

The PKK claimed that two leading members of the KDP politburo, Nechirvan Barzani and Sami Abdal Rahman, had called the PKK a "terrorist" organization over Turkish TV in early August 1995.[40] Cemil (Cuma) Bayık—often referred to as the number two person in the PKK hierarchy and the commander of its military wing, the People's Liberation Army of Kurdistan (ARGK)—personally visited Barzani in an attempt to have the KDP repudiate the accusation that the PKK was "terrorist." When Barzani refused, the PKK retaliated.

In its weekly paper *Welat*—published in the PUK-held Iraqi Kurdistan capital Irbil—the PKK explained that it was attacking the KDP because it refused to join the fight for a "greater Kurdistan" and added that Barzani's party had "to be wiped out because it was backing Turkey's bid to crush the PKK rebels."[41] Öcalan himself condemned as an "act of treason" the Drogheda agreement between the KDP and PUK aimed at preventing the PKK from launching cross border attacks from Iraqi Kurdistan against targets in Turkey.[42]

In a lengthy interview the PKK leader termed Barzani's peshmergas (fighters), "primitive nationalist forces"[43] who "have for 40 years slaughtered Kurdish patriotic forces for their own narrow tribal interests and in league with the Turkish intelligence services." Barzani's "collaborationist forces" were guilty of a "betrayal of the people of the north" [the Turkish Kurds] and had committed "an unforgivable crime" by developing "relations with Turkey" and putting "themselves under the command of its special forces." In reference to Turkey's village guard program of some sixty-seven thousand Turkish Kurdish supporters of Ankara, Öcalan also accused the KDP of having "played a key role in the development of the village guard system in Bohtan" [the area in Turkish Kurdistan south of Lake Van that extends to the Iraqi border] and of having "tried to set up a village guard party . . . to strangle our struggle."

The PKK leader maintained that these actions had "prevented many areas becoming liberated zones" and "killed many [PKK] patriots and our most respected fighters." By attacking the KDP now, the PKK "will play a significant role in putting an end to this" and "open the way for the people of south [Iraqi] Kurdistan to move towards a federation." He also added that "we do not expect the PUK to oppose these developments very much."

In another interview on MED TV—the pro-PKK TV channel that began broadcasting to Kurdistan from Britain in the spring of 1995—Öcalan further developed his theme on how "the notorious collaborationist policy of the KDP was the most basic internal reason why, during the past 40 years, the Kurdish national liberation movement failed to develop."[44] The PKK leader asserted that his conflict with the KDP "started in the 1970s" when "patriotic revolutionaries from Turkish Kurdistan went there—we can include the Faik Bucak incident of 1965[45] in that, too—and asked for support and solidarity." The KDP, however, "has considered the elimination of contemporary and patriotic policies and their leaders as one of its main missions."

Öcalan then explained that "of course, it was impossible for us to accept this because we wanted to take progressive steps." Not only did the KDP reject the PKK's position, but it also "wanted to implement Turkey's demands in northern Kurdistan as well. In 1985, Barzani asked us to stop. He said: "Your armed struggle is not timely." Öcalan further maintained that "recently the KDP wanted to implement against our forces in the south the policy it had implemented against patriots earlier. With difficulty, we managed to save our forces from this danger." Öcalan's reference was to the proposed KDP role in policing the Turkish-Iraqi border to prevent PKK infiltration into Turkey.

The Atrus refugee UN camp near Dohuk and the Turkish border in KDP-controlled territory also played a significant role in the outbreak of conflict between the PKK and KDP. In May 1994, at the same time that serious fighting broke out between the KDP and PUK, the PKK encouraged some twenty thousand Turkish Kurds to flee the strife raging in Turkey for sanctuary in northern

Iraq. Not only was this viewed as a propagandistic ploy against Turkish repression but also as a chance to establish shelter for PKK fighters amid the thousands of women and children protected by the UN. In the long run, moreover, these Kurdish refugees from Turkey could serve as the first step in establishing a Kurdish federation in northern Iraq under PKK control. Reports at the time indicated that Barzani was wary of the refugee influx, while Talabani favored it.[46]

Once fighting broke out between the PKK and KDP, Turkish Kurds took eight UN and other humanitarian workers in the Atrus camp hostage against possible attack from the KDP. Eventually, however, Barzani's *peshmerga*s managed to search the camp and supposedly uncovered some PKK fighters, arms and equipment. The KDP declared that "it is high treason to aim weapons at the legitimate Kurdish administration in the region, the KDP"[47] and that the PKK attacks "confirmed that Öcalan is the enemy of Kurds"[48] and constituted "terrorist and criminal behavior."[49]

Barzani himself claimed that, contrary to Öcalan's accusations of KDP betrayal in the past, "had it not been for the party's [KDP's] assistance, the PKK would not have managed to stand on its feet."[50] However, "no sooner had they [the PKK] sensed that they are once again standing on solid ground than they broke their promise and disavowed values." The "ungrateful PKK has forgotten all the support and assistance the party [KDP] offered them in 1980 when they fled Turkey following the military coup."

Turning to the present situation the KDP leader maintained that the Drogheda principles of August 1995 used by the PKK "as an excuse to justify their aggression" was "a peace agreement the Kurdish people and all their friends have welcomed." As to the specific PKK charges that the KDP was supporting Turkey, Barzani maintained that he had "not asked for any Turkish assistance despite the Turkish Government's offer. . . . We are committed to safeguarding only our people's security and not that of others." He added, however, that "we respect relations with all neighbors and we do not permit that their security be threatened from our territory."

While Turkey, implicitly at least, supported the KDP against their common PKK enemy, it seemed likely that both Iran and Syria were supporting the PKK because neither wanted to allow Turkish influence to expand in northern Iraq. What is more, neither Iran nor Syria wished to see the U.S.-brokered peace talks between the KDP and PUK succeed because this would extend U.S. influence in the region. Supporting the PKK would be a way to sabotage the U.S.-sponsored peace process. Finally, the PUK could not help but see the PKK-KDP struggle as in effect a second front against its KDP enemy.[51]

Although by late October 1995 the KDP was claiming that most of the Dohuk region and Khwakurt to the east had been cleared of the PKK[52] it was difficult to believe that Barzani's *peshmerga*s could have crushed in a few short months an organization that Turkey had been unable to in more than eleven years of warfare. A further reckoning between the two Kurdish enemies seemed likely.

Given this Byzantine background of implicit alliance politics as well as more than twenty years of intra-Kurdish rivalry between the different actors, the PKK-KDP fighting came as little surprise. It was difficult, however, to see how this latest round of hostilities had solved anything. The basic underlying problems remained. The cease-fire that was announced in early December 1995, therefore, seemed more likely a pause than any final denouement.

NOTES

1. On divisions in Kurdish society, Martin van Bruinessen, *Agha, Shaikh and State: The Social and Political Structures of Kurdistan* (London: 1992); Gerard Chaliand, ed., *People without a Country: The Kurds and Kurdistan* (London: 1980); Nader Entessar, *Kurdish Ethnonationalism* (Boulder: 1992); Amir Hassanpour, *Nationalism and Language in Kurdistan, 1918-1985* (San Francisco: 1992); Mehrdad R. Izady, *The Kurds: A Concise Handbook* (Washington: 1992); Philip G. Kreyenbroek and Stefan Sperl, eds., *The Kurds: A Contemporary Overview* (London: 1992); David McDowall, *A Modern History of the Kurds* (London: 1996); and Robert Olson, *The Emergence of Kurdish Nationalism and the Sheikh Said Rebellion, 1880-1925* (Austin: 1989).

2. The KDP was established on 16 August 1946 by the legendary Iraqi Kurdish leader Mulla Mustafa Barzani (1903-79). Currently led by his son Mas`ud Barzani (1946-), it has been described as rightist, conservative, feudal, tribal and nationalist and is associated with the Kurmanji-speaking area of northwestern Iraqi Kurdistan. For further analyses, see Edmund Ghareeb, *The Kurdish Question in Iraq* (Syracuse: 1981), 35-41; Michael M. Gunter, *The Kurds of Iraq: Tragedy and Hope* (New York: 1992), 17-24; Sa`ad Jawad, *Iraq and the Kurdish Question, 1958-1970* (London: 1981), 296-300, 315-20; and McDowall, *Modern History of the Kurds,* 343-47.

3. The KDP was established by Jalal Talabani (1933-) in Damascus on 1 June 1975 following the collapse of Mulla Mustafa Barzani's revolt against Baghdad the previous March. It has been described as leftist, socialist and progressive and is associated with the Sorani-speaking area of southeastern Iraqi Kurdistan. For further analyses, see Entessar, *Kurdish Ethnonationalism,* 78-80 and 130-33; and McDowall, *Modern History of the Kurds,* 342-47.

4. The PKK was formally established on 27 November 1978 by Abdullah (Apo) Öcalan (1948-). It has been characterized as Marxist and stridently nationalist. For further analyses, see Ismet G. Imset, *The PKK: A Report on Separatist Violence in Turkey (1973-1992)* (Ankara: 1992); and Ahmet Ersever, "Kurds, PKK and A. Öcalan" (a lengthy manuscript available over the Internet), 1992. The Turkish Chamber of Commerce and Commodity Exchange (TOBB), under the directorship of Doğu Ergil, published the "Southeast Report" in August 1995. Also see Michael M. Gunter, *The Kurds in Turkey: A Political Dilemma* (Boulder: 1990); Michael M. Gunter, *The Changing Kurdish Problem in Turkey* (London: 1994); Henri J. Barkey, "Turkey's Kurdish Dilemma," *Survival* 35 (winter 1993), 51-70; Hamit Bozarslan, "Political Aspects of the Kurdish Problem in Contemporary Turkey," in *The Kurds: A Contemporary Overview,* ed. Philip G. Kreyenbroek and Stefan

Sperl (London: 1992), 95-114; and Philip Robins, "The Overlord State: Turkish Policy and the Kurdish Issue," *International Affairs* 69 (Oct. 1993), 657-76.

5. This and the following data were taken from Ismet G. Imset, "PKK: Deception of Terror (Countering Stability in Turkey), Part II," *Briefing* (Ankara), 6 June 1988, 20.

6. "On Elections, PKK, Independence," *Milliyet*, 23 Feb. 1992; as cited in *Foreign Broadcast Information Service—Western Europe*, 26 Feb. 1992, 26. Hereafter cited as *FBIS-WEU*.

7. This and the following citation appear in Imset, "PKK: Deception of Terror."

8. "A Good-Will Gesture: But at What Cost?" *Briefing*, 12 Sept. 1988, 6.

9. "Will the PKK Be a Regional Issue?" *Briefing*, 14 March 1988, 11.

10. "Talabani's Meeting with PKK Leader Reported," *Hürriyet*, 22 Dec. 1991, 16; as cited in *FBIS-WEU*, 27 Dec. 1991, 12.

11. Turkey now sought to protect and, in effect, promote the Iraqi Kurds for a variety of reasons. If the Iraqi Kurds were dependent on Turkish goodwill, Turkey might be able to influence them from establishing their own state, which could conceivably have a dangerous demonstration effect on the Turkish Kurds. Additionally, an unfriendly Iraqi Kurdish state might begin aiding the PKK or even make territorial claims on Turkey's Kurdish region. On the other hand, by supporting the Iraqi Kurds Turkey might influence them to be pro-Turkish and thus help to solve its own Kurdish problem more readily. Furthermore, if Saddam Hussein were to crush the Kurds again, Turkey might have to face hordes of destabilizing Kurdish refugees once more. Finally, being looked upon as the protector of the Iraqi Kurds would win Turkey respect and support in the West, where Turkey sought eventual membership in the European Union.

12. "Formation of PKK-Affiliated Party Reported," *Cumhuriyet*, 1 Nov. 1991, 10; as cited in *FBIS-WEU*, 18 Dec. 1991, 55.

13. Cited in "Iraqi Kurds Reportedly to Bloc Terrorist Attacks," Ankara TRT Television Network in Turkish, 1600 GMT, 8 April 1992; as cited in *FBIS-WEU*, 9 April (1992), 43.

14. "Talabani Calls on PKK To End Armed Action," Ankara Anatolia in Turkish, 1415 GMT, 18 Oct. 1991; as cited in *FBIS-WEU*, 21 Oct. 1991, 58.

15. This and the following citation were taken from "Meets with Demirel," Ankara TRT Television Network in Turkish, 1600 GMT, 9 June 1992: as cited in *FBIS-WEU*, 11 June 1992, 42.

16. Cited in "Talabani Calls on PKK to End Armed Action."

17. "PKK Said to Suspend Armed Activity Until March," *Günaydın* (Istanbul), 28 Nov. 1991, 8; as cited in *FBIS-WEU*, 3 Dec. 1991, 50.

18. Ismet G. Imset, "PKK Promises No More Military Attacks," *Turkish Daily News* (henceforth *TDN*), 10 Dec. 1991, 1, 11; as cited in *FBIS-WEU*, 16 Dec. 1991, 42.

19. Ismet G. Imset, "Further on Interview," *TDN*, 28 Nov. 1991, 5; as cited in *FBIS-WEU*, 5 Dec. 1991, 40.

20. Ismet G. Imset, "Cease-Fire Announcement Causing PKK Confusion," *TDN*, 19 Dec. 1991, 1, 11; as cited in *FBIS-WEU*, 26 Dec. 1991, 25.

21. This and the following citations are taken from "PKK's Öcalan on Turkish, U.S., Syrian Policies," *2000 Ikibin'e Doğru* (Istanbul), 22 March 1992, 18-29; as cited in *FBIS-WEU*, 23 April 1992, 28.

22. This and following citation, ibid., 29.

23. Cited in "Talabani Comments on Ankara, Talks, PKK," *TDN*, 16 June 1992, 2; as cited in *FBIS-WEU*, 29 June 1992, 54.

24. "Talabani: Iraq Preparing for War Against Turkey," Ankara TRT Television Network in Turkey, 1600 GMT, 14 June 1992; as cited in *FBIS-WEU*, 15 June 1992, 39.

25. "DPK Political Bureau Criticizes PKK, Ankara," (Clandestine) Voice of the Iraqi People in Arabic, 1700 GMT, 25 March 1992; as cited in *Foreign Broadcast Information Service-Near East & South Asia*, 26 March 1992, 15. Hereafter cited as *FBIS-NES*.

26. "Barzani Arrives, Criticizes PKK Savagery," Ankara Radyoları Network in Turkey, 2000 GMT, 30 March 1992; as cited in *FBIS-WEU*, 31 March 1992, 27.

27. "PKK Denounces Barzani as Collaborator," *Hürriyet*, 24 Feb. 1992, 14; as cited in *FBIS-WEU*, 28 Feb. 1992, 44.

28. This and the following citation were taken from "Öcalan Said To Order Deaths of Barzani, Talabani," *Tercuman* (Istanbul), 24 Jan. 1992, 11; as cited in *FBIS-WEU*, 27 Jan. 1992, 43.

29. "Öcalan Interviewed on Foreign Support for PKK," *Milliyet*, 26 March 1992, 14; as cited in *FBIS-WEU*, 30 March 1992, 36.

30. Abdullah Öcalan, "The Outlook for Political Struggle and the Autonomy Talks in Southern Kurdistan," *Serxwebun* (Germany), July 1991, 1, 7-11; as cited in *FBIS-WEU* 29 Aug. 1991, 42.

31. "Öcalan Interviewed on Foreign Support for PKK."

32. The following analysis is largely based on Ismet G. Imset, "Analysis," *TDN*, 10 Aug. 1992, 1, 12; as cited in *FBIS-WEU*, 18 Aug. 1992, 40-42; and Ismet G. Imset, "Ankara Still Silent on PKK Blockade," *TDN*, 12 Aug. 1992, 1, 12; as cited in *FBIS-WEU*, 19 Aug. 1992, 27-28.

33. Cited in: "KDP's Barzani Interviewed on Federation, Plans," *Al-Akhbar*, 22 Nov. 1992, 4; as cited in *FBIS-NES*, 1 Dec. 1992, 26.

34. "Talabani Interviewed on Agreement with PKK," *Nokta* (Istanbul), 29 Nov. 1992, 10-21; as cited in *FBIS-NES*, 14 Dec. 1992, 21.

35. This and the following citation were taken from "Kurdistan Government Statement Criticizes PKK," (Clandestine) Voice of the People of Kurdistan in Arab, 1700 GMT, 5 Aug. 1992; as cited in *FBIS-NES*, 7 Aug. 1992, 20.

36. Cited in "Iraqi Kurdistan Prime Minister Interviewed," *Avanti* (Rome), 31 Oct. 1992, 16; as cited in *FBIS-NES*, 4 Nov. 1992, 21. Barzani similarly argued that the PKK was "supported by Iran, Iraq, and Syria, which are all against Kurdish independence." Cited in Jim Muir, "Iraqi Kurds Question Aims of Turkish Incursion into Iraq," *Christian Science Monitor*, 9 Nov. 1992, 4.

37. Cited in "Operation Kills 2,000 Guerrillas," Paris AFP in English, 1126 GMT, 4 Nov. 1992; as cited in *FBIS-WEU*, 4 Nov. 1992, 30. Also see Chris Hedges, " An Odd Alliance Subdues Turkey's Rebels," *New York Times*, 24 Nov. 1992, A1, A8.

38. Cited in "Sabah Reports Chief of General Staff Interview," *Sabah* (Istanbul), 7 April 1993, 16; as cited in *FBIS-WEU*, 13 April 1993, 41.

39. This scaled down figure was given to me by Hoshyar Zebari, a member of the KDP politburo with responsibility for foreign relations, when I spoke at length with him in Irbil, Iraqi Kurdistan on 17 August 1993. Nevertheless, Zebari still emphasized that there had been serious fighting the previous October.

40. Kani Xulam, representative of the American Kurdish Information Network (PKK affiliate), interview, Washington, D.C. 8 Dec. 1995.

41. "Kurds Accuse Iran, Syria of Backing PKK To Ruin Truce," Paris AFP in English, 2307 GMT, 2 Sept. 1995; as cited in *FBIS-NES*, 7 Sept. 1995, 46.

42. "Öcalan on Reasons Behind Weekend Attacks," Paris AFP in English, 0807 GMT, 29 Aug. 1995; as cited in *FBIS-NES*, 30 Aug. 1995, 51.

43. This and the following citations were taken from "A Political and Military Challenge: PKK Operation Against the KDP in South Kurdistan," *Kurdistan Report* (London/PKK affiliate) 22 (Sept./Oct. 1995): 25-7.

44. This and the following citations and data were taken from "MED TV Interviews PKK's Abdullah Öcalan," London MED TV Television in Turkish, 1630 GMT, 18 Sept. 1995; as cited in *FBIS-WEU*, 22 Sept. 1995, 37.

45. Bucak was a Turkish Kurdish lawyer from Urfa in Turkey who headed the Kurdish Democratic Party (KDP) of Turkey. Following his murder, the party split into two hostile groups which fled to Iraqi Kurdistan. There, under circumstances which remain obscure, both of the new leaders (Dr. Şivan [Sait Kırmızıtoprak] and Sait Elçi) were killed and their organizations eliminated. Some say that Mulla Mustafa Barzani executed one of them, while others say that it was the result of provocation by the Turkish intelligence service, the MIT (Milli İstıbarat Teşkilatı).

46. Uğur Şefkat, "PKK's Plan on Northern Iraq," *Sabah*, 15 May 1994, 25; as cited in *FBIS-WEU*, 1 June 1994, 67.

47. "KDP Appeals to PKK Fighters to Surrender," (Clandestine) Voice of Iraqi Kurdistan in Arabic, 1815 GMT, 3 Sept. 1995; as cited in *FBIS-NES*, 7 Sept. 1995, 43.

48. Cited in Bayram Baran *et al.*, "We Met Mas`ud Barzani at the Battle Front," *Zaman* (Istanbul), 1 Sept. 1995, 11; as cited in *FBIS-WEU*, 5 Sept. 1995, 30.

49. "KDP Radio Reports PKK Surprise Attack," (Clandestine) Voice of Iraqi Kurdistan in Arabic, 1810 GMT, 26 Aug. 1995; as cited in *FBIS-NES*, 29 Aug. 1995, 44.

50. This and the following citations were taken from "Kurdish Leader on Victories Over PKK," (Clandestine) Voice of Iraqi Kurdistan in Arabic, 1820 GMT, 22 Oct. 1995; as cited in *FBIS-NES*, 26 Oct. 1995, 44.

51. This author's thinking on these points was made clearer by an interview with Dr. Najmaldin O. Karim, the president of the Kurdish National Congress (KNC) of North America and a well-connected observer of the events, Washington, D.C., 9 Dec. 1995. The conclusion drawn here, of course, is solely that of the author.

52. Hoshyar Zebari (KDP spokesman), "Press Release," Salahuddin, Iraqi Kurdistan, 23 Oct. 1995.

Part 2

THE KURDISH NATIONALIST MOVEMENT AND ITS IMPACT ON TURKEY'S FOREIGN POLICY

4

UNDER THE GUN: TURKISH FOREIGN POLICY AND THE KURDISH QUESTION

Henri J. Barkey

For the past twelve years, the Turkish state has been grappling with a Kurdish insurrection that shows no sign of dissipating despite the enormous resources committed to its defeat by Ankara. While this rebellion is primarily domestic in origin, it is casting a long shadow on the formulation and conduct of Turkish foreign policy. This is not to say that all of Turkey's foreign policy priorities have become subservient to this issue or that other countries' perception of and behavior toward Ankara is determined by it. The prolongation and deepening of the Kurdish insurrection, however, could potentially bring about this result.

There are four principal reasons that account for the (re)emergence of the Kurdish question and its potential impact on Turkey's foreign relations. First and foremost, the continued rebellion in the southeast of the country represents an existential challenge to the state. It not only contradicts the ideology that has been dominant since the beginning of the republic regarding the existence of one harmonious nation, but a successful rebellion could also possibly force a change in the boundaries and/or organization of the state.

Second, because of the dispersion of traditional Kurdish territories among at least four states—Turkey, Iraq, Iran and Syria—the Kurdish question cannot always be contained within the territorial limits of one state. In addition to its appeal across Kurdish communities, the temptation for neighboring states to take advantage of the other's minority problem to score tactical or strategic gains is especially enhanced during periods of local unrest. Syria's support for the PKK falls into this category.

A third reason for the internationalization of Turkey's Kurdish problem is the emergence of an active Kurdish diaspora, especially in Europe. The politicization of a large and concentrated group of Kurdish activists has helped heighten the visibility of the issue and has also provided the various Kurdish political organizations in Turkey with financial and other forms of critical support.

Finally, the transformation of international political balances in the aftermath of the Soviet Union's demise have rekindled some of the long-dormant ethnic tensions around the globe. Turkey is not an exception. In the post–cold war environment, the reemergence of the Kurdish question has helped undermine Turkey's efforts at clearly defining its priorities. To be sure, the Kurdish question is not the only reason for the lack of coherence in Turkey's foreign policy. Turkey is not alone among mid-level powers whose firmly established cold war position has been undermined by the Gorbachev reforms. But, in the aftermath of a systemic transformation, the Kurdish question, with all its attendant implications for the unity of the Turkish state, has put Turkish foreign policy on the defensive. This chapter seeks to demonstrate the impact of the Kurdish question on the formulation and implementation of Turkish foreign policy.

About the Origins

Not unlike other ethnic conflicts, the Kurdish question in Turkey has deep roots and evokes strong passions on either side of the issue. The causes and evolution of the conflict itself, however, are beyond the scope of this chapter, as are Kurdish viewpoints. The making of Turkish foreign policy, by contrast, is clearly determined by the different views held by state authorities and populace at large.

The Kurdish question, while new to the Turkish population, especially those living in central and western parts of the country, is, nevertheless, an old one for the state. The present insurrection is not the first one. During the Turkish nationalist revolt against the foreign occupation of Anatolia that led to the inception of the republic and, soon after, to its independence, Kurds in Turkey rebelled. The most important of the rebellions, the Sheik Said rebellion of 1925, set the tone for future government reaction. It was decisively repressed, its leaders executed and many of their followers exiled. Other rebellions erupted periodically, with the 1930 Ağrı and 1937 Dersim revolts being the more notable ones, which were equally suppressed with much bloodshed. From 1937 onward, however, there were no other significant revolts. This absence of organized Kurdish violence did not represent an end to Kurdish political activity, which underwent a transformation of sorts as it subsumed itself into Turkish politics. But the absence of violence did not reduce state concerns as Kurdish activists were closely monitored and often hounded. Government authorities in Ankara, without openly articulating them, put into effect measures that were designed to curb potential Kurdish secessionary or other types of activities.

The primary objective of state policy became the assimilation of the Kurds into the larger Turkish ethnicity. The use of the word *Kurd* in the press and elsewhere was abandoned, as were any overt manifestations of Kurdish cultural expression. Kurds and Kurdishness were, in effect, officially transformed into non-entities. The policy of assimilation contained both a repressive and an inclusionary dimension. The latter consisted of opening the doors of the state to all those who accepted the dominant Turkish identity. This was applicable not just to Kurds but also other Muslim minorities that either hailed from abroad, such as the Bosnians or Circassians, or from Turkey itself, such as the Lazs of northeast Black Sea region.

Immediately with independence, the domestic Kurdish question made its impact felt on foreign policy. The Sheikh Said rebellion convinced Ankara not to pursue its claim over the oil-rich Mosul area that the British had decided would become part of modern Iraq. In fact, Turkish leaders were convinced that the Sheikh Said rebellion had been fomented by the British in an attempt to demonstrate the difficulties involved in ruling over a large Kurdish minority, to thus deter the Turks from pursuing their claim to Mosul. Soon after the conclusion of the Sheikh Said rebellion, relations with Iran deteriorated as a new set of Kurdish rebels frequently crossed the border from Iran to mount raids. In turn, Turkish hot pursuit operations angered Tehran. Ultimately, the two countries succeeded in managing the tensions by signing a series of agreements, including a 1932 treaty regulating the borders.

Although the abandonment of the claim to Mosul was significant, it is in the 1980s that the Kurdish question achieved an unprecedented preeminence in foreign policy formulation. The recent reemergence of the Kurdish issue in Turkey was the product of a confluence of two sets of developments, one domestic and the other international. Domestically it was the failure of the Turkish political left. This failure manifested itself in what the Kurds perceived as their coalition allies' disregard for their plight as well as the successful 1980 military coup that targeted the political left, both Turkish and Kurdish variants, in an attempt to eradicate it. The disappointment of the Kurds coincided first with the 1980-88 Iran-Iraq war and later with the 1991 Gulf war. The long-lasting struggle between Iraq and Iran resulted in a decline in the Iraqi state's authority over its northern provinces, where not only traditional Iraqi Kurdish groups, some with the help of Iran, began to roam freely but also Turkey's Kurds found the area a good location for basing and training themselves beyond the easy reach of their own state's military. The Gulf war and the ensuing Kurdish drama in Iraq, which had hundreds of thousands of Kurds fleeing Saddam's revenge in the aftermath of their ill-fated rebellion, focused the attention of the world, including Turkey—one of the two destinations for these refugees—on the unresolved nature of the Kurdish issue in the Middle East.

The PKK, the Kurdistan Workers' Party, which has emerged as the deadliest and most formidable of the Kurdish organizations, has its origins in the twin failure of the Turkish left and Saddam Hussein's wars against his neighbors. The organization found resonance and support among the Kurds of Turkey because it not only articulated long-held grievances of those Kurds who either had resisted or had been ignored by the state's assimilationist policies, but also because in offering strong military resistance to the Turkish state it succeeded in triggering a repressive counteraction by the state. In turn, the prowess of the PKK and the repression further politicized the region's peasantry. Not inconsequential in the early days of the PKK was the support it received from a Syrian government anxious to defeat or set back Turkish intentions regarding the mammoth Southeastern Anatolian Project, known as the GAP, that threatened to significantly reduce the flow of the Euphrates.

Internationalizing the Problem

The resurgence of the Kurdish question in Turkey has been a difficult one for the Turkish public to accept. Unaware of the depth of the Kurdish resentment, the large majority of Turks had taken for granted the state's official discourse on one homogeneous ethnicity residing in Turkey. In this discourse, Bosnians, Albanians, Circassians and many other non-Turkish minorities were added to the Turkish melting pot to be redefined. To the extent that it was cognizant of a Kurdish identity, the Kurds were viewed by the majority as recalcitrant, backward and, yet, "Turkish." At the origin of the confusion over ethnic identity lies the Atatürk's own, perhaps deliberate, confusion over this issue: At different moments Turkishness was based on citizenship, Islam or race. There is an irony, as one author has suggested, that the emergence of the PKK and its terror tactics in the 1980s did more to define Turkish identity than seventy years of republican policies aimed at the homogenization of the population.[1]

Primarily because the state's discourse had ignored the Kurds, their resurgence as a problem was attributed to the meddling of foreign elements. To the extent that the Syrians have actively nurtured the PKK, foreign interference has been extensive. It is not only the Syrians but the Iranians and, at times, Saddam Hussein who have flirted with the PKK, offering it support and sanctuary. Turks have also bitterly complained about their age-old nemesis, the Greeks, offering the PKK at the very least political support if not materiel as well. But the most puzzling of the accusations have been those directed at the United States and Turkey's other western allies. The tenacity of the PKK and the inability of the much-heralded Turkish army to defeat the "terrorists," despite its yearly promises to eradicate them, have allowed the construction of conspiracy theories that have captured the imagination of both the public and many of its elected politicians. Hardly a week goes by that a foreign western power is not accused of meddling in Turkish domestic affairs or inciting the Kurds to rebel in order to carve up Turkey.[2] Such discourse, which brands any criticism coming from abroad as a threat to the integrity of the state, has resulted in alienating the Turkish public from its allies and has hamstrung the foreign policy professionals in their dealings with them.

Turkey's Kurdish Policy

The state's response to the Kurdish insurrection has varied between denial and repression.[3] As the insurrection has gathered steam, so has the state's repressive apparatus. A series of institutional measures together with extra legal ones were put into effect. Not only was a state of emergency declared in the mostly Kurdish regions, but a system of village guards was invented that sought to take advantage of intra-Kurdish divisions by arming those pro-regime Kurds against the PKK and the Kurds of questionable loyalties. While these measures, combined with an increased deployment of the military and the gendarmerie, were aimed at defeating the PKK, they inadvertently provoked the local population and contributed to the swelling of the PKK's ranks. With the exception of the latter years of President Özal's rule, when alternative political strategies were considered, including overtures to Iraqi Kurdish leaders and even the opening of radio and television stations broadcasting in Kurdish, the state has pursued a primarily military formula.

With Özal's death (17 April 1993) the alternative strategies were abandoned as the regime in Ankara hardened its line. It banned pro-Kurdish political parties on the pretext that they were associated with the PKK. The same fate befell newspapers and publishers. Intellectuals found themselves in prison charged under the infamous law against terrorism that liberally construes most forms of speech on this issue as aiding and abetting terrorism. The state also stepped up its campaign of village destruction in the southeast with the aim of denying the PKK bases of support but in the process created a large refugee population that moved into the cities of the south and southeast, swelling their populations. Ankara also undertook a more aggressive policy with respect to northern Iraq, where it has always suspected the PKK of maintaining bases and preparing attacks; successive air raids were followed by large and small incursions into the area, often with the help of at least one of the two Iraqi Kurdish groups dominant in the region, the KDP or the PUK.

After the death of Özal, the state tried to equate all Kurdish aspirations with PKK activities; by harassing and persecuting non-PKK moderate Kurdish political organizations, associations and intellectuals, it increasingly sought to polarize the issues of ethnicity, language and civil rights. In so doing it has elevated the PKK and raised its profile. This is not accidental; by associating all Kurdish activities with the PKK it has aimed at delegitimizing all Kurdish aspirations in the eyes of both the domestic Turkish public and foreign audiences. In effect, it is far easier for Ankara to devise a PKK-focused policy than to forge links with those disaffected Kurds living in Turkey who have not expressed much sympathy for the PKK and its activities. The risk in Ankara's policy is that it will alienate increasing numbers of Turkish Kurds and drive them into the arms of the PKK. In view of the "existential" nature of the problem for Ankara, it is not surprising that it is willing to take such risks.

Turkey has been caught in the horns of a dilemma as far as the PKK is concerned. On the one hand, it perceives the organization as a dangerous enemy that has managed to inflict significant damage. On the other hand, it has come to believe its own propaganda about the PKK's lack of support and relatively small size. As a result the state has overestimated the military dimensions of the conflict while underestimating its political potential. This has allowed the PKK to cash in on its "military" success for political gains. In the long run, the more successful the PKK is politically, the less important its military campaign will be.

FOREIGN POLICY AND THE KURDS

What are Turkey's primary objectives in the a post—cold war environment?[4] The emergence of the Central Asian republics and Azerbaijan from Soviet rule created at first unrealistic expectations in the Turkish imagination. However, the realization quickly set in: These states would simply treat Turkey as a first among equals and not as a leader of a new political-economic bloc, hence the twenty-first century is unlikely to become the "Turkish Century." This has enabled Ankara to return to the basics of its foreign policy even though Central Asia remains a potentially important source of oil and gas as well as a market for Turkish industry. Ever since its accession to NATO, Turkey has followed a primarily pro-Western orientation. It needed the protection of the United States and its allies against the rising power of the Soviet Union. It is with the European Community that it has developed the most extensive economic relations, and the presence of close to two million hold-ers of Turkish passports in Germany alone further binds it to the West.

While Turkey's Islamic character has become more pronounced in recent years, the heyday of its economic ties with the Middle East appear to have passed. The extensive trade links forged in the early 1980s were the result of unusual cir-cumstances created by the Iran-Iraq war, and these relations, not surprisingly, have stabilized at a level commensurate with both the level of development of the region and the comparative advantages offered by Turkey.

The orientation of Turkish foreign policy increasingly exhibits the same level of confusion as its domestic approach to the question of identity. Those who primarily interpret Turkish identity as Islamic have pushed toward closer integra-tion with the Middle East, while the racialist view supports greater efforts in Central Asia and the Caucasus.

The dominant strain in Turkish foreign policy, which has advocated closer integration with the West, has suffered the most from the rise of Kurdish nation-alism in Turkey. As long as the Kurdish issue was under wraps, the dominant pro-West element's belief in principles of secularism and citizenship blended well with those of the West, despite the fact that the Turks have at times kept the West at arm's length and have generally been uneasy about the extent of their relation-ship with the United States. In fact, until the Özal years, Turkish foreign policy was, for the most part, unimaginative and averse to risk.[5] Still, as Ziya Öniş points out, there was a "remarkable degree of consensus" about the desirability of mem-bership in the European Community (EC) in 1987 when Turkey applied to join.[6] As Turkey prepares to enter into a customs union with the European Union, a step still far from full membership, it has reluctantly agreed under pressure to introduce reforms in its penal code that are designed to soften some of the restrictions on freedom of speech. These changes, as almost everyone accepts, are also specifically aimed at allowing Kurds to express themselves somewhat more freely.

As far as foreign policy is concerned, Ankara has extended its domestic practice of associating anything Kurdish with the PKK to this domain as well. While it has succeeded in equating the PKK with terrorism and other ills in the minds of U.S. citizens and most Europeans, it has also steadfastly refused to acknowledge the existence of moderate Kurdish groups. Ankara will be facing difficulty in the future because of the proliferation of such groups, which will emerge as a result of two developments. First, the PKK itself will spawn groups and associations such as the present Kurdistan parliament in exile (KPE) in order to put the Turkish government on the defensive. It will also engage in many more initiatives, such as the cease-fire announced on the eve of the 24 December 1995 national elections, designed to slowly build up momentum in its favor. Increasing diplomatic consciousness among Kurds will result in both the PKK feeling politically more confident and, therefore, more inclined to experiment with political options as well as non-PKK groups emerging to fill in the space between the PKK and the political center. One can even argue that the moderation of the PKK may result from the successful Turkish campaign to demonize it. Such developments will likely bring more attention and sympathy for the plight of the Kurds in Turkey and hence more criticism of Ankara's policies.

A closer examination of the four principal areas of Turkish foreign policy interest—its geopolitical role and standing, its economic relations, its regional role and standing and its relations with Central Asia and Azerbaijan allows us to assess the full impact of the Kurdish question.

GEOPOLITICAL ROLE AND STANDING

The most critical factor in Turkey's geopolitical standing is its relations with the United States, the predominant and only superpower. President Özal was the first to clearly chart a new course in Turkish-American relations when he aligned his country, despite intense domestic opposition to his actions, along the multinational coalition facing Saddam Hussein. Özal, just as in the Kurdish question, was more willing to pursue policy choices outside the conventional and, perhaps because he had resided in the United States, was less willing to demonize the United States and the West. However, with his death, Turkish foreign policy assumed its previous stance of close, yet "distant," friendship.

Despite the disappearance of the Soviet Union, U.S. policy toward Turkey has remained very supportive. Following the Gulf war it pushed Kuwait and Saudi Arabia to compensate Ankara for the losses it had incurred during the war as a result of the shutdown of the Iraqi oil pipeline traversing Turkish territory and the collapse of transit traffic in the southeast. The United States provided significant military supplies to Turkey for free as it ran down its European stocks (Greece was another beneficiary of this policy) and, perhaps most importantly, it successfully lobbied vigorously the European Union members to improve the conditions for Turkey's accession to a customs union. Recently, the United States has moved away from its pro-Russian policy and supported Turkish demands that Azeri oil (and later Kazakh oil as well) be transported not through the Russian Black Sea port of Novorossiysk but rather through the Anatolian mainland to the Mediterranean.

Paradoxically, the Kurdish question may have helped Turkey's relations with the United States in the short-run. On the PKK, U.S. policy has mimicked Turkey's: In branding the PKK a terrorist organization at every possible occasion, the United States has demonstrated its unwavering support for Turkey's basic position in this regard.[7] In the absence of the Kurdish insurrection, it is also unlikely that Ankara would have faced such difficulties in its attempt to join the European Customs Union and, therefore, the intensive and successful U.S. lobbying would have been unnecessary. The United States shares some of the credit in helping surmount these obstacles in the 13 December 1995 vote in the European Parliament, especially in view of the strong opposition to Turkey's human rights violations. However, despite the decidedly pro-Turkish positions of the recent U.S. administrations, the Kurdish question intrudes on the U.S.-Turkish dialogue in two areas: in regard to the policy toward Iraq, and northern Iraq in particular, and concerning human rights violations.

Ironically, it was the United States' sense of obligation to Özal's Gulf war stance that ultimately led to what is now called Operation Provide Comfort (OPC), a round-the-clock military protective shield for the Kurds of northern Iraq. The joint military task force—composed of U.S., British and French aircraft as well as a small contingent of ground troops, which includes Turks—was created so as to enable the hundreds of thousands of Kurdish refugees that had sought shelter along the Turkish and Iranian borders after the collapse of their rebellion at the end of the Gulf war to return to their homes. Subject to six-month renewals by the Turkish parliament, the OPC has become one of the more contentious issues in the bilateral relations with the United States.

Turkish uneasiness with the de facto autonomous entity in northern Iraq run by the Kurds is at the source of the resentment toward OPC. Primarily because the entity in northern Iraq is perceived to have acquired attributes that can potentially influence Kurds living in Turkey, the continued presence of OPC gets grudging approval from the Turkish establishment. In fact, many, including the former head of state and junta leader, Kenan Evren, political parties and journalists have openly advocated the removal of the force. The military itself has done little to bolster the fortunes of OPC, preferring to let the mission hang in the balance until the parliamentary vote. By contrast, the foreign ministry is cognizant of the negative repercussions the cancellation of the OPC would have on U.S.-Turkish relations, especially if it were to be followed by an Iraqi advance toward the north. The ministry also understands that the removal of the umbrella over northern Iraq would likely result in a significant refugee flow duplicating the conditions that gave rise to OPC in the first place.

The United States has been careful to continually reiterate its policy that it respects the territorial integrity of Iraq; with the exception of senior diplomats and others well acquainted with U.S. politics, this is a claim that convinces few in Turkey. The upsurge in fighting among the two Kurdish factions in northern Iraq has somewhat reduced Turkish anxieties since it demonstrates the inability of the Kurds to run their own affairs.[8] The United States has made sure that Turkey was directly involved in the negotiations it sponsored in Ireland in the fall of 1995 to reconcile the Iraqi Kurdish factions. But the complete breakdown of order in northern Iraq potentially helps the PKK, which can operate with a greater degree of freedom.

This fear of PKK support in northern Iraq also fuels Ankara's continued uneasiness with the autonomous region and, therefore, until recently it openly advocated a return to the status quo ante that prevailed before the Gulf war. In fact, Ankara has made its displeasure obvious at any arrangement that would secure a federal or even an autonomous region for the Kurds in a post-Saddam Iraq. Also claiming that the embargo on Iraq has disproportionately harmed citizens of the southeast, an argument used to explain away some support for the PKK, Ankara has demanded that it be eased. While Turkey has pulled back from an open disagreement with U.S. positions on Iraq, it is clear that it would not be opposed to Saddam's return to northern Iraq. The U. S. has sought to help Turkey recoup losses it incurred during the Gulf war by not only requesting aid from the Saudis but by agreeing to the one-time flushing of the Kirkuk-Yumurtalık pipeline, through which Iraq transported its oil to the Mediterranean and Turkey. The U.S. has also insisted that most of the oil Iraq is allowed to sell under UN Resolution 986 be shipped through the Turkish pipeline network.

Unlike some of the Europeans, the United States has been more tolerant of Turkish incursions into northern Iraq in pursuit of the PKK, including the large March/April 1995 one noted for its duration and the extent of the operation—thirty-five thousand men. While this U.S. support was appreciated in Ankara, the basic interests of the United States and Turkey in Iraq cannot be reconciled; for the United States, Saddam Hussein remains the primary threat to the region and its interests, whereas from Turkey's perspective the existence of the Kurdish entity poses a long-term threat too great to ignore. At the heart of this divergence lies two different interpretations of the Kurdish problem in Turkey.

However, as reflected in State Department reports on human rights violations, the U.S. has become alarmed at the repression applied to Kurds in Turkey. The Kurdish question was first mentioned in the department's 1988 report.[9] Since then, the reports have chronicled state actions in greater detail, all the while criticizing the PKK for its share of atrocities. Nevertheless, the State Department reports have become an important tool for those in Congress anxious to reduce the level of aid to Turkey or those opposed to Turkey because of the latter's invasion of Cyprus or those who dislike being associated with levels of repression unbecoming a U.S. ally and NATO member. Similarly, the nongovernmental groups concentrating on human rights have accelerated their criticism of Turkish policies. The beginning of the Arab-Israeli peace process and the dissolution of the Soviet Union have also allowed human rights activists to focus more on previously neglected questions such as the Kurdish one in Turkey. One of their more notable successes was achieved when they managed to block the sale of cluster bombs to Turkey.

Because the Kurdish issue evokes the worst fears among the Turkish public and leadership, the current U.S. administration has chosen to pursue a policy intended to bolster Turkey's confidence in the post—cold war environment with the hope that a Turkey that is more firmly footed in both NATO and the European Union, even if this is limited to a customs union, will be able to take steps to accommodate some of the Kurdish demands. The threat of destabilization that the prolongation of the Kurdish question poses for Turkey is particularly worrisome to the United States. With its diminished strategic importance, Turkey remains a valued ally and, perhaps more important, at a time when the Arab-Israeli conflict is finally on the verge of being resolved, the Unites States does not want the emergence of another long-standing ethnic conflict that could encompass other regional actors. Turkey's weakness does not bode well for NATO even if the primary enemy against which it was constituted has left the scene.

Can the United States indirectly create the conditions conducive for the Turkish leadership to engage in political reforms that are inclusive in character and, therefore, accommodate some of the moderate Kurdish demands? Despite the Unites States' efforts on Turkey's behalf, Turkish uneasiness remains strong; suspicions that the United States may be harboring a secret agenda are strengthened by the conflicting messages that emanate from Washington, especially during periods of intense legislature-executive squabbling. This attitude is best captured by a foreign policy watcher: "If we put aside the improvement in our relations with the U.S. since 1991 . . . Western European and U.S. policies have given rise to the isolation of Turkey in the international scene."[10] What is the source of this sense of isolation? In part it is not new; Turkey has always felt it did not receive its fair share of attention. On the other hand, Ankara has interpreted Western reactions to both the Armenian-Azeri and the Bosnian conflict as the abandonment of *its* own positions without cognizance of the inherent contradictions between those and its positions on other issues, such as the Kurdish or the question of ethnic Turks in Bulgaria or Greece. Surrounded by states that have troublesome relations with Turkey, Ankara has a demonstrated ability to exaggerate its own vulnerabilities.

Foreign Economic Relations

Turkey's most important economic relations are with the European Union.[11] By abandoning its inward-oriented economic policies in the early 1980s, Turkey has succeeded in not only diversifying its exports but also in becoming an important market for direct foreign investment. The U.S. Commerce Department has included it in its list of the ten Big Emerging Markets that warrant special attention because of their potential for expanding trade relations. Turkey's economic progress and its proximate location to Europe have given an added impetus to its primary trade links with Europe, which have blossomed.

At a time when trade blocs account for an increasing share of world trade, Turkey needs to firmly locate itself in one. This is the reason the achievement of a customs union agreement with Europe has been such a priority for recent Turkish governments—even though they would have preferred to become full members of the European Union. Yet it is in the realization of the customs union agreement that the Kurdish issue has made itself felt most acutely. The European Parliament made it clear that it would not sanction Turkey's accession to the Customs Union until certain basic modifications were made to the laws governing the criminalization of speech and constitutional provisions that represented roadblocks in the furthering of the democratization process. While some members of the European Parliament would have preferred to push Turkey to make more concessions, such as the release of jailed DEP (pro-Kurdish Democracy Party) parliamentarians, others were clearly satisfied with the constitutional changes, though minor, implemented earlier in 1995 and the modification of the infamous Article 8 of the penal code, which has been used to effectively prohibit any serious discussion of many controversial issues, but, in particular, the Kurdish one.[12]

However minor the European demands, they represented an obvious interference in the domestic affairs of a state and one with which many of the same countries have had extensive military relations. Still, given the importance of the Customs Union, Ankara was willing to pay the price to join. While there were parliamentarians and others who, in the name of greater democratization, advocated deeper changes in these provisions, the recalcitrance to alter them lasted until the very last moment. If Ankara delayed some of the changes until the last moment, it was for tactical reasons; the sooner these were implemented the greater the likelihood that the Europeans could demand further concessions. In either case, the discomfort with having to adhere to external pressures was made amply evident.

Progress toward becoming part of the Customs Union was almost derailed by the massive Turkish incursion into northern Iraq in March and April 1995. The scope and duration of the operation had to be reduced because of the intense criticism coming from Europe. In fact, Ankara waited until after the ministerial council of the European Union voted to give the go-ahead for the customs union before invading northern Iraq.

Will admission into the Customs Union increase or decrease the pressure Turkey will feel from the European Union member states with regard to democratization and the Kurdish issue? Although the Europeans no longer have the Customs Union as a carrot to dangle in front of Ankara, the fact remains that for Turkey this is an interim step: the ultimate goal is full membership. This very desire will render Ankara vulnerable to criticisms. More important, membership in the Customs Union, as a further step toward the Europeanization of Turkey, will inevitably mean that Europeans will feel freer to criticize Turkey for human rights violations.[13] Events on the ground will also help shape the nature of the European concern; continued harsh treatment of the Kurds will also encourage further European criticism. Already, Germany has been forced by domestic critics to suspend arms deliveries to Turkey. While these were eventually resumed, the suspension itself demonstrated the potential capabilities of domestic lobbies.

While Turkey was actively pushing for inclusion into the Customs Union, it did not shy away from confrontations with European Union member states over the Kurdish issue. Both Belgium and Holland were severely criticized for allowing the Kurdish parliament in exile to gather for meetings in their respective capitals. In the case of Holland, Turkey even placed the Hague on its "red list," meant, presumably, as a retaliation and a sign that arms purchases from that country would be reduced. Ankara has overreacted to the parliament in exile, which has subsequently met in Austria and most recently in Moscow. The great consternation with which these meetings are received in Ankara has obliged Turkish leaders to initiate political demarches that far exceed the severity of the political embarrassment that may be caused by these meetings of the parliament in exile.[14] Ironically, these demarches have served to attract far greater attention to the question.

This is reminiscent of the mid 1980s when Turkish foreign policy almost came to a standstill as a result of the campaign by Armenians, especially in the United States and France, to have the Armenian massacres of World War I officially commemorated. Then, U.S. "congressional supporters of Turkey [were] bewildered that security assistance seem[ed] less important to the Turkish government than the Armenian question."[15] The Kurdish question, admittedly, is far more threatening to Turkish state interests, but the single-minded manner in which it has come to dominate the calculations of its decision makers leaves little room for discussion between supporters of Turkey who are critical of its government's policies and the Turkish establishment.

The presence of a Kurdish diaspora abroad and, particularly, in Europe only serves to accentuate the problem because, once politically mobilized, these groups will help sustain the pressure on Ankara. Although there is a far larger number of Turks residing in Europe than there are Kurds, the latter have the advantage of being underdogs and mobilizing in support of a cause. In fact, the PKK has been far more successful in organizing the Kurds of Germany, who perhaps number five hundred thousand out of a total Turkish/Kurdish community that approaches 2 million, than it has the Kurds of Turkey. Despite the German government's ban on the organization, the PKK has staged large demonstrations, collects and extorts funds and recruits fighters. With the rise in intercommunal conflict, the Kurdish question increasingly becomes more of a domestic problem for the German government, which is powerless to resolve it. Therefore, in the long run, it is likely that the German government will seek to influence Ankara to adopt a more accommodationist stance at home. In the short run, to counter the spread of intercommunal violence, Bonn even dispatched a high-ranking intelligence advisor to Chancellor Kohl to meet with PKK leader Abdullah Öcalan in Syria.[16]

THE REGIONAL ROLE

Surrounded by states that are either hostile or potentially hostile to it, Turkey's foreign policy is perhaps destined to be distracted and incoherent. The elimination of cold war era inhibitions on state action and the proliferation of new actors has further complicated Ankara's task. In fact, Turkey has discovered that its Kurdish problem has benefited its neighbors with which it has had long-standing disputes by providing them with an opportunity to embarrass or even harass Ankara.[17] The most obvious example is Syria, which has actively supported the PKK and specifically given shelter to its leader, Abdullah Öcalan. For Greece, which has feared Turkey and has long sought to contain its military power and has been at odds with Ankara over the divided island of Cyprus, the Kurds represent a welcome source of Turkish weakness that can be readily exploited. Similarly, for Iran, which regards Turkey as a Muslim state in the service of its nemesis, the United States, the Kurdish insurrection not only distracts Ankara but makes it solicitous of Tehran's cooperation for border security.

Turkey has yet to discover that it is plagued by a delayed form of post-empire politics; it had hitherto been sheltered from the backlash to Ottoman rule in territories formerly controlled by the Ottomans. The changes engendered by the end of the cold war, however, have revived old antipathies and insecurities that target Turkey as the self-proclaimed successor to that empire. In addition, the Kurds, by virtue of their dispersal among the four states, have become a regional problem. The temptation for the different states to use their neighbors' Kurds in pursuit of their regional ambitions is matched only by the willingness with which the Kurds have accepted assistance from neighboring states as a means of eluding the limits imposed by state boundaries.[18]

In the long run, the impact of the Turkish-Syrian divide is far more damaging to Turkey's role in the region. In addition to harboring a long-held resentment over the loss of Alexandretta to Turkey in 1939, Syria has increasingly worried about Turkish attempts at developing the southeast through the GAP, the Southeastern Anatolia Project, which envisages the construction of dams and irrigation networks on both the Euphrates and Tigris. This project has already diminished the downstream flow of water and, in the future, will also impact its quality, as fertilizer use is augmented and some of the fertilizer-rich water seeps back into the river. Despite their long-standing differences, the issue of water is one that unites Syria and Iraq, since Iraq too is at risk given its dependence on both of these rivers. The water problem resonates elsewhere in the Arab world, where the issue has the potential of uniting a number of states behind Syria and Iraq. Egypt, for one, faces exactly the same dilemma with the river Nile. In early January 1996, the Turkish government reacted very negatively to the declaration issued in Damascus by seven Arab countries, including Egypt, calling on Turkey to provide Syria with a "just" share of the Euphrates water.[19]

Although Syria and Iran have cooperated with Turkey over northern Iraq, they are deeply mistrustful of Ankara's intentions,[20] as is Ankara of theirs. The resurgence of ethnic politics, the diminished importance attached to the inviolability of state boundaries and the precedent set by cases such as the former Yugoslavia are threatening to Middle Eastern states that have just witnessed the Iran-Iraq and Gulf wars, where territorial changes were clearly among the aims of the aggressor. Even though none of these states would like to see an independent Kurdish state established in northern Iraq, five years after the conclusion of the Gulf war, Saddam's resilience has perpetuated the status quo. With the emerging divisions among the Kurds of northern Iraq, Turkey has increasingly relied on Barzani's faction, the KDP, whose territory abuts the Turkish frontier, to contain PKK activities. The subtle shift in Turkey's post-Özal strategy, moving away from a refusal to cooperate with the Kurds of Iraq to a strategy of almost exclusive reliance on the KDP, may have initiated a new conflict of proxies in the region. The outburst of severe PKK-KDP fighting in northern Iraq in fall 1995 may be an attempt by the Syrians, who have a great deal of influence over the PKK, to check the growing influence of Turkey in the area. Similarly, Iran's decision to send a large number of armed Iraqi Shiites of the Badr brigade into northern Iraq to bolster the anti-KDP forces and even serve as a balance of sorts indicates the growing direct involvement of the neighboring states in the workings of the enclave.[21]

Syrian support for the PKK has brought numerous calls for a more activist policy toward Damascus from the Turkish press as well as parliamentarians, including members of the ruling party, the True Path Party (DYP) of Prime Minister Tansu Çiller. Two factors have acted as constraints: the fear of creating an anti-Turkish backlash in the Arab world and the impact such a course of action would have on the Syrian leg of the U.S.-sponsored Arab-Israeli peace process.[22] On the other hand, the peace process has allowed Turkey to effect a rapprochement with Israel; although this was long desired by Israel, it is Turkey that has the greater stake in this new relationship. Israel, in Ankara's eyes, can serve as a means of increasing pressure on Damascus and also curry favor with Washington. Similarly, as long as the peace process between Israel and Syria remains deadlocked, Israel can correspondingly make use of the same card. These tactics, however, are of limited use to either side, in part because Arabs are aware that even the talk on cooperation against terrorism articulated by both sides in their joint meetings carries different meanings since Turkish and Israeli views of Arab and Kurdish terrorism vary widely.[23] Also, in the context of a regionwide peace treaty, Israeli interests will significantly diverge from the alliances in the "periphery" that had characterized the thrust of its regional policy during most of its existence.[24] The Syrians may be playing a similar game by improving their relations with Greece. Turkey warned Damascus not to enter into an alliance with Greece and was reported not to have found convincing Syrian assurances that it would not give Greece any bases on its territory.[25]

The Turkish-Iraqi relationship deteriorated with the onset of the Gulf crisis as pipelines carrying Iraqi crude to the Mediterranean were ordered to shut down by Özal, who correctly anticipated UN Security Council resolutions. In fact, Özal may have accelerated a process of estrangement that began in the waning days of the Iran-Iraq war when Iraqis bitterly complained of Turkish trade and business practices and Turks of Iraqis's tendency to accumulate trade arrears. Iraqi concerns regarding the GAP project further accentuated the uneasiness as Baghdad refused to extend Ankara the cooperation that had allowed Turkish troops to cross into northern Iraq in hot pursuit operations against the PKK.[26] Recently, despite Turkish efforts to get the Iraqi Kurds to negotiate with the regime in Baghdad, the U.S.-sponsored intra-Kurdish negotiations in Ireland, in which the Turks participated as active observers, have unnerved the Iraqis.

Convinced of the effects of regional demonstration toward the Kurds, Turkey is faced with difficult choices with respect to Iraq: while its ardent wish is that the Iraqis regain complete control of their territory, the continued status quo increases doubts about the viability of a future Iraq.[27] Hence, Ankara's fears of the unknown are intensified. Driven by its concern to control the PKK, Ankara is being slowly drawn into the management of the enclave. Should there be a change in the regime in Baghdad, Turkey will find it difficult not to use its accumulated clout to influence the overall outcome in Iraq and perhaps antagonize not just Iraqis, Kurds and Arabs, but also other Arab states.

In other words, Turkey may find it very difficult to extricate itself from northern Iraq. Unable to determine events in northern Iraq, faced with increased pressure from domestic and foreign—regional and international—sources to alter its policy on the Kurds, Ankara may genuinely become isolated. Turkey fears two other possible scenarios in Iraq: the replacement of the Iraqi Ba'ath by a Syrian Ba'ath, or Baghdad's submission to Iranian influence given the majority Shiite population in that country. It is then that Turkey would be in need of European and U.S. support. In effect, Turkish foreign policy will have effected a full circle because of the Kurdish question. Having tried to go alone, it will have to seek support from those states that have in fact been its friends all along.

RELATIONS WITH CENTRAL ASIA AND AZERBAIJAN

The impact of the Kurdish question is only indirectly felt in Turkey's relations with Central Asian states. The Central Asians care little about the issue and are generally staunchly supportive of any Turkish government. In view of the presence of the significant and sometimes troublesome Russian minority in their midst, the leaders of Central Asia sympathize with the plight of Ankara; however, the Kurdish issue affects Ankara's relations with them in three distinct ways.

First, it represents a distraction for Turkish foreign policy makers, who have to expend a great deal of energy and resources on this issue: it is in the resulting significant opportunity costs that the impact of the Kurdish problem can best be observed, in the form of delays in the approval of or wrangling over membership in the customs union, resulting in inharmonious relations with its principal allies. The issue has also somewhat sullied Turkey's image as a model for these states.

Second, the continued insurrection in the east and southeastern provinces does cast a long shadow on the security and to a lesser extent on the feasibility of the pipeline projects envisaged by Turkey to bring in Azeri and Kazakh oil and Turkmen gas. An undefeated PKK could conceivably create severe problems for long-term maintenance of such pipelines, although it could not stop them altogether from operating and transporting the oil and gas.

Finally, and most important, the Kurdish insurrection provides the Russians, who have watched with great uneasiness Turkey's economic and political moves in Central Asia to supplant them, with a card to exploit. Moscow has been particularly angered by Turkish moves to obtain international support for the construction of Azeri and Kazakh pipelines bypassing Russian territory and emptying in the Turkish port of Dörtyol in the Mediterranean. Because of Turkish sensitivities over the Kurds, Moscow was successful in muting Ankara's criticisms over its attack on Grozny. In addition, periodic Russian actions, such as the organization of Kurdish conferences on its territory, serve as constant reminders of Moscow's potential reach.

Similarly, the Iranian regime, fearful of Turkish irredentist ambitions in Azerbaijan has used the PKK as a way of reminding Ankara of its own vulnerabilities. Iranian anxieties reached a peak with the ascendancy of Abulfaz Elçibey and his nationalist Popular Front in Baku. Elçibey, who did not hide his dream of unifying all Azeris, was enthusiastically backed by Ankara. His downfall, engineered in part by Moscow, account for the increased, but measured, Iranian cooperation with Ankara along the their common border.[28]

CONCLUSION

The internationalization of Turkey's Kurdish problem was the result of both accident and design. The changing international strategic balances and their ensuing impact on regional ones were beyond the control of Ankara, which had since the constitution of the republic tried very hard to contain its Kurdish problem. However, once the Kurdish insurrection gained momentum—with the initial help of foreign powers, notably Syria—Ankara found itself on the defensive. Forced to acknowledge the existence of an issue it had tried so hard to cover up but one that also presented a severe threat to its conceptualization of state structure and organization, the Ankara government decided to externalize the problem.

Turkey's importance to the West, in general, has not been diminished by the repercussions of the Kurdish problem. The Europeans' overwhelming vote

(343 for, 149 against, 36 abstentions) in favor of Customs Union membership on 13 December 1995 and the United States' general pro-Turkey attitude are indications of this. But the Kurdish problem is a dynamic one and has the potential of changing directions and affecting Turkey's foreign policy.

Refusing to accept any share of the responsibility for the insurrection, Ankara blamed external powers—friends and foes alike—for the emergence of the problem. The strategy to equate Kurdish demands with the PKK has worked domestically by solidifying Turkish, as opposed to Turkish and Kurdish, opinion behind itself. In the long run, this may backfire. Internationally, this strategy has produced even more limited results. While the PKK has been almost universally branded as a terrorist organization, the strategy of aggressively attacking the "Kurdish cause" is increasingly bearing the wrong results. It has created a quagmire in Ankara's negotiations with the European Union, creating the occasion for genuine foreign interference in Turkish domestic matters. As a result, the Kurds hae won a degree of legitimacy they previously did not enjoy. From Russia, Syria, Iran and Greece, who are ready and willing to use the issue against Ankara, to its friends in Europe and the United States, for whom the Kurds may increasingly appear as underdogs and therefore create a moral dilemma, the government's strategy has enabled all to become active in Turkish and Kurdish politics. In so doing, Ankara has transformed the Kurdish issue into Turkey's greatest vulnerability. In effect, the Ankara government is increasingly facing the possibility of being imprisoned in a cage of its own making.

Notes

1. Mümtaz'er Türkone, "Kürt Kimliği: Çözüm Nerede?" *Türkiye Günlüğü* 33, (March-April 1995):31.

2. A typical example of this attitude is conveyed by Ismet Sezgin who, in a March 1992 interview with the interior minister, simply stated that in the southeast, "the West is trying to achieve what it could not with Sèvres [the 1920 Sèvres Treaty]. The aim is to create a Marxist-Leninst autonomous Kurdish state." Reprinted in Ahmet Taner Kışlalı, *Atatürk'e Saldırmanın Dayanılmaz Hafifliği* (Ankara: Imge Kitabevi, 1994), 295.

3. For a detailed analysis of Turkish domestic policy, see Henri J. Barkey, "Turkey's Kurdish Dilemma," *Survival* 35, no. 4 (winter 1993-94); and Philip Robins, "The Overlord State: Turkish Policy and the Kurdish Issue," *International Affairs* 69, no. 4 (1993).

4. On post-cold war Turkish foreign policy, see Kemal Kirişci, "The End of the Cold War and Turkish (In) Security," Boğaziçi University Research Paper, ISS/POLS 94-1 (Istanbul: 1994).

5. This is not to say that there were not any disagreements with the West and, in particular, the United States. The Cyprus question is probably the single most important disagreement, which ultimately led to the U.S. embargo on the sale of arms to Turkey. For an analysis of U.S.-Turkish relations, see George Harris, *Troubled Alliance* (Washington: 1980); Henri J. Barkey, "An Alliance of Convenience: Turkish-American Relations in the Post-War Era," *Orient* 33, no. 3 (Sept. 1992).

6. Ziya Öniş, "Turkey in the Post-Cold War Era: In Search of Identity," *Middle East Journal* 49, no. 1 (winter 1995): 53.

7. The United States even promised to provide technical assistance to help "Turkey monitor its mountainous border with Iraq against infiltration by separatist Kurdish rebels." *Reuters*, 1 Nov. 1995.

8. On the other hand, the Kurds of northern Iraq have been subjected to a double embargo: one imposed by the UN on all of Iraq, and another by the regime in Baghdad. Hence, their ability to survive as long as they have can be viewed as a success in spite of the breakdown in communications between the two predominant factions led by strong-willed leaders.

9. Turan Yavuz, *ABD'nin Kürt Kardı* (The U.S.'s Kurdish Card) (Istanbul: 1993), 102-4.

10. Hasan Köni, "Yeni Uluslararası Düzende Türk-Amerikan Ilişkileri," (Turkish-U.S. Relations in the New International Order) *Yeni Türkiye* 1, no. 3 (March-April 1995): 432.

11. In 1993, 59.1 percent of Turkish exports were destined for OECD markets, whereas 67.9 percent of imports came from these same markets. Europe's share of total exports and imports for the same year were 47.5 and 44 percent, respectively. TÜSIAD, *The Turkish Economy* (Istanbul: 1994), 159, 161.

12. Even the modification of Article 8 does not amount to a significant qualitative change; jail sentences will be reduced, more monetary penalties will be assessed and judges will have greater latitude in sentences.

13. That membership in the customs union will increase European vigilance over Turkey's human rights performance is also echoed by European diplomats. See Ilnur Çevik, "Lobbying: Left-wing leaders in Britain and Germany are trying to convince their parliamentarians to vote favorably." *Turkish Daily News*, 15 Nov. 15, 1995.

14. Similarly, Turkish leaders were mobilized to block the possible selectioning of the jailed Kurdish member of parliament, Leyla Zana, as the 1995 recipient of the Nobel Peace prize. She did, however, win the European Parliament's Sakharov prize, causing embarassment to Turkish leaders.

15. Ellen Laipson, "U.S.-Turkey: Friendly Friction," *Journal of Defense Diplomacy* 3, no. 9 (Sept. 1985): 26.

16. The visit by the offical from the Office for the Protection of the Constitution came in the immediate aftermath of a similar visit bt a member of the German Parliament. *Reuters*, 25 Nov. 1995. Both of these visits have predictably infuriated the Ankara government.

17. See Robert Olson, "The Kurdish Question and Turkey's Foreign Policy, 1991-1995: From the Gulf War to the Incursion into Iraq," *Journal of South Asian and Middle Eastern Studies* 29, no. 1 (fall 1995): 1-30.

18. Hamit Bozarslan, "La régionalisation du problème kurde," in *La nouvelle dynamique au Moyen Orient: Les relations entre l'Orient Arabe et la Turquie* ed. Elisabeth Picard (Paris: L'Harmattan, 1993), 184.

19. They also accused Turkey of dirtying the same waters. *Hürriyet*, 2 Jan. 1996.

20. Some of the Arab concern was provoked by a comment made by President Demirel following the March/April military incursion into northern Iraq, when he was quoted as having called for border modifications between the two countries and reviving, at least in some Arab minds, the question of Mosul, which in 1926 Turkey conceded to England and indirectly to Iraqi sovereignty. See "Arabs alarmed by Demirel's call for redrawing the Iraq-Turkey border," *Mideast Mirror*, 4 May 1995, 14-19.

21. Arab unease about the Turkish role in northern Iraq was reflected in an unsigned editorial in the Saudi Arabia's pan-Arab daily *Ashraq al-Awsat*, which termed Ankara's cooperation with the KDP "occupation by proxy," *Mideast Mirror*, 23 May 1995, 20.

22. There was one unpublicized 1994 Turkish raid across the border into Kamishli in Syria against a PKK installation designed to warn the Syrians of Turkish impatience.

23. For an in-depth analysis of current Arab thinking on Turkey, see Mohammeed Nouredden, "Can Turkey Become Part of the 'New Middle East?'" from *al Hayat*, reproduced in the *Mideast Mirror*, 25 Aug. 1995, 8-13.

24. One arena of potential Israeli-Turkish cooperation is in trade and economic exchanges in general. Contrary to the Arab perceptions that Turkey represents a competitor for Israel and despite the relatively low level of bilateral trade, the two economies increasingly complement each other. In turn, Turkish-Israeli trade will flourish as relations between the two continue to expand.

25. *Cumhuriyet*, 9 Nov. 1995. Turkish Syrian relations took a turn for the worse following an incursion by a large PKK contigent from Syria and Syrian foreign minister Faruk al-Shaara's reported comments, which classified PKK activities as "resistance" and not terroristic. *Cumhuriyet*, 28 Nov. 1995.

26. Even before the end of the Iran-Iraq war, the Iraqis made their displeasure with Turkish air raids on the their territory known to visiting high-ranking Turkish officers. Necip Torumtay, *Orgeneral Torumtay'ın Anıları* (Istanbul: 1993), 86-87.

27. In 1984 the Turkish government objected to Iraq's plans to give the Kurds of northern Iraq any autonomy, and the Iraqis, who were not enthusiastic about the idea in the first place, may have used the Turkish pressure to tell the Iraqi Kurds that they had changed their mind on the issue. See Mehmet Ali Birand, *Apo ve PKK* (Istanbul: 1992), 130-32.

28. For an analysis of Turkish-Iranian relations, see Atila Eralp, "Facing the Iranian Challenge: Turkey's Relations with Iran after the Islamic Revolution," paper presented at The Reluctant Neighbor: Analyzing Turkey's Role in the Middle East, United States Institute of Peace, 1-2 June 1994, Washington; and Henri J. Barkey, "Iran and Turkey: Confrontation across an Ideological Divide," in Alvin Z. Rubinstein and Oles Smolansky, eds., *Regional Power Rivalries in the New Eurasia* (New York: M.E. Sharpe, 1995).

5

THE KURDISH QUESTION AND TURKEY'S FOREIGN POLICY TOWARD SYRIA, IRAN, RUSSIA AND IRAQ SINCE THE GULF WAR[1]

Robert Olson

This chapter addresses the Kurdish question and the Kurdish problem and the role that they play in the foreign policy of Turkey, especially in its relations with Iraq, Iran, Syria and Russia.[2] The Kurdish problem in this context refers to the challenge of Kurdish nationalism within Turkey itself. Four countries— Turkey, Iraq, Iran and Syria—have Kurdish problems, but the stress here is on Turkey's Kurdish problem. The Kurdish question refers generally to the interstate dynamics among these four states; but, as I argue in the course of this chapter, it has spread beyond these four countries since the Gulf war of 1991. In this article, Russia will be included as a player within the wider parameters of the Kurdish question. It is clear that, since the Gulf war, the Kurds and their political future have been high on the agenda of the world community. I argue in this chapter, however, that the saliency of the Kurdish question, in the sense of international support for some kind of Kurdish autonomous entity in northern Iraq, let alone an independent Kurdish state, has diminished during the past two years or so. The major reason for this diminution has been the challenge of the Kurdish nationalist movement, spearheaded by the PKK, a Kurdish nationalist guerrilla organization active in Turkey, which stepped up its military campaign against the Turkish government following the Gulf war. PKK is an acronym for *Partia Karkaren Kurdistan* or Kurdistan Workers' Party.[3] The PKK became the most potent expression of Kurdish nationalism in Turkey after it launched its guerrilla against the government in 1984. Its role grew exponentially after the Gulf war.

The Kurds are estimated to number some 20 to 25 million people, living largely in four Middle East countries: Turkey, which is estimated to have a population of 10 to 12 million; Iran, with 5 to 6 million; Iraq, with 3.5 million; and Syria, with 1 million. Some seventy to eighty thousand Kurds also live in Armenia and in Azerbaijan. Recent reports suggest that between three hundred thousand and 1 million Kurds live within the Russian Federation.[4] Since the bulk of Kurds live in contiguous areas of east and southeast Turkey, north and northeast Iraq, north and northwest Iran and in east and northeast Syria, they have possessed a sense of self, community and shared space since medieval times at least. This sense of identity was reinforced by the emergence of nationalist movements in the last two decades of the nineteenth century. The Kurds consider themselves to be direct descendants of the ancient Medes (although modern scholarship doubts this), who, because of military conquests, defeats and collapses of empires, began to migrate and locate themselves around two thousand years ago in the mountain fastnesses of the present states of Turkey, Iran, Iraq and Syria. From these strategic and almost impregnable locations, the Kurds were able to preserve their communities while at the same time participating in the great Armenian, Greek, Byzantine, Arab, Turkish, Iranian and Ottoman empires that dominated this region's history right up to the collapse and partition of the Ottoman empire at the end of World War I. The Kurds were promised the possibility of an independent state in articles 62 and 64 of the Treaty of Sèvres signed on 10 August 1920.

But there was to be no Kurdish state. The main reason for this was the emergence of a strong Turkish nationalist state in the aftermath of World War I and the subsequent suppression of Kurdish nationalist revolts in 1925, 1930 and 1937-38. There was not to be another Kurdish nationalist challenge to the Turkish state until the emergence of the PKK in the early 1980s. The Kurdish movement in Iran was also contained by a strong nationalist government in Iran during the interwar and post–World War II periods. The one exception was the brief one-year period in 1946, when the Kurds were able to establish a nationalist government in Mahabad before it fell to the vicissitudes of the emerging cold war. It was only with the commencement of the Islamic revolution in Iran in 1978 and the 1980s that the Kurds in Iran were once again able to press vigorously their demands for more cultural and political autonomy. The Iraqi Kurds' situation was substantially different from that of the Kurds in Turkey or Iran because Great Britain, which became the mandatory power in Iraq in 1920, supported, in varying degrees, Kurdish nationalist demands for cultural rights and local political administrative autonomy. The British never advocated or supported an independent state in Iraq during the period from 1920 to 1958 when they controlled the country: they supported Kurdish cultural and some limited political autonomy in Iraq mainly as a counterpoise to Arab nationalism and the government, largely Sunni and Arab, in Baghdad. Ever since the British were expelled from Iraq in 1958, the Kurds in the north of Iraq and the Iraqi government have been, intermittently, at war.[5]

It was only in the wake of the 1991 Gulf war that the Kurds in Iraq seemed to have gained an opportunity to establish an independent state or, at least, an autonomous entity federated with the rest of Iraq, as a result of the Allied policies, led by the United States and Europe, to topple Saddam Hussein from power. To achieve their goal the Allied forces supported a Kurdish insurrection against his regime. The defeat of the Kurdish insurrection by government forces and the subsequent flight of the Kurds to the mountainous regions bordering Iran and Turkey, especially the latter, created further support in the West for some kind of sanctuary for the Kurds in northern Iraq. Of course, the Kurds desired to make this "safe zone" as autonomous as possible. I will argue that the perceived intent of the Kurds to create an independent state in northern Iraq led Turkey to conclude a series of national security agreements between itself, Iran and Syria and also led to a brief rapprochement with Iraq starting in 1993.

TURKEY'S RELATIONS WITH SYRIA

On 19-20 November 1993, Major General Adnan Badr al-Hasan, Syrian interior ministry chief of security, just after Turkey and Syria signed a security protocol regarding the PKK and other "terrorists," stated in an interview that Syria would not be a thoroughfare for "those who are against Turkey's interest."[6] A few days later, Nasir Kaddur, Syrian state minister for security, in a television interview referring to the security protocol, stated that Syria had "begun to ban the PKK on President Hafiz al-Asad's orders." Kaddur added that PKK leader Abdullah Öcalan and other "terrorists" would not be allowed to use Syrian territory or pass through Syria for operations against Turkey. The security chief noted that some PKK members had already been arrested. He implied further that henceforth Öcalan would be unwelcome in Syria. Kaddur concluded his interview by saying, "Turkey's stability and integrity is important for Syria and the region. Therefore there is no room for any groups perpetrating terrorism and causing trouble for Turkey."[7] Turkish officials were undoubtedly delighted to hear the Syrian security chief characterize the PKK as a terrorist organization. This was the first time that a high-ranking Syrian official had done so and marked a significant departure in the foreign policy of Syria, which had supported the PKK since it commenced its guerrilla activities in 1984.

On 23 August, Syria participated on the foreign minister level in a summit conference held in Damascus with Iran and Turkey in which the Kurdish question figured prominently. The three foreign ministers, Ali Akbar Velayati of Iran, Faruk al-Shar'a of Syria and Mümtaz Soysal of Turkey, who was to become officially foreign minister on 27 August, expressed their unalterable opposition to the fragmentation of Iraq and vehemently opposed to the planned elections in 1995 in northern Iraq, which they declared would contribute to the fragmentation of that country. The ministers, especially Soysal, expressed their displeasure at not being invited to attend the Kurdish Conference held on 23 July in Paris, although officials from Great Britain, France and the United States did attend.

At the Damascus summit, al-Shar'a did not specifically denounce the PKK as a terrorist organization as Turkey demanded, but he did say that Syria was adamantly opposed to the fragmentation of Middle East countries, an apparent reference to the Kurdish nationalist challenge to Turkey as well as to Iraq. In his turn, Soysal announced at the summit that Turkey would soon place new restrictions, especially on representatives of nongovernmental organizations (NGOs), on entries into Iraq at the Habur/Khabur crossing, the main entry point between Turkey and Iraq, located at the town of Cizre (Jazirat Ibn ʾUmar) on the Turkish side of the border.[8] Some two weeks later the Turkish government did announce that it was closing the Habur crossing to representatives of human rights organizations and members of foreign parliaments. Only personnel connected to UN programs in northern Iraq and Turkish and Iraqi journalists would be allowed passage. A Turkish authority was quoted as saying:"Northern Iraq is our back yard. Of course, we will control who comes and goes."[9]

The August summit meeting in Damascus made clear the direct connection between the Kurdish question and the distribution of the Euphrates river waters. The Turks emphasized that they would not pursue earnest negotiations on the water question until Syria assured them that they would no longer support PKK activities or shelter Abdallah Öcalan. Until agreement was reached, Ankara stressed that it would be difficult to move forward on other problems such as the distribution of the Orontes River (*Asi* in Turkish and *al-ʾAsi* in Arabic), which flows through Syria before entering Turkey's Hatay province. The Turks want an agreement that will prohibit the Syrians from severely restricting the Orontes' flow before it enters Hatay. Ankara also indicated that it sought indemnification for property in Syria belonging to Turkish citizens, some cases of which go back prior to World War I. The Syrians are also interested in putting the question of the sovereignty of Hatay/Alexandretta on the agenda. Hatay was a province of Syria prior to being annexed by Turkey in 1939, with the support of the European powers, in return for Turkey's hoped for neutrality in the increasingly bitter conflict between Germany and its European neighbors. The Turkish foreign minister stated, however, that the two countries should try to solve the least intractable problems first. Some Turkish editorial writers declared that the August summit marked "a new era" in Turkish-Syrian relations. All three foreign ministers declared their unalterable opposition to the creation of an independent Kurdish state in northern Iraq. Prior to the Damascus summit and just after being appointed foreign minister, Soysal announced publicly that he believed that it was the West's intention to establish an independent state in northern Iraq.[10]

In late 1994 and early 1995 relations between Turkey and Syria took a brief upswing. On 5 December, Yalım Erez, president of Turkey's chamber of commerce and stock market and a close adviser of prime minister Tansu Çiller, led a one-hundred-person delegation to Damascus to engage in trade discussions. Syrian foreign minister Muhammad Imadi made it clear that Syria was interested in improving trade relations with Turkey, especially if Syria's $300 million trade deficit with Turkey could be reduced, and he suggested that one way to reduce the trade deficit would be for Turkey to import phosphates from Syria, which had an abundance for export, rather than from Tunisia. Erez indicated that Turkey would strive to reduce the trade deficit. Turkish press editorials were largely in favor of improved relations with Syria. Ankara was hopeful that, when signed, a peace agreement would open up greater trade opportunities for Turkish trade and business ventures, especially for its construction companies in Syria, Lebanon, the West Bank and Gaza. The Turkish delegation stated emphatically that their country wanted to participate in the reconstruction and development in the Arab region. Editors close to government circles stressed that better relations with Syria were a key to Turkey's participation in the "millions" that would be spent on reconstruction and development in the region and that if Ankara and Damascus did not improve their relations, the West would "eat all of the pasta (desert)."[11]

By February 1995, despite differences over the issue of Damascus' continued support for the PKK and the agreement that greater trade was desirable, the amount of water released by Turkey from its upriver dams on the Euphrates remained a bitter issue between the two capitals. In early February 1995, however, Prime Minister Çiller announced that Turkey was ready to sign a "water protocol" with Syria guaranteeing a flow of at least 500 million cubic meters per second, if Damascus would abandon its "protection of PKK terrorists."[12]

By mid-summer, however, reports that the PKK was attempting to establish an organizational structure in Hatay once again soured what seemed to be improving relations. In July the commander of the People's Liberation Army of Kurdistan (ARGK), the military wing of the PKK, announced that PKK guerrillas were engaging in operations in the Taurus mountains and in Hatay. The commander stated that the PKK first stationed forces in these regions in 1994. He claimed that Turkish intelligence first became aware of the PKK presence in early 1995 and that the Turkish National Security Council met to discuss methods of eliminating the PKK presence and decided to send "thousands of soldiers to the region and hoped to achieve a victory over us [ARGK] by means of military operations. Because they could not achieve such a victory, they built up a system of contra-guerrillas and village guards in urban centers such as Çukurova, Hatay and Adana." The commander went on to report that in the first six months of 1995, ARGK killed twenty-five Turkish soldiers, village guards and fascists, which, in the PKK lingo refers to those individuals and groups who collaborate with the Turkish military and security apparatuses. The ARGK spokesman said only two of its fighters had been killed. He added that the Turkish people had shown a great deal of interest in the struggle of the PKK.[13]

The story of the PKK presence in Hatay first broke in the Turkish press on 17 September. *Hürriyet* reported on that date that Abdullah Öcalan had proclaimed that he "would turn Hatay into Bohtan." Bohtan is the area south of Lake Van, extending into areas in northern Iraq, in which bloody battles have occurred during the past decade between the PKK and the Turkish armed forces. Hatay, too, said Öcalan, "must be turned into a bloody lake."[14]

According to *Hürriyet*, the PKK first attempted to infiltrate into the Adana, Mersin and Hatay regions in the early 1990s but won over only a few recruits in the hinterlands of Adana and Mersin. By the early 1990s these cities were already swelled with Kurds fleeing the scorched earth policies of the Turkish armed forces in the southeast. But the PKK had tough sledding in Hatay because of the tight security blanket thrown over the entire region by the Turkish security apparatuses. In spite of setbacks, the PKK persisted in trying to establish themselves in the region, as Hatay shares a border with Syria, where the PKK have sanctuary. The PKK operatives tried to ensconce themselves along the road from Lataqiya in Syria to Samadağ, a village in the Amanus mountains in Hatay. This is a road used heavily by smugglers and drug traffickers, which the PKK hoped to exploit to their advantage.

There are no reliable figures regarding the ethnic and religious profile of Hatay, so an estimation of its demographic composition has to be based on guesswork. The population does include a large number of Arabs, both Sunni and Alevi/Alawite. The Turkish population is predominately Sunni. The Kurdish population that has taken refuge in the province during the past decade is probably largely Sunni as well, but may include 15 to 20 percent Alevis, which is approximately the proportion of Alevis among the Kurdish population of Turkey. As mentioned above, Hatay shares a border with the Syrian province of Lataqiya, which has a predominately Alawite/Alevi population. The Alawites of Syria have been in control of the higher echelons of the Syrian Government since 1970. Hafiz al-Asad, the president of Syria, is an Alawite.

The *Hürriyet* account emphasized that the PKK hoped to exploit the religious and ethnic diversity of Hatay. One of the first operations of the PKK was to attack the Sunni-Turkomen villages. When the Turkish government then armed the Turkomen, the PKK countered with propaganda that the state was arming Sunnis against Alevis—Arab, Turk and Kurd. When, again according to *Hürriyet*, the PKK found themselves unable to exploit the religious and ethnic differences, they attempted to ingratiate themselves with the local population by purchasing food provisions at prices substantially higher than the market price. All transactions were carried out in German marks. Prices were high. For example, one egg sold for two marks or 65,000 Turkish lira; a 50-kilo sack of flour was going for 1,000 marks or 33 million lira. By their largess the PKK hoped to establish support and receive protection from the indigenous population.

In addition to exploiting the different religious and ethnic groups in Hatay, the PKK, the *Hürriyet* alleged, also tried to take advantage of the traditionally strong leftist sentiments in Hatay by proclaiming themselves a Marxist organization, while they abandoned this strategy in the southeast to portray themselves as a moderate leftist-Islamist–oriented organization to take advantage of the Islamist upsurge among segments of the population during the previous decade. Reports of further clashes between the PKK and Turkish armed forces during the first days of December 1995 suggest that there was truth in the comments of the ARGK commander and in the report in *Hürriyet*.

If the above mentioned reports are correct, they indicate the PKK's intention to expand its guerrilla war from the region of the southeast to the shores of the Mediterranean. An increase in guerrilla war in Hatay would suggest that the PKK is willing, bold enough or feels sufficiently compelled, whether from perceived weakness or strength, to take its war against Ankara out of the southeast region, which is predominately Kurdish. The choice of Hatay is as significant as it is sensitive. The province was part of Syria until 1939, and its sovereignty is still a contentious issue between Turkey and Syria and one of the sore spots in their relationship. The attempt of the PKK to enlist the minority Alevi/Alawite, especially Arab, and economically marginalized population against the dominant Sunni and Turkish population is bound to create more friction between the two capitals. Reports in the summer of 1995 of the PKK's attempts to move into Hatay further iced relations between the two countries. When the PKK attacked the KDP in northern Iraq on 25 August as a result of its unhappiness with the results of the first Drogheda conference, Turkey was quick to announce that Damascus, as well as Iran, encouraged the PKK to attack.

It would be easy to understand Turkish suspicions that Damascus is behind the PKK's attempts to establish bases in Hatay. But the PKK's movement into Hatay, if proved to be true and to be substantial, is bound to plunge relations between the two countries to another nadir. Such a development would further confirm Ankara's position that Damascus supports the PKK and the Kurdish nationalist movement in Turkey as instruments to weaken politically, militarily and diplomatically its big northern neighbor.

It is beyond the scope of this chapter to discuss all of the reasons for Syria's slight change of policy vis-à-vis the PKK in 1993-94, but obviously its continued negotiations with Israel and with the United State and its desire to participate in the Middle East peace process have played major roles in this change of policy. Anti-terrorist remarks and positions were also obviously preparation for the summit meeting between President al-Asad and President Clinton in Geneva, Switzerland, 16 January 1993. Syria no doubt thought its anti-terrorism remarks would result in its removal from the U.S. State Department's list of countries supporting terrorism and bring with it the benefits that would entail. The removal of Syria from the list was again discussed by President al-Asad and U.S. Secretary of State Warren Christopher during meetings in July and December 1994, March 1995, and in 1996. Improved relations between Turkey and Syria depend a good deal on the Middle East peace process. If Syria does not sign a peace accord with Israel, it will obviously be less amenable to allowing Turkish companies to participate in the reconstruction and development of the region.

There is, however, another dimension to Syria's anti-terrorism remarks with reference to the PKK. This is the realization on the part of Syria that Europe and the United States do not want the destabilization or weakening of Turkey as a result of Syrian support for the PKK. When the Arab states, the Palestinians and Israel finalize their peace negotiations, Syria may well have a role to play in the interregional sharing of water schemes, which now abound. Any pipeline carrying water from the upper reaches of the Euphrates and the Ceyhan and Seyhan rivers located in south central Turkey would have to traverse Syrian territory. Syria will want to extract as much diplomatic, political and economic leverage as possible from such a potentiality. Such a role demands, however, that it no longer pursue policies against the course of wider regional water, trade and economic agreements and geostrategic understandings. In turn, this would mean less support of PKK activities against Turkey. Another aspect of such policies is that Syria would be less able to use the Kurdish card against the Ba'thist regime in Baghdad. In short, the emerging geopolitic and geostrategic trends in the Middle East indicate that Syria's continuing support of the PKK may in the future be less of an asset in achieving its foreign policy goals.

The issue of Syria's support of the PKK reared its head again in late 1995, when Öcalan had contacts with high-ranking German political and intelligence officials in Damascus. On 30 September, Heinrich Lummer, a political ally of Chancellor Helmut Kohl, met with the PKK leader in the Syrian capital. After the Lummer visit, German media announced that several high-ranking intelligence officials had met with Öcalan before Lummer's visit.[15] The stated reason for the German visit was to discuss German concerns that PKK demonstrations and political activities in Germany were creating more disorder than Germany thought tolerable. The Germans also brought to Öcalan's attention their unhappiness with the PKK's involvement in drug trafficking in Germany. For his part, Öcalan stressed his desire that Germany recognize the PKK as a legitimate entity and that it stop characterizing PKK as a terrorist organization. The fact that Damascus was the site of such negotiations, which, if they come to fruition, would prove very detrimental to Turkey's policy of delegitimizing the PKK by referring to it as a terrorist organization, is notable.

One of the major questions concerning Turkish-Syrian relations in 1995 and 1996 is: If Syria's headquartering of Öcalan in Syria and its support for the PKK is so strong, and if one of Syria's objectives is to support the PKK as a bona fide nationalist organization, why doesn't Ankara take stronger actions, even military ones, against Syria? The answer seems to be twofold: Ankara undoubtedly does not want to attack a major Arab country, especially just as it seems closer to signing a peace agreement with Israel. Such an action would hurt Turkey's relations with the entire Arab world, albeit in varying degrees. The second reason seems to be that even if such an attack were carried out, it might be ineffective. An ill-planned attack on the PKK in Syria could yield little in the way of destruction of PKK facilities. On the other hand, it could produce a diplomatic brouhaha that could persist for some time. At the end of 1995, Syria's sheltering of Öcalan and its support for the PKK, and especially its support for the PKK move into Hatay, remained the principle reason for the sour state of relations between the two countries.

TURKEY'S RELATIONS WITH IRAN

In 1993 and early 1994 a rapprochement between Turkey and Iran over the mutual challenge of Kurdish nationalism, especially from the PKK, continued. In May and June 1994, the diplomatic and national security meetings were frequent. By 1 September 1994 approximately ten major meetings had taken place. The two countries signed a joint security protocol on 30 November 1993. The protocol stipulated that neither country would permit any terrorist organization [read PKK] to exist on its territory. Golam Husseini Bolandijian of the Iranian delegation and the authorized representative of President Rafsanjani stated that Iran would take military measures against the PKK. The 7 December 1993 issue of the Turkish conservative newspaper, *Sabah*, had a banner headline proclaiming, "Iran issues order for PKK members to be shot." Bolandijian reportedly stated: "Iran has issued an order for any PKK member to be shot regardless of whether they are wearing PKK uniforms or are smugglers." The article concluded, "At the end of seven [security] meetings between the Iranian and Turkish delegations a protocol to take action against terrorism was signed."

On 4 May 1994, Turkish interior minister Nahit Menteşe announced that Iran had turned over to Turkey twenty-eight members of the PKK, ten of whom were corpses. On 13 June, Ankara requested of visiting Iranian interior minister, Mohammad Besharati, that Turkey be allowed to bomb PKK bases located around the areas of Mounts Ararat and Tendürek in and near Iranian territory. On 14 June, President Süleyman Demirel even took time out from his summer vacation to announce that Ankara and Tehran had agreed to cooperate against the PKK, and the Turkish press announced on 16 June that Iran had given permission to Turkey to bomb PKK bases located in Iranian territory. The 16 June declaration centered on three major points of agreement: to prevent the passage of PKK members from northern Iraq to Iran; to prevent PKK passage to Armenia and hence to Russia; and—a Turkish request—to bomb roads in Iranian territory that were used by the PKK to replenish supplies for the camps in Iran from which it launched attacks against Turkey. In a press conference Besharati did not officially acknowledge that Iran would give permission to Turkey to bomb PKK bases located in Iranian territory, but he did state that Iran would cooperate with Turkey in every way against "their common enemies." In return, Ankara announced that it would move "against" the *Mujahidin-i-Halq* opposition to the Iran government in Turkey. Menteşe stated that Turkey would not allow any group operating from Turkish territory "to give harm" to the Iranian government.

The national security concerns between Turkey and Iran over the Kurds were given prominence when President Demirel met with President Rafsanjani on 15-27 July, the first visit by a Turkish president to Iran in decades. In press inter-

·views prior to the meeting, Rafsanjani gave assurances that Iran was fully cooperating with Turkey against the PKK, and he stated that the creation of a Kurdish state was "impossible."[16] Although Rafsanjani did make a point of claiming that the Islamic Republic had solved its Kurdish problem within the "spirit of Islam," this reply was probably meant to imply his approval of the religiously oriented Welfare (Refah) Party (WP) in Turkey, which is in opposition to Demirel's True Path (*Doğu Yolu*) Party (TPP). The Demirel-Rafsanjani meeting received wide coverage in both the Iranian and the Turkish press, but it was more limited in Turkey because of the hullabaloo over the disclosure of Prime Minister Tansu Çiller's and her husband's personal wealth and the fact that the couple had some four or five million dollars invested in real estate in the United States. Foreign Minister Hikmet Çetin was also forced to resign during Demirel's visit in Tehran. While it is still unclear as to all of the reasons compelling Çetin's resignation, his handling of the Kurdish question and Turkey's Kurdish problem and its many manifestations may well have played a role in his forced resignation. Çetin himself is an ethnic Kurd and perceived to be "soft" on the Kurdish issue. Nahit Menteşe, the Turkish interior minister, stated that he was confident the new security agreements between the two countries as well as agreements with Syria would lead to the capture of PKK leader Öcalan, who, like the recently apprehended Carlos the Jackal, could not escape justice forever.[17]

Turkish and Iranian relations continued to improve in early 1995. Much of the improvement centered on Iran's potential participation in an international consortium of companies and countries slated to build a natural gas pipeline estimated to cost $6 billion from Turkmenistan to Turkey. In its initial stages, one proposed route for the pipeline was to cross 1,200 kilometers of Iranian territory after traversing the Caspian Sea. Iran was to finance the portion of the pipeline that would cross its territory in exchange for a percentage of the total gas transferred.[18] Immediately in the wake of the national gas pipeline negotiations, Iran moved to settle a $200 million debt it had with Turkish exporters.[19]

The importance of the Iranian route for the proposed pipeline and a projected trunk line through Turkey is clear: It would mean even greater cooperation between Turkey and Iran against the Kurds. Since the pipeline would have to cross regions largely inhabited by Kurds in both Iran and Turkey, this would engender even closer national security cooperation between Ankara and Tehran to prevent Kurdish and Iranian opposition forces, such as the *Mujahidin-i-halq*, from sabotaging the pipeline.

The emphasis placed on preventing the emergence of an independent Kurdish state in northern Iraq was again the major topic of discussion by the foreign ministers of Turkey, Iran and Syria on 8 September in Tehran, during their 7th Triparitite meeting since the Gulf war. At the meeting, the three foreign ministers reaffirmed their previous proclamations: They were opposed to the division of Iraq's territorial integrity; they were against "terrorism" but gave no names; and they were all three concerned about the stockpiling of weapons in northern Iraq.[20]

When Iranian Minister of Economic and Financial affairs, Morteza Mohammad Khan, met with President Demirel on 7 November 1995, the president stated that he fully agreed with the decisions reached at the 7th Tripartite talks held in Tehran. He remarked, "Western countries intended to form a Kurdish government with the help of separatists."[21] Demirel also repeated that Turkey and Iran are not in competition with each other. In turn, Mohammad Khan stressed the need for greater economic cooperation between the two countries. On 1 December, the Turkish Foreign Ministry's undersecretary Onur Oymen visited Iran and held talks with President Rafsanjani in which the President noted the good relations between Tehran and Ankara, but he, too, indicated Iran's desire for more economic cooperation.

The national security agreements between Turkey and Iran are important in several ways. They indicate the serious challenge of Kurdish nationalism, especially of the PKK to Turkey, to both countries; they suggest that Ankara and Tehran are probably more willing than heretofore to cooperate regarding their respective policies toward countries in the Caucasus, especially Armenia, Azerbaijan and the accompanying problem of Norgorno-Karabagh and, by extension, the increasingly strong role and presence of Russia in the region; they may indicate that the two countries are also prepared to be more cooperative in their policies toward the Central Asian states and; 4) they point to the need for Turkey to maintain close coordination with Iran in order to prevent the emergence of an independent Kurdish state in northern Iraq and all of the geopolitical and geostrategic headaches that this would bring to the two capitals.

From the Gulf war to the end of 1995, Turkish and Iranian relations regarding the Kurdish question went through many fluctuations. In spite of the cooperation evinced by the numbers Tripartite meetings among the big three—Iran, Turkey and Syria—the emergence of areas in northern Iraq no longer under the control or authority of Baghad means necessarily greater competition between Ankara and Tehran in that space. The problem is where the lines of the two countries' spheres of influence will be drawn. This very problem was exacerbated from 1994 to 1995, as the two largest Kurdish nationalist groups, the KDP and the PUK, respectively, drew closer to Turkey and Iran as the result of their internecine fighting.

An example of the creation of spheres of influence in Iraqi Kurdistan was the reported agreement of Jalal Talabani to allow amassing of three to five thousand troops (some sources put the figures much lower) consisting of *Shi'a* who had earlier fled Iraq and are now under the control of Ayatollah Bakr al-Hakim, a member of the Supreme Assembly for the Islamic Revolution in Iraq (SAIRI).[22] Talabani announced that the force would be used in joint operations with his *peshmergas* against Saddam Hussein. Safa'in Diza'i, the KDP's representative in Ankara, emphasized that the KDP had nothing to do with the deployment, which was entirely Talabani's decision. He noted further the KDP was following closely developments in the PUK-controlled region, which by the end of 1995 included half of the territory of northern Iraq and 70 percent of the regions' population. Diza'i noted further that the decision to deploy Iranian troops in northern Iraq should have been a decision of the Iraqi National Congress (INC) and not solely that of the PUK.

Aziz Kader, leader of the Turkomen in northern Iraq, claimed that the force was paid for entirely by Iran and that Talabani requested the force as a result of the increasingly close relations between the KDP and Turkey, a development feared equally by Tehran. PUK and Iranian fears increased after the PKK attacked KDP forces on 25 August 1995, and the KDP was compelled to coordinate many of its military operations against the PKK with Turkey.

The deployment of troops ostensibly under the control of an Iranian Ayatollah in the PUK-controlled territory of northern Iraq indicated a further diminution of the agreements reached at the Drogheda conferences in Ireland in August and September. The major result of the first conference was that the PKK used it as a reason to attack the KDP, which it characterized as a puppet of the United States and Turkey. Öcalan was also apparently impatient to test whether some the Kurds in Bahdinan, the KDP-controlled area in northern Iraq, were as unhappy with Barzani as he thought. The PUK was also unhappy with aspects of the Drogheda conference, but it did not come to the aid of the KDP when it was attacked by the PKK on 25 August. It is not clear just why Talabani felt the need for the Iranian-controlled reinforcement of his *peshmergas,* unless he believes that they will be useful if the KDP attacks his forces, if and when they repel the PKK challenge. He might also find the Badr brigade, as the Iranian force is called, useful in reducing further the territory held by the KDP.

In conclusion, it can be said that since the Gulf war, Turkish-Iranian relations have improved overall and that the geopolitical necessity of the two capitals to cooperate against the growth and spread of Kurdish nationalism has been an essential factor in their relationship. The creation of an independent and internationally recognized state in northern Iraq is perceived by the two states as a potential disaster and a challenge to the two states as presently constituted, physically and ideologically. Both countries have substantial Kurdish problems within their own borders. In the case of Turkey, the Kurdish nationalism movement is the preeminent factor in both domestic and foreign policies. In Iran the Kurdish question is inextricably linked with the Azerbaijan question.[23] Given the fact that neither country deems it militarily or politically possible to subdue the Kurds in all of northern Iraq, both countries seem, at the end of 1995, to have adopted a policy of carving out respective spheres of influence in Iraqi Kurdistan.

In this regard, another reason for Talabani's acceptance of the Iranian Badr brigade, other than his announced reasons, is that he hopes to send a signal to Tehran that he wants closer economic relations and more trade between the PUK-controlled area and Iran. Since fighting between the KDP and PUK broke out over disagreement on how to allocate the money received for the truck traffic entering the KDP-controlled territory in northern Iraq from Turkey at the Habur crossing, it seems possible that Talabani hopes to increase his revenues by fostering greater trade with Iran. Thus, there is an emerging situation in which the KDP-controlled territory is being brought under the Turkish sphere of economic as well as political influence and the PUK-controlled territory is being tied economically and politically more closely with Iran. In return for reducing the barriers for a greater flow of trade, Tehran might well have demanded from the PUK leader an Iranian presence in his region for its own geopolitical reasons. For the first time Iran has acknowledged sending troops into Iraq since the Iraq-Iran cease-fire of August 1988, and Iran at the end of 1995 and in early 1996 was challenging a bit more aggressively the United States and European "dual containment" policy in the Gulf region.

TURKEY'S RELATIONS WITH RUSSIA

In 1994 and early 1995, the Kurdish question also began to figure strongly in Turkey's relations with Russia. The Turks protested when they learned that Moscow would be the site of an international conference to discuss the problems of the Kurds in the Russian Federation, whose population was estimated at 1 million, and the Kurds of Turkey. The tensions between the two capitals increased in January 1995 when Ali Yiğit and Necdat Buldan, two former Kurdish members of the Turkish parliament who had fled to Europe to escape imprisonment, visited Moscow in order to the ascertain Russian authorities' views regarding the possibility of establishing a Kurdistan parliament in exile (KPE) in Moscow. Attempts to establish the parliament in Brussels had been rejected by the Belgian government. While the Russian foreign ministry stated that Russians would not "open their arms to the PKK," they did seem inclined to allow a Kurdish House (Kürt Evi), in which the PKK would obviously participate, to be established in Moscow. The Turks were not satisfied with the Russian foreign ministry statement; a large portrait of Abdullah Öcalan, the PKK leader, hung over the speakers' table. The Moscow conference rang alarm bells in Ankara, and exactly one week later Turkish Interior Minister, Nahit Menteşe, and a coterie of other high-ranking national security officials were in Moscow. After two days of negotiations, Turkey and Russia signed a "Protocol to Prevent Terrorism" in which the two countries agreed to exchange intelligence information to prevent "terrorism." The Russian interior minister stated that the PKK would "not be a legal organization in Russia."[24]

In late February, two more high-ranking Russian delegations visited Turkey in order to strengthen further intelligence cooperation between the two countries. Turkey's efforts to curtail PKK operations in the Russian Federation were high on the agenda. Yevgeny Primakov, head of the Russian foreign intelligence service, and Sergei Stepashin, head of the Russian Federation counterintelligence service, arrived in Ankara, accompanied by five high-ranking Russian generals. Before becoming director of the Russian Federation intelligence service, Primakov was the top national security advisor to former Soviet Premier Mikhail Gorbachev; earlier Primakov had been a journalist for *Pravda* and an analyst of Middle East politics. One of the leading Turkish newspapers reported that the main topic of discussion was that, in return for Turkish support for its policies in Chechnya, Russia would not allow the PKK or a Kurdish House to be set up in Moscow.[25] The Russians reportedly received a promise on the part of the Turks that Ankara would not allow volunteers to go and fight in Chechnya and would not sell arms to the Chechens. The Russians also wanted Turkey to exercise its influence on Dzhokar Dudayev, the Chechen president, and his advisors so that they would agree to negotiate with the Russians. In return the Russians promised they would not allow any "activities" in Russia against Turkey.

The agreement between the two countries included other matters, such as cooperation against international drug trafficking, but it was clear that the main topic of discussion was Russian succor to the Kurdish nationalist movement and particularly to PKK efforts to establish offices in Moscow and other cities within the Russian Federation. In return for their not recognizing the KPE, the Russians demanded that Ankara proclaim Russia's war against Chechnya an "internal affair."[26] The agreement seemed to imply that Turkey would take a low profile regarding Russian efforts to reassert its presence in the entire Caucasus region, including Azerbaijan and Armenia and those two countries' conflict over Norgorno-Karabagh. Less than one month after the security and intelligence agreements, Russia commenced its beefed-up pacification of Chechnya, and Turkey mounted a large attack into northern Iraq.

The ferocious Russian attack on Chechnya, which continued throughout 1995 and 1996, brought loud protests from the Turkish government, although some of them seemed intended only for public consumption. In spite of its protests and undoubtedly real consternation, Ankara seemed to abide by the January and February agreements, as did Moscow. There were, however, continuing disagreements between the two capitals. On 16 March, in a media interview in Baku, Walter Shoniya, the Russian ambassador to Azerbaijan, noted that "Turkey has been fighting the Kurds for ten years and the Russians have said nothing. . . . If the Turks want to help the Chechens, when they talk to Dudayev every day on the telephone, one day let them [the Turks] say, 'Surrender'; that is how the Chechens will be saved from war."[27] On 24 April two members of the KPE, Rustam Broyev and Asiri Şerif, after being rebuffed by the Russian administration in their attempts to establish a Kurdish office in Moscow, sought support from members of the Duma. Mikail Burlakov, a member of Vladamir Zhirinovsky's Liberal Democratic Party, stated that he supported the Kurdish cause. He said that the Turkish army was annihilating the Kurds in northern Iraq and added, "We don't see Turkey as an independent country but rather as a pawn of NATO and we request that Turkey be thrown out of the alliance because of its aggression" [against the Kurds].[28]

On 17 July the Turkish press reported that Russia would send Albert Chernishev, one of its top diplomats, who had spent seven years in Turkey as Russian ambassador in the late 1980s and early 1990s and is quite fluent in Turkish.

Chernishev's mission was to request that Turkey curtail the activities of the Caucasian and Chechnya solidarity associations in Turkey, which were supporting the Chechens by sending them food, arms and volunteers. There were also unconfirmed reports that Turkey was training Chechens within Turkey itself. Chernishev arrived in Ankara on 20 July and proclaimed there was no "Chechen question between Turkey and Russia." But he added, obviously referring to the Kurdish question and Turkey's war against the Kurds, "We must understand one another. People who live in glass houses shouldn't throw stones."[29] Chernishev stressed this point by saying it in Turkish. After meeting with Foreign Minister Erdal İnönü and President Demirel, the Russian envoy stated that his anxieties regarding Turkey's policy toward the war in Chechnya had disappeared. He announced that the Turkish government had assured him that the Caucasian and Chechnya solidarity associations would not be able to harm relations between Turkey and Russia. Chernishev noted that Turkey had received similar assurances that Russia would not allow Kurdish organizations sympathetic to the PKK to operate in Russia. He emphasized that Russia and Turkey had a profound understanding between themselves on the subject of the Chechens and the Kurds. The Russian envoy concluded his remarks, again in Turkish, by saying, "Turkey and Russia are in the same boat. If the boat sinks, we both sink. It is necessary that we find the means for both of us to stay on the surface."[30]

Turkish-Russian relations took a nosedive in October and November 1995, when members of the Russia Duma, led by Viktor Ustinov, director of the Duma's Geopolitical Affairs Committee, agreed to host on 30 October through 1 November, a third international conference of the KPE. The conference was not officially recognized by the Yeltsin government, but it appeared to the Turks that the conference would not have taken place if the Russian foreign ministry had not given its tacit approval. The Turkish foreign ministry labeled the affair as a "deep wound that only Russia can bandage."[31] The Turkish press called the conference an act of "Russian treachery."[32] Russian perfidy was compounded by the fact that four former Kurdish members—Ali Yiğit, Nizamittin Toğuç, Remzi Kartal and Mahmut Kılıç—of the Turkish Parliament who had fled Turkey in 1994 under threat of being jailed, were in attendance. This semiofficial recognition of the KPE broke the agreements that had been reached in February and July.

The harshness of Ustinov's words suggested deep dissatisfaction with Turkey's support of the Chechens. Ustinov stated boldly that the Lausanne Treaty of 1923, which did not mention the Kurds, unlike the Treaty of Sèvres, signed in 1920 in which articles 62 and 64 recognized the conditions for the possibility of the creation of a Kurdish state, should be canceled. "The Lausanne Treaty," he said, "has given birth to unjust consequences." Furthermore, Ustinov continued, "If Turkey, for the sake of Chechnya, is meddling in Russia's affairs, we know how to prevent it."[33] By this he apparently meant that Russia well knew that the Achilles heel of all of Turkey's foreign and domestic policies is its preoccupation with the consolidation and spread of Kurdish nationalism. Official Russian recognition of the KPE would be a significant victory for the PKK, which has strong representation in the KPE, and would open the doors to recognition of other CIS states. The KPE has already been recognized officially by the Netherlands and has its headquarters in The Hague. Major conferences of organizations affiliated with the KPE have been held in Switzerland, Austria, Sweden and Norway. Although Yeltsin spokesmen and the Russian foreign ministry denied official support, KPE president Yaşar Kaya deepened Ankara's suspicions when he stated at a news conference at the end of the meeting that although the Russian foreign ministry announced that the conference was illegal, it had done nothing to stop the conference and had not interfered with the proceedings. Kaya said the KPE received "help" from many countries, even though those countries did not recognize the PKK as a "state."

The Turkish foreign ministry made it clear that it was "unsatisfied" with the Russian response. It stated that the "healing of the wound" opened by the KPE conference was Moscow's responsibility. If Russia "did not bandage the wound," Turkey would be obliged to take actions that were "inescapable."[34] The Turks were as good as their word. On 4 November, Ankara announced that it would begin to concentrate troops on its borders with Armenia and Georgia in order to pressure Russia to abide by the Conventional Forces Reduction Agreement (CFRA), in which Russia agreed to reduce its forces on NATO's northern and southern flanks. Russia was supposed to have carried out these the reductions by 17 November 1995, but it has continued to delay the agreed reductions on the southern flank of NATO, i.e. Turkey. The Turks requested that President Clinton bring their concerns to the attention of President Yeltsin when the two met in New York in late October. According to the Turks, Clinton did not raise the issue because he did not want to offend either Turkey or Russia.

The Turks could have hardly been surprised by Clinton's action. Ankara already knew by the time of the Clinton-Yeltsin meeting that the Americans would not put pressure on Russia to meet the concerns of the Turks. In a September meeting of NATO's defense ministers, in which Russia participated, Turkey received little support from its NATO allies for its request that Moscow abide by the CFRA. Pavel Grachev, the Russian defense minister, made a speech in which he said that he saw nothing in Russian actions that should offend the Turks. Grachev made the argument that the South Caucasian countries were happy (he did not mention Chechnya!) with the number of Russian troops deployed in the region. He saw no reason for the reduction of forces called for in the CFRA. In the communiqué issued after the meeting, Turkish officials were unable to place in the text a "reminder" to the effect that the CFRA was being violated in the "wings" of NATO. The reminder referred obviously to the southern wing, since the reduction of forces in the northern wing were being carried out, albeit somewhat reluctantly.[35]

In mid-January 1996 the Chechnya question again intruded directly into Turkish-Russian relations. On 16 January a Turkish ferryboat plying the route between Trabzon, a Turkish town on the northern coast of the Black Sea, and Sochi, a Russian resort town on in the Crimea, was hijacked by nine individuals, all, apparently, of Turkish citizenship, but all of Caucasus origin—Abkazian, Circassian (Cherkess) and Adegyian. While the hijackers claimed not be connected directly with the Chechen resistance forces of General Dudayev, they were all, apparently, members of the Chechen-Caucasus Solidarity Association (CCSA), which has some ten thousand active members in Turkey and claims to represent the 2 to 3 million people of Caucasus descent living in Turkey. The CCSA is the very organization whose activities on the part of Chechnya high-ranking Russian officials tried to get Ankara to curtail during the high-level meetings held between the two countries in 1995.

The ferryboat hijacking did not seem to affect the 1995 security agreements. The presidents of Turkey and Russia made charges and countercharges during the incident, which reflected the chill in relations between the two countries regarding their respective policies in the Caucasus, Central Asia and the Balkans. Yeltsin accused Turkey of prolonging the incident in order to give the Chechens more favorable international exposure, especially in the wake of the brutal Russian attack on the village of Pevomoskoye, in Daghestan, which the Russians had destroyed just prior to the hijacking. The Russians justified the destruction of Pevomoskoye as necessary to dislodge the Chechens there, who had taken several hundred of the townspeople hostage in a hospital in an attempt to use them as bargaining tools to negotiate a solution to the Russian war in Chechnya. Ankara replied to Yeltsin's charge that it needed more time to bring the hijacking to an end without bloodshed, which it managed to do on 19 January.[36]

There is strong support for the Chechens in Turkey. The CCSA is very active and lobbies strongly for Chechnya. But the dilemma of Turkey was epitomized by Doğan Güreş, the former Chief of the General Staff of the Turkish armed forces. Güreş' mother was Chechen, and he still claims to speak the language. He acknowledged the legitimacy of the Chechens' cause, but he said that Turkey could not abide the hijacking because according to international law it was a terrorist act. The Turkish media seemed to take their cue from Güreş and after his remark referred to the hijackers as "terrorists." The discourse used against the PKK foe now of necessity had to be used against friend.

The Kurdish question and the Chechen question have played important roles in Russian-Turkish relations in the 1990s and continue to do so. Russian control of Chechnya is vital if it is to maintain control of the Caucasus and of Central Asia. Loss of Russian control of Chechnya would greatly encourage the nationalist forces in the Caucausus, especially in the republics and regions that are predominately Muslim. The north Caucasian republics of Daghestan, Chechnya-Ingushetia, Kabardino-Balkar, Karachai-Cherkess, Adygeya and Azerbaijan are predominately Muslim, and, if organized into a united North Caucasian Front, they would form a Muslim belt across the northern Caucausus separating the

Christian republics of Georgia and Armenia from Russia. Such a development would make Armenia and Georgia not only dependent on their relations with their northern Caucasian neighbors but on the big Muslim states of Turkey and Iran to the west and south.

The Russian war against Chechnya caused deep fissures in the Russian government, fissures which at times challenged Yeltsin's hold on power. It created deep divisions in the military and between the armed forces and the civilian government. The war demonstrated the weakness of the Russian armed forces and the insubordination that was rife in all ranks. The war also strained relations between Russia and the West and encouraged European and American groups who wished to expand NATO eastward. The Russian officials who advocated war against the Chechens—Sergi Stepashin, federal counterintelligence service head; Oleg Soskovets, first deputy prime minister; Nikolai Yegorov, deputy prime minister; Oleg Lobov, security council secretary; Alexsandr Korzhakov, head of Yeltsin's private security—also had major roles in formulating Russia's policy toward Turkey and the Kurds and in determining the potential routes of the gas and oil pipelines. Michael McFaul argues that the difference between those officials eager to prosecute the war against Chechnya and the traditional core of Russia's reformers may have created a divide that cannot be bridged.[37] In addition, like Turkey's war against the Kurds, Russia's war against Chechnya proved to be expensive. By May some estimates put the cost of the war at $6 billion, a figure close to what the Turks were estimated to be spending in their war against the PKK.[38] The cost of the war and the corruption it entailed imperiled further Russia's economic and political reforms. Turkey has been unable to take advantage of the Russian predicament in Chechnya because of its own war against the PKK and the cost of its efforts to suppress the Kurdish nationalist movement in Turkey, which reached new heights in 1995.

In short, the challenge of the PKK and of Kurdish nationalism has dominated Turkey's political agenda, both foreign and domestic, throughout the 1990s. The larger interstate Kurdish question and the Turkish policy toward the Kurds in northern Iraq added to the maelstrom.[39] The point I wish to stress here is that the great strain and challenge of the PKK and of Kurdish nationalism to the Turkish state and the costs of suppressing them has affected greatly Turkish relations with Russia. It is not a coincidence that Russia sent Albert Chernishev, a former Turkish speaking Russian ambassador, to Ankara at the height of the Russian onslaught on Grozny. Chernishev, perhaps more than any other Russian diplomat, is deeply aware of the profound consequences of the Kurdish problem in Turkey and its affects on Turkish domestic and foreign policies. He was acutely aware of the fear of Turkish officials that Russia will officially recognize the KPE and allow Kurdish nationalists to establish offices in Moscow and in other cities of the CIS. Russian recognition of the KPE would open the floodgate to a number of other countries, especially European, to recognize the KPE. Turkey wanted to avoid this possibility at all costs. And, as mentioned above, the price of Russian nonrecognition of the KPE was Turkish noninterference in Russia's war against Chechnya.

There is no doubt that the challenge of the PKK and of the Kurdish nationalist movement in Turkey has restricted severely Turkey's ability to play a strong role, even diplomatically, in the Balkans, especially in the Bosnia conflict, in Europe, in the Caucasus and in Central Asia. It is in Turkey's interests to reduce Russian military and political presence in the Caucasus and in Central Asia and Azerbaijan.[40] Chechnya'a Declaration of Independence in autumn 1991 provided an excellent opportunity for Turkey to lessen the presence and authority of Russia in the Caucasus, but it was unable to take advantage of this opportunity because of its war against the PKK and against the Kurdish nationalist movement and its challenge to the Turkish state as presently constituted.[41] At the end of 1995, Russia was able to play its "Kurdish card" much more effectively against Turkey than Turkey was able to use the "Chechen card" against Russia.

TURKEY'S RELATIONS WITH IRAQ

Turkey's relations with Baghdad began to improve in 1993 from their icy state in the aftermath of the Gulf war, a trend that gathered momentum throughout 1994 and early 1995. As early as December 1992, Bülent Ecevit, the Democratic Left Party (DLP) leader, conducted talks with Iraqi leaders in Baghdad. This is the same Ecevit who announced on 1 August 1994 that "the fundamental goal of the United States was to create an autonomous (*özerk*) region in southeastern Turkey."[42] In April 1993, Ankara established diplomatic relations with Iraq at the level of chargé d'affaires with ambassadorial rank. Economic, business and even military delegations, both official and unofficial, came and went continuously between the two capitals in 1993, 1994 and early 1995. Even the assassination of Cağlar Yücel, administrative attaché of the Turkish embassy, in Baghdad on 11 December 1993 did not affect developing relations between the two governments. There were no allegations by Ankara that the Iraqi government was involved in the assassination. Neither government wanted the assassination to impede ongoing negotiations to improve trading and economic cooperation. By early 1994 both capitals were pressing the UN and other governments, including the United States, to allow the reopening of the two oil pipelines running from Iraq through Turkey.

Prime Minister Tansu Çiller pushed hard in her talks with U.S. officials during her October 1993 visit to Washington to allow the pipelines to be reopened under some formula allowed by the UN sanctions. In spite of U.S. reluctance to grant such permission, negotiations between Ankara and Baghdad and other parties regarding the reopening of the pipelines continued from 1994 into 1996. Iraq apparently hoped that negotiations to open the oil pipelines would also open the way to better relations between the two countries on a host of other issues, in spite of profound Iraq resentment of Turkey's influence in northern Iraq and its deep suspicions of Turkey's intentions. The most pressing problem between the countries was and is, of course, the Kurdish question.

By summer 1994 the tempo of meetings and consultations between Baghdad and Ankara were becoming daily events. In late June, Murat Karayalçın, assistant prime minister and leader of the Social Democrat Party (SDP), which was the main coalition partner with Çiller's TPP until its merger with the Republican Peoples' Party (RPP) in February 1995, visited Baghdad and had extensive talks with the highest-level Iraqi officials, including Saddam Hussein.[43] Karayalçın undertook the visit in spite of opposition from members of his own party, especially those from Turkey's east and southeastern provinces, some of whom are of Kurdish ethnicity. Some six weeks after Karayalçın's visit, the Habur/Khabur crossing, as mentioned earlier, was officially opened on 28 August. While trucks from Turkey going to Iraq were declared to be carrying only food and medicine, as allowed by UN sanctions, it was widely reported that they were transporting other goods and materials as well. The Turkish press reported that the trucks were returning from Iraq carrying two to three tons of oil per truck.

During the last days of August there were more high level meetings between Turkish officials, including powerful members of Turkey's business community. The meeting was of particular importance because the Turkish delegation was led once again by Yalım Erez, which emphasized that the trip had the blessing of the government. Erez was accompanied by seventy-seven well-connected businessmen, which suggested further the Turkish government's conviction that Saddam Hussein was going to remain in power for the foreseeable future, contrary to the U.S. position that he would not be able to do so. This U.S. position was the officially proclaimed reason for maintaining U.S. support of the Provide Comfort force in southeastern Turkey, whose role is to monitor the UN imposed "no-fly" zone over northern Iraq.

The Erez delegation came to significant understandings with Iraq, and the two governments signed a protocol stipulating that Turkish businessmen would be given every opportunity to do business in Iraq; that Iraq wished to buy all kinds of goods and materials from Turkey; that, because of Iraq's lack of hard currency and funds, the bulk of the trade would be bartered; and that acceptance of the above was dependent on the Turkish government's approval. It seemed clear that Iraqi oil would be bartered for Turkish goods. At the conclusion of Erez's stay, Prime Minister Çiller was invited to visit Iraq, and Taha Yasin Ramadan, one of Saddam Hussein's chief advisers and the person who extended the invitation, indicated his desire to visit Turkey—and the sooner the better.[44]

In another goodwill gesture to Baghdad, Turkey's foreign ministry announced on 11 September that all persons entering Iraq from Turkey, with the exception of UN personnel involved in the distribution of aid in northern Iraq, diplomats, foreign journalists in Turkey, Turkish and Iraqi journalists and Turkish and Iraqi citizens, would have to obtain a visa from Iraqi authorities. Kurds who were identified as being from Iraq would also be allowed passage. In those cases in which Iraq was unable to grant a visa, right of entry was to be determined by Turkish authorities.[45]

Turkey's opening to Iraq was met with approval in the media. Editorial writers proclaimed that by its actions Ankara was sending the strong signal that Baghdad was "the owner" of northern Iraq. It was another in a series of actions to persuade the Kurds to abandon their attempts to establish an independent state in northern Iraq. The editorials stated that Ankara's actions were also a signal to the Western countries to abandon their desire to establish an independent Kurdish state in northern Iraq and, furthermore, that all Western efforts to aid the PKK should cease. At the same time, Turkey claimed that it had suffered $20 billion in lost trade as a result of the UN sanctions. In a recent article, Eric Rouleau, a former French ambassador to Turkey and a well informed analyst of Turkish and Middle East affairs, put the figure at "between $10 and $20 billion."[46] Approval was especially strong on both the left and the right. Bülent Ecevit, leader of the DLP, and Necmettin Erbakan, the leader of the WP, voiced their strong approval of the government's new policy. But government spokesman and one of the principal architect's of the opening to Baghad, Undersecretary of State Özdem Sanberk, stressed that Turkey's negotiations with Baghdad were "conducted in close consultation with our Western allies. . . . Turkey is acting as a catalyst and is in a unique position to play such a regional role."[47] Sanberk's remarks suggested that Europe and the United States were, at least, informed of the content of the negotiations, if not privy to every detail. Sanberk's remarks gave the further implication that most countries in Europe were not opposed to an easing of the sanctions.

Sanberk's remarks were echoed by Rouleau. In a statement to the Turkish media in early September, Rouleau stated that Turkey's policy of easing the embargo against Iraq was not contrary to the policy that the UN and its Provide Comfort force was pursuing in northern Iraq. Rouleau stated that Turkey's policy was aimed at preventing the Balkanization of the countries of the Middle East and that this policy had the support of Europe as well as other countries. The former ambassador suggested that the main purpose of Provide Comfort was largely to reduce the influence of Baghdad in northern Iraq. Rouleau stressed that Provide Comfort did nothing but watch the fierce fighting among contending Kurdish forces, especially those of Jalal Talabani and Ma'sud Barzani, that had taken place in August, in which hundreds had been killed. Rouleau speculated that the United States' strong position against the easing of sanctions was no longer aimed at toppling Saddam Hussein from power but rather indicated U.S. anxiety that the reentry of Iraqi oil into the world oil market would cause oil prices to fall and would make it difficult for the two major producers, Saudi Arabia and Kuwait, to repay some $30 billion they owed the United States for arms purchased after the Gulf war. Another reason for U.S. opposition, in Rouleau's view, was that lower oil prices would increase the competitiveness of the United States' two major economic rivals: Germany and Japan, both of whom lack oil resources of their own.[48] Given the fact that Turkey and the United States have close political relations and cooperate on intelligence matters concerning the Middle East, it seems likely that the United States was informed of Turkish intentions to reduce substantially the embargo sanctions against Iraq. This, in turn, makes Rouleau's comments credible.

In late 1994 and early 1995 Turkey and Iraq continued to improve their relations. Iraqi deputy foreign minister Tariq Aziz was invited by Foreign Minister Mümtaz Soysal to visit Turkey in late December. Aziz's visit was, however, subsequently canceled because of Soysal's resignation and his replacement by Murat Karayalçın, deputy minister and head of the SDP. There was speculation that U.S. pressure had contributed to the cancellation of Aziz's visit.

But high-ranking Iraqi visitors kept coming. Iraqi foreign minister Muhammad Sa'id al-Sahhaf arrived in Turkey 9 February 1995. This was the first visit by an Iraqi foreign minister to Turkey since the Gulf war. At a press conference al-Sahhaf stated that Iraq and Turkey were continuing to negotiate to achieve agreement on the opening of the oil pipelines. Both foreign ministers emphasized their countries' desire for better relations. Karayalçın reiterated Turkey's support for Iraq's territorial integrity.[49] Editorials in the Turkish press stressed that after four years America had not brought peace to the area; only Turkey and Iraq would be able to do so.

One of the issues discussed during al-Sahhaf's visit was undoubtedly the national security positions that the two governments would take against the fighting between the KDP and PUK forces in northern Iraq. Unable to reach agreement as to the distribution of power and attempting to consolidate their respective political and territorial positions before the UN-proposed elections in the spring or early summer of 1995 in the Kurdish-controlled zone in northern Iraq, serious clashes between the two groups started in December 1994 and continued throughout 1996. It was reported that seven to eight hundred people had been killed in the clashes. By March 1995 it appeared that northern Iraq had been divided into three parts, with the KDP in possession of much of the territory north of the 36th parallel and the PUK pushed almost completely to the south of the 36th parallel. Major fighting occurred in and around Arbil. Subsequent KDP possession of the region of Arbil, with the exception of the city itself, virtually excluded the PUK from territory north of the 36th parallel. A third area of northern Iraq, south of the 36th parallel and east of the territory controlled by the PUK and adjacent to Iran, was in the hands of the Islamic Movement of Kurdistan (IMK), which has close ties with Iran.[50] The IMK was subsequently defeated and the territory it controlled was taken over by the PUK. The rift between the two Kurdish groups seemed to become irreparable when Barzani accused the PUK of setting off a bomb in the money changers' market in Zakho on 28 February, killing seventy-six people, eleven of them children. Barzani claimed that the bombing was a heinous act and that the KDP had evidence that Talabani was behind the explosion. The KDP leader charged the PUK with seeking revenge for their defeat at the hands of KDP forces during the previous two months.[51]

The fighting between the rival Kurdish groups, however, illustrates the dilemma of Turkey. Fighting between the two major Kurdish organizations and the weakening of one posed the inevitable challenge that the weaker of the two would seek closer cooperation with the PKK. Indeed, Ankara accused PUK leader Jafar Talabani of exactly that. While Talabani denied the accusation, it was conceivable that it would be in the PUK's interest, given the setback that it was receiving at the hands of the KDP, to seek closer relations with the PKK. In late February 1995, Talabani appealed to Turkey not to compel the Kurds to negotiate with Baghdad and demanded that Turkey close the Habur/Khabur border crossing. Talabani claimed that Ankara was putting great pressure on the Kurds in northern Iraq to negotiate with Baghdad. He also stated that if the PKK was a close ally of the PUK, it would have come to the PUK's aid in its clashes with the KDP. Despite Talabani's denials of a close relationship with the PKK, Ankara remained firm in its belief that the two Kurdish organizations were in close contact and cooperating with one another.[52]

The second demand of Talabani was that Turkey close the Habur/Khabur crossing. He claimed that fifteen hundred vehicles, mostly trucks, some with trailers, carrying 2 to 3 tons of food, pharmaceuticals and other materials on their entry into Iraq and 2 to 3 tons of oil on their return were crossing the border every day. He asserted that the KDP was assessing a tax on all of this traffic and that the collected revenue was being used by the KDP to buy the weapons that were fueling the fight against the PUK. In return, Ankara announced that it would reduce the number of trucks crossing the border, although by the early spring of 1996 there seemed to have been no reduction this traffic.

By the spring of 1995, the eventual consequences of the fighting between the DKP and the PUK were unclear. But the de facto partition of northern Iraq into two parts seems to have sounded the death knell for the possibility of creating a unified automonous Kurdish region in northern Iraq, at least, in the short term.[53] The partition could herald a situation in which the Kurmanj-speaking area of most of the northern portion of Iraq, under the control of the KDP, will increasingly come under the influence of Turkey and the portion south of the 36th parallel, Sorani-speaking and under the control of the PUK, will draw closer to Iran. Ironically, the areas proclaimed as safe havens for the Kurds in 1991 would fall almost completely under the control of the KDP and, thus, indirectly under the influence of Turkey. The area of northern Iraq under KDP control could come to resemble the security zone that Israel established in southern Lebanon in 1978. The establishment of such a zone in northern Iraq would create the buffer between the PKK and the PUK forces that Turkey desires for its perceived national security needs. The hostility of the PKK and the PUK toward the KDP and of the PUK toward the KDP would also make the KDP more dependent on Turkey. Baghdad may find itself impelled to accept a Turkish-influenced KDP region north of the 36th parallel. Such an agreement might mean that the PUK-controlled regions would be more vulnerable to pressure and attacks from Baghdad. Indeed, in early March

1995 there were reports that Iraqi forces were reinforcing their positions and deploying tanks and equipment in the vicinity of the city of Kifri, which is controlled by the PUK.[54] PUK leader Talabani claimed on 4 March that Iraqi airplanes were bombing towns in and around Kifri and that Arbil was also bombed. He stated that it was Iraq's intention to recapture the province of Kirkuk, which, with the exception of the city itself, was under the control of the PUK. Kirkuk city is south of the 36th parallel and is controlled by Baghdad's forces.[55]

The KDP claimed that Talabani exaggerated the Iraqi government build up in order to enhance the PUK's position in the inter-Kurdish power struggle and as a face-saving excuse for the PUK's military defeats at the hands of the KDP in recent fighting.[56]

It was in the context of the inter-Kurdish war between the KDP and the PUK that in late March 1995 Turkey sent a reported thirty-five thousand troops, accompanied by dozens of tanks and aircraft, some 25 to 35 miles into northern Iraq along a 150-mile front. Ironically, the territory included nearly the entire region that was declared a safe haven for the Kurds of northern Iraq by the Allied forces in 1991.[57] The attack was the largest since 1992, when Turkey launched a similar attack against PKK bases. The biggest difference between the 1992 and the 1995 attacks is that in the 1992 attack Turkey had the cooperation of the KDP and the PUK. The 1995 attack had only the support of the KDP. The preoccupation of the KDP and the PUK with their internecine fighting had allowed the PKK to further consolidate its bases and presence in northern Iraq, from which it launched attacks into Turkey. This was a situation completely unacceptable to Ankara. Even without the deteriorating circumstances of the inter-Kurdish fighting, it seemed likely as early as fall 1994 that Turkey would send large forces into northern Iraq in the spring. Turkish military and intelligence officials had made numerous comments to the press that PKK bases in northern Iraq had to be "cleaned out" if Turkey was ever to have "security." The inter-Kurdish fighting from December 1994 throughout 1995 provided Turkey with a golden opportunity to move militarily into northern Iraq. The big question posed once again by the invasion was: What kind of military and, by extension, political presence would Turkey maintain in northern Iraq? It seems most likely that eventually the bulk of Turkey's military forces will pull out of Iraq and deploy along the international border. It also seems likely, given Ankara's political need to emphasize that it has dealt a severe blow to the PKK, that substantial liaison troops, commandos and intelligence personnel will remain in portions of northern Iraq for some time to come. At the end of 1995, hundreds of Turkish military and intelligence personnel remained in northern Iraq. It would be accurate to say that they were "stationed" there in agreement with the KDP.

The improvement of relations with Turkey, albeit meager, on the part of Saddam Hussein's regime may indicate that while Baghdad is resentful of Turkey's relationship with the leaders of the Kurdish Regional Government (KRG), especially with the KDP, and its influence in northern Iraq, Baghdad does not think that Turkey wants to annex or militarily occupy northern Iraq but rather that it wants to remain the dominant political influence there. If this is Baghdad's position, the Iraqi leadership may think it can conduct negotiations with Turkey on a number of issues other than the political status of northern Iraq. A further improvement in relations between the countries, which seemed in the offing in 1996, could well mean that Ankara would tolerate the Iraqi regime's incremental attempts to regain territory on the southern fringes of the KRG as long as Turkey's dominant political and military position in the north and its relationship with the KRG leadership of Ma'sud Barzani and Jalal Talabani is not jeopardized. Such a relationship between Turkey and Iraq would effectively neutralize the leadership of Talabani and Barzani, unless the PUK seeks a closer political and military alliance with the PKK. This would imply recognition on the part of Baghdad that Turkey's position in northern Iraq was dictated by its need to control the Kurdish national movement within Turkey itself and not a desire on the part of Turkey to militarily occupy northern Iraq.[58] Thus the policies of Turkey since the Gulf war have come full circle: from unequivocal support for the West and the United States to tepid rapprochement with Iraq as well as with Syria and Iran—a rapprochement, however, that was largely driven by Ankara's needs to constrain the Kurdish nationalist movement in both its intrastate and its interstate dimensions. It is ironic that Turkey is compelled to favor a policy of lifting the sanctions against Saddam Hussein, whom it tried, along with its Western allies, to topple from power during the course of the Gulf war. But the increased activities of the PKK after the Gulf war and the great expense of combating the Kurdish nationalists in Turkey, many of whom find sanctuary in northern Iraq and Iran, compelled Turkey to seek some accommodation with its southern neighbors.

On 28 October 1995, Turkey's parliament voted to extend the mandate for Provide Comfort for another three months instead of the usual six months. But developments in 1995, especially the large Turkish attack into northern Iraq in March 1995, suggest that Provide Comfort has become little more than a flaccid symbol of the internationalism represented by the Allied coalition in its war effort against Iraq in 1991. Its main purpose by the end of 1995 seemed to be to act as a deterrent to any attempts by Saddam Hussein to challenge the consolidating status quo in northern Iraq. If Turkey seeks to establish its own national security zone in northern Iraq, Provide Comfort can be seen as a mechanism supporting such a development. Developments in 1994 and 1995 demonstrated to Ankara that Barzani and Talabani, largely as a result of their own disputes, were unable to do this. Whether Provide Comfort should be extended beyond 1996 will be a hotly debated issue in Turkey, especially since a vote against its extension would be contrary to U.S. policies in the region. The future of Provide Comfort could be affected by the new government that will come to power after the 24 December 1995 election. In 1995, the UN, under pressure from the United States, agreed to extend the economic sanctions on Iraq until the demands of the United States and Great Britain are met: that Baghdad return all property stolen from Kuwait, account for missing Kuwaitis, and stop mistreating citizens in the north and south of the country, the latter including thousands of people living the marshes in the south of the country. But it seems likely that the United States will agree to ease the oil embargo sanctions in 1996.

By August 1995 Baghdad began to show dissatisfaction with what it viewed as Turkey's increasing presence and role in northern Iraq. On 19 August, Baghdad announced that it was closing its consulate in Istanbul. Iraq also requested that Turkey close its consulate in Mosul. This was a sharp blow to Ankara, as the Mosul consulate served as its major contact with the Turkomen population in northern Iraq, numbering five hundred thousand or so. In addition, Iraq announced a reduction in staff at its embassy in Ankara and requested that Turkey reduce the number of staff at its embassy in Baghdad. While Iraqi officials stated that the the closures and cutbacks were due to lack of funds, it seemed clear that Ankara's lack of response to a series of diplomatic initiatives by Baghdad, including one to lift the UN-imposed economic sanctions and open the oil pipeline, was the real reason.[59]

On 4 September, Mümtaz Soysal, who had served as Turkey's foreign minister for six months in 1994, paid a quick visit to Baghdad. The main reason for his visit has to quiet Baghdad's fears regarding Turkey's long-term objectives in northern Iraq. Baghdad was upset by the Drogheda conference held in August under the auspices of the United States to settle differences between the two warring Kurdish factions. Baghdad's ire was raised by the fact that Turkey was also an invited participant. No Syrian, Iranian or Iraqi representatives were invited to attend. Turkey's increasingly enhanced role as a arbiter of the disposition of power in northern Iraq posed a challenge to any hope that Baghdad may still entertain of regaining influence in the region. Soysal was apparently sent because during his stint as foreign minister he was an advocate of greater cooperation with Baghdad in order to prevent the emergence of an strong Kurdish political entity in northern Iraq. Soysal's visit seemed to have little effect, however, on the policy that was being pursued by the government.[60] Relations between the two countries were soured further throughout 1995 by Demirel's sporadic statements that the international boundary between Turkey and Iraq should·be changed, and he left no doubt that the change should be southward.

By late 1995 other factors were mitigating the need on the part of Turkey for improving relations with Iraq. On 9 October, it was announced that the Azerbaijani International Oil Consortium (AIOC) had agreed to transport some of the oil from its Caspian fields through Georgia to Turkey. Turkey had to fight to secure the route in the face of strong Russian opposition. But with the strong support of the United States, one of the routes for the Azerbaijani oil was seemingly secured for Turkey. The possibility of obtaining long-term oil supplies from the Caspian oil fields will lessen Ankara's need to improve relations with Baghdad in order to secure oil from that country. It also reduces Turkey's need to expend its diplomatic capital to try to get the oil pipelines from Iraq to Turkey reopened. At the end of

1995, with the potential of satisfying a good portion of its oil needs from the Azerbaijan and Caspian oil and natural gas fields, the most important factor impelling Turkey to better relations with Baghdad, other than the need to control the Kurdish nationalist movement, was somewhat reduced.

The end of the cold war had made Turkey a less significant military ally for the West. However, Turkey will obviously want to keep as close military and economic relations as possible with Europe and the United States. Its admission to the European Customs Union (ECU) on 13 December by the overwhelming vote of 343 in favor, 149 against and 36 abstentions demonstrates the solidity of the increasingly strong economic and trading relations between Turkey and Europe. The vote also emphasizes, as Philip Robins writes in his contribution to this volume, that the impact of the Kurdish issue on European-Turkish relations is "more apparent than real." The vote states emphatically Europe's desire to have Turkey as a trading and economic partner in the EU. But the profound dimensions of the Kurdish question may mean that Turkey will still have to consider carefully its Western-oriented military and defensive alliances. The Kurdish question demands that Turkey pay closer attention to its relations with Syria, Iran, Iraq and, even Russia, than it has in the past. There is some irony in the fact that Turkey's trade with its Arab neighbors and with Iran represents only 17 or 18 percent of its total trade, whereas its trade with the OCED countries is over 60 percent. Turkey's admission into the ECU means that this percentage may well shift even more in favor of European trade. Without the alarms and worries of the Kurdish question, there would be less need to foster closer relations with Syria, Iraq and Iran.

In late December 1994, Prime Minister Tansu Çiller, responding angrily to Greek statements that it would veto Turkey's entry into the ECU, stated: "Beware, Turkey is coming with its 60 million people, and behind them with the 200 million Turkish speaking people."[61] In the end Greece was unable to prevent Turkey's admission into the customs union, but neither has Turkey been able to resolve its Kurdish problem and the interstate Kurdish question. As I have argued in this chapter, the voices of the 260 million Turkish people have been made less audible by the cacophony of some 23 million Kurdish voices.

NOTES

1. I wish to thank Hafeez Malik, editor of *Journal of South Asian and Middle Eastern Studies* for permission to reuse material here that first appeared in *Journal of South Asian and Middle Eastern Studies* 19, no. 1 (fall 1995). For some preliminary comments on this subject see my "The Kurdish Question Four Years On: The Policies of Turkey, Syria, Iran and Iraq," *Middle East Policy* 3, no. 3 (1994), 136-44.

2. For the role of Turkish foreign policy in the immediate aftermath of the Gulf war see my "The Creation of a Kurdish State in the 1990's?" *Journal of South Asian and Middle Eastern Studies* 15, no.4 (summer 1992), 1-25; "The Kurdish question in the aftermath of

the Gulf war: geopolitical and geostrategic changes in the Middle East," *Third World Quarterly* 13, no. 3 (1992), 475-99; "The Kurdish Question and Geopolitic and Geostrategic Changes in the Middle East After the Gulf War," *Journal of South Asian and Middle Eastern Studies* 17, no. 4 (summer 1994), 49-67. Also see Henri J. Barkey, "Turkey's Kurdish Dilemma," *Survival* 35, no. 4 (winter 1993), 51-70; Philip Robins, "The overlord state: Turkish policy and the Kurdish issue," *International Affairs* 69, no. 4 (October 1993), 657-71; Nevzat Soğuk, "A Study of the Historico Cultural Reasons for Turkey's Inconclusive Democracy," *New Political Science* 26 (fall 1993), 89-116.

    3. The most detailed study of the PKK is that of Ismet Imset, "The PKK: a report on separatist violence in Turkey, 1973-1992" (Ankara, 1992). This book is not scholarly, but it is informative. It is written by a Turkish journalist who closely followed the development of the PKK. Also see Michael Gunter, *The Kurds in Turkey: A Political Dilemma* (Boulder, 1990), especially pages, 57-96; Martin van Bruinessen, "Between Guerrilla War and Political Murder: The Workers' Party of Kurdistan," *Middle East Report*, no. 153 (July-Aug. 1988), 40-42; 44-46, 50.

    4. Kurdish sources claim the Kurdish population in 1990 was 27.4 million with the following distribution: Turkey, 14.3 million; Iran, 6.7 million; Iraq, 4.7 million; Syria, 1.4 million and members of the Russian Federation, 300,000. The respective percentage of Kurds among the total population of the above countries is: 25 percent for Turkey; 12 percent for Iran; 25 percent for Iraq; 12 percent for Syria. See *Kurdish Times* 4 (1992), 21.

    5. The literature on these developments is voluminous. I shall here merely cite some general accounts of this period, which provide the necessary bibliographies to a detail study of the period. Nader Entessar, *Kurdish Ethnonationalism* (Boulder, 1992) provides coverage of the Kurdish nationalism movements in Iran, Iraq and Turkey from World War I to the early 1990s; Michael M. Gunter, *The Kurds of Iraq: Tragedy and Hope* (New York, 1992) focuses on Iraq. See also the sources cited in note 2 above.

    6. *Newspot*, no. 93/24, 2 Dec. 1993, 4.

    7. *Newspot*, no. 93/25, 21 Dec. 1993, 4.

    8. *Hürriyet*, 23 Aug. 1994.

    9. *Hürriyet*, 11 Sept. 1994.

    10. *Hürriyet*, 24 Aug. 1994.

    11. *Hürriyet*, 4-6 Dece. 1994.

    12. *Hürriyet*, 11 Feb. 1995. As of the writing of this chapter no agreement over the flow of water had been reached.

    13. *Kurdistan Report*, no. 22 (Sept.-Oct. 1995), 25.

    14. *Hürriyet*, 17 Sept. 1995.

    15. *Hürriyet*, 22-26 Nov. 1995.

    16. *Hürriyet*, 22 July 1994.

    17. Carlos the Jackal, the pseudonym of Ilich Ramirez Sanchez, well known terrorist, was delivered to the French government by the government of Sudan on 15 August.

    18. *Hürriyet*, 10 Jan. 1995.

    19. *Hürriyet*, 3 Feb. 1995.

    20. *Ettela'at*, 16 Sept. 1995.

    21. *Ettela'at*, 10 Nov. 1995.

    22. *Hürriyet*, 3 Nov. 1995; *Iran Times*, 1 Dec. 1995.

    23. For the connection between the Kurdish question and the Azerbaijan question see my "The Kurdish Question and the Kurdish Problem: Some Geopolitical and Geostrategic Comparisons," in *Les Kurdes et les Etats*, a special issue of *Peuples Méiterranéens*, no. 68-69 (July-Dec. 1994), 231-41.

24. *Hürriyet*, 25 Jan. 1995.

25. *Hürriyet*, 24 Feb. 1995.

26. *Hürriyet*, 24 Feb. 1995.

27. *Hürriyet*, 17 March 1995.

28. *Hürriyet*, 25 April 1995.

29. *Hürriyet*, 21 July 1995.

30. Ibid.

31. *Hürriyet*, 2 Nov. 1995.

32. *Hürriyet*, 3 Nov. 1995.

33. *Hürriyet*, 1 Nov. 1995.

34. *Hürriyet*, 2 Nov. 1995.

35. *Hürriyet*, 30 Nov. 1995.

36. The hijacking dominated the Turkish media from 16-21 January. I read accounts in *Hürriyet* and *Cumhuriyet*.

37. Michael McFaul, "Russian Politics after Chechnya," *Foreign Affairs*, no. 99 (summer 1995), 149-68. McFaul also cites "career advancement" as the main factor influencing the Russian "party of war."

38. Holly Burkhalter, *Christian Science Monitor*, 8 May 1995. McFaul puts the cost of the war at $5 billion as of 1 March 1995.

39. An example of the preoccupation of the Turkish government was the issuing of a report entitled *The Southeast Report: Diagnoses and Remedies. Southeast* in Turkish parlance is a euphemism for the Kurdish problem. The report was published in *Hürriyet* in serialized form from 14 August to 6 September. The report is purported to have been prepared for the government under the aegis of the Turkish chambers of commerce and stock markets, the president of which is Yalım Erez, a close advisor and confidant of Prime Minister Tansu Çiller and himself an ethnic Kurd. The research team that prepared the report was headed by Professor Doğu Ergil, an academic who teaches at Ankara University and has long been interested in the "Eastern Question." Throughout August and September the report and the discussion of it in the press and in private think tanks created a brouhaha. Allegations regarding the provenance of the report, its political intentions, the validity of the data base and the reliability of the research methodology employed continued throughout the remainder of 1995. Some oppositional political leaders claimed that the report was the brainchild of the United States, through which it was laying the foundation to later establish an independent Kurdish state in southeast Turkey and in northern Iraq. The purpose of the report was to persuade the Turkish government and the Turkish people of the necessity of granting the Kurds cultural and a large measure of political autonomy in the southeast.

40. Ebulfez Elçibey, the former pro-Turkish president of Azerbaijan, in his first interview with a Turkish reporter, on 18 September 1995, criticized Turkey for not supporting him during the rebellion of Suret Hüseyinov, which led to his deposition and eventual replacement by the pro-Russian Haidar Aliyev, the current president of Azerbaijan. Elçibey stated that he received no support from Turkey during the rebellion and that he was still "angry at Turkey." Furthermore, said the former president, "Russia is simply a blown-up balloon. It put all of its resources against the war in Chechnya. What did it accomplish? Nothing. Turkey must not be so timid in supporting the Turkic republics and must be in the forefront. Turkey today is pursuing the same hesitant policy against Russia that it has pursued for centuries." (*Hürriyet*, 10 Sept. 1995.

41. The dilemmas, contradictions and paradoxes of Russian-Turkish relations are poignantly illustrated by reports that Turkish construction companies will be heavily in-

volved in the reconstruction of Grozny. The problems on the domestic front also continued to mount. In the fall of 1995, Turkey began to experience a shortage of meat as a result of its policy of emptying the villages of the southeast. The resulting flight of the population to larger towns and cities left no one to tend the flocks of livestock that are one of the main exports of southeastern Turkey to the urban areas in the west. In 1995 and 1996 Turkey was compelled to import millions of tons of meat. The skyrocketing cost of meat resulted in more criticism of the government's policy toward the PKK and the Kurdish nationalist movement.

42. *Hürriyet*, 1 Aug. 1994,

43. *Hürriyet*, 28 June, 1994.

44. *Hürriyet*, 30 Aug. 1994).

45. *Hürriyet*, 15 Sept. 1994.

46. Eric Rouleau, "America's Unyielding Policy Toward Iraq," *Foreign Affairs* 75, no. 1 (Jan.-Feb. 1995), 70.

47. *The Christian Science Monitor,* 8 Sept. 1994.

48. *Hürriyet*, 2 Sept. 1994. Rouleau made essentially the same argument in his article in *Foreign Affairs* quoted above, with the exception that he did not mention that lower oil prices would increase the competitiveness of Germany and Japan, the United States' two most important economic competitors.

49. *Newspot*, 24 Feb. 1995.

50. *Hürriyet*, 16 Feb. 1995.

51. *Hürriyet*, 7 March 1995.

52. *Hürriyet*, 23 Feb. 1995.

53. The long-term possiblities, however, seem better as Hamit Bozarslan suggests in this contribution.

54. *Hürriyet*, 4 March 1995.

55. *Hürriyet*, 5 March 1995.

56. *Middle East International,* no. 496, 17 March 1995.

57. For some of the first accounts of the invasion see *New York Times*, 21, 22, 23 March 1995, and the article by Sami Kohen, 23 March 1995.

58. Such a development of relations between Ankara and Baghdad would imply that the future of Iraq vis-à-vis its Kurdish problem and the Kurdish question is not as dire as some have predicted. In this regard see, Graham Fuller, "Iraq in the Next Decade: Will Iraq Survive Until 2002?" Rand, N-3591-DAG, 1993 (Santa Monica, Calif., 1993).

59. *Hürriyet*, 20 Aug. 1995.

60. *Hürriyet*, 5 Sept. 1995.

61. *The Christian Science Monitor,* 27 Dec. 1995.

6

MORE APPARENT THAN REAL? THE IMPACT OF THE KURDISH ISSUE ON EURO-TURKISH RELATIONS[1]

Philip Robins

In February 1994 a meeting on Turkish foreign policy was convened at Chatham House, the home of the Royal Institute of International Affairs, in London. The organizers at the Institute had expected the audience to be addressed by one speaker, Professor Emre Gönensay, advisor to the Turkish prime minister. In reality, a large official delegation of Turkish personalities turned up[2] and collectively insisted that the meeting be addressed in turn by five of their number, to the evident embarrassment of Professor Gönensay. Furthermore, when the Turkish team did take the lectern they ignored the scheduled subject of the meeting and, instead, each speaker insisted on addressing an aspect of the country's Kurdish problem. After the meeting, the Turkish ambassador to London apologized personally to the chairman of the event[3], pleading that Ankara had sent instructions to take every opportunity to put forth its side of the story on the issue.

Although only an anecdote, this story illustrates some of the dynamics in the Euro-Kurdish-Turkish relationship as they had appeared by the beginning of 1994. First, it shows to what extent the Kurdish issue had emerged as a major problem in relations between the state of Turkey and some of the leading members of the European Union. Second, it shows how a small number of European cities had become the focus of debate on Turkey's Kurdish problem. Third, it indicates how ill prepared the Turkish government is to resist the increasingly well organized and professional publicity machine in support of Turkey's Kurdish nationalist movement. In the case of the meeting at Chatham House, the Turkish officials, who can usually be relied upon to observe scrupulously any pre-agreed ground rules, effectively hijacked the meeting. In doing so, they risked offending an important institution, which hitherto had shown itself interested in cultivating close links with Ankara.[4] In doing so, their ploy backfired; the distinguished audience that had assembled to hear a lecture and discussion on Turkish foreign policy was greatly irritated at the change in substance of the meeting.

Taking this vignette as its point of departure, this chapter aims to explore the relationship between Western Europe and Turkey, in the light of the Kurdish issue. Western Europe will be analyzed both in terms of individual states and as a collective in the guise of the European Union (EU).[5] This chapter will consider why the Kurdish issue, as the story above indicates, has emerged as a significant problem in bilateral relations. It will also consider Western European responses toward Turkey over the issue. Finally, it will consider whether the Kurdish issue, for all the rhetoric and newspaper headlines, has actually damaged in a material sense the relationship between Turkey, the leading European states and the EU. In other words, has the Kurdish issue really been a barrier in Euro-Turkish relations, or has its impact been more apparent than real?

THE EMERGENCE OF THE KURDISH ISSUE

The intrusion of the Kurdish issue into relations between Turkey and the EU is a relatively recent phenomenon. Prior to the mid 1980s there was little popular consciousness in the continent of Europe as to the Kurdish people. A threshold in popularizing the Kurdish issue in Western Europe was the use of chemical weapons by the Iraqi military against the Kurdish town of Halabja. The gas attack took place shortly after the Iraqi army had lost control of the town in 1987. Revelations about the use of chemical weapons, together with the painful death suffered by some five thousand victims, elicited great sympathy for the Kurds.

This image of the defenseless Kurd at the mercy of the repressive states of the region received a powerful boost in the aftermath of the international coalition's victory against Iraq in February 1991. Fearing a new gas attack as the Iraqi state struggled to repress uprisings across the country, hundreds of thousands of Kurds fled Iraqi Kurdistan in panic. Some 750,000 of them ended up on the Turkish border. Though Turkey was the passive object of this exodus, unfavorable publicity almost inevitably attached itself to Ankara. While the Turkish government resisted the massive influx of Kurdish refugees for fear of the demographic and economic implications of their possible semi-permanent residence,[6] journalists at the scene became ever more impatient with Turkey's handling of the affair. Criticism was particularly sharp over Ankara's priority of *raison d'etat* over humanitarianism.

Though the flight of Iraqi Kurds to Turkey after the Gulf war was brought to a satisfactory and speedy end, the news reporting of the event as a whole helped to enforce popular cultural stereotypes in Western Europe about Turkey and the Turks. Turkey's reluctance to allow the Iraqi Kurdish refugees to come down from the mountain ridges reinforced a view of Turks as heartless and brutal, underpinned by historical images of Ottoman repression. The images of the Turks perpetuated in popular Western culture, through films like *Lawrence of Arabia* and *Midnight Express*, were confirmed.

The tendency to equate these images of callous violence by the Turks with images of the Kurds as victims was further reinforced by two trends: the growing Kurdish insurgency in southeastern Turkey against the Turkish state and the growing presence of an effective Kurdish lobby in Western Europe. The Kurdish insurgency inside Turkey commenced in 1984 at the instigation of the Kurdistan Workers' Party (PKK). When it began, the PKK was small in size and extremist in ideology—in short, a fringe organization with little prospect of success.[7] Its rise was facilitated and accelerated by the Turkish state in the 1980s, which, in the wake of the generals' hard-line policy against the Kurds, helped to eradicate the center ground in Kurdish politics. The result was political polarization. Increasingly, Kurds in the troubled areas of Turkey were forced to face a stark choice: support either a repressive state or a militant body committed to violence as a mechanism to bring about political change.

Since 1989 the insurgency has grown in strength, as have the casualties sustained by, in all probability, all sides.[8] During the first decade of fighting, around fourteen thousand people were killed. In 1995 a U.S. State Department report estimated the number of the PKK's full-time guerrillas at ten to fifteen thousand, some five to six thousand based inside Turkey, with a further sixty to seventy-five thousand part-time operatives.[9] Such figures suggest that, for all the claims of imminent eradication from Ankara, the PKK's ability to sustain the insurgency remains substantial.

As the insurgency has grown more serious and the brutal methods used by the PKK more widespread, the Turkish state has resorted to instruments commensurate with what the military and much of the political establishment regard as a challenge to the very integrity of the state. These instruments have included the increased use of sometimes extended cross-border raids into northern Iraq,[10] the application of intensive and often indiscriminate conventional firepower on civilian areas within Turkey,[11] the forced relocation of villagers followed by the destruction of their former dwelling places,[12] and the introduction of death squads targeting Kurdish political activities in the southeast.[13] All of these acts have become widely known among human rights activists in Western Europe. The scale of the insurgency and the widespread nature of the methods used to try to suppress it have resulted in a growing fusion of human rights questions with the Kurdish issue. While other human rights abuses, such as the near routine use of torture in some police stations,[14] clearly do continue to take place in Turkey and while the victims are certainly not exclusively Kurdish, during the 1990s it has become increasingly difficult to separate the Kurdish issue from the human rights issue. Liberal Turks who argue that all citizens of Turkey suffer from human rights abuses and a democratic deficit and that such problems are not confined to

Turkey's Kurds find the argument increasingly difficult to sustain, especially to an international audience.

The second factor that has helped to bolster the image of Turks as oppressors and the Kurds as victims is the growing Kurdish expatriate presence in Western Europe and its increasingly sophisticated political organizations, especially with regard to the use of information. Again, the Turkish state has to take much of the blame. It was the state's uncompromising policies and brutal methods that forced many Turkish Kurds to flee. Even those who had not been subject to systemic persecution or who were merely economic migrants found a receptive atmosphere in Western Europe to their applications for political asylum, based on the activities of the Turkish state throughout much of the 1980s.

Consequently, there is now a substantial presence of Turkish Kurds in the countries of Western Europe. Of course, it is near impossible to calculate how many arrived for political reasons. Indeed, it is difficult to establish what percentage of the Turkish community living in Europe is Kurdish, for reasons similar to the difficulty of judging the size of the Kurdish population in Turkey itself, which explains why estimates have differed so widely. In Germany, for example, statistics for the number of Turkish Kurds in the country have ranged from seventy-five[15] to four hundred thousand.[16] The PKK is believed to have some forty-eight hundred activists in Germany.[17] In Britain, official sources put the number of Kurdish refugees at twenty thousand.[18] The number of Kurds in France is estimated at sixty thousand.[19]

Of greater importance than the numbers involved is the effectiveness of the organization of the Turkish Kurds in Western Europe and the extent to which their bodies are funded. There are, of course, a plethora of Kurdish expatriate organizations in Europe. It is, however, interesting to note that the organizational plurality among the Kurds is largely a characteristic of Iraqi Kurdish communities. While there are many different bodies among Turkey's Kurdish émigrés, including social, cultural, media and political organizations, the best organized and most effective appear to be those linked to the PKK, often indirectly through affiliated organizations such as its predominantly political wing, the National Liberation Front of Kurdistan (ERNK).

A few disparate examples will help support the point. At the political level, the Kurdish parliament in exile (KPE) convened in The Hague in April 1995 was dominated by the PKK.[20] In Brussels, the former Democracy Party (DEP) MPs in exile, having effectively admitted their close links with the PKK, have established a "DEP Solidarity Office" in the Belgian capital. The PKK has pursued a policy of trying to open representative offices across the continent. ERNK offices are now to be found in Athens, Copenhagen and Madrid in Western Europe, while Kurdistan solidarity and information centers, associated with the PKK, are found elsewhere, such as in London. In the media field, the PKK news agency, *Kurd Ha,* was a constant source of information on the Kurdish issue in Turkey; in April 1995 the MED-TV station was set up principally to broadcast to Turkey's Kurds from Brussels.

A number of factors may be advanced to explain the rapid emergence of the PKK as the dominant political organization among Turkey's Kurds. One set of factors refers to the political situation in Turkey. With moderate Kurdish organizations not allowed to function normally, the suppression of two Kurdish parliamentary parties—the Democracy Party (DEP) and the Peoples Labor Party (HEP)—in less than a year[21] and the armed operations of the PKK as the only force capable of resisting the Turkish state, there is no convincing alternative political vehicle for Kurdish nationalists from Turkey to support. A second set of factors relates to the organizational nature and methods of the PKK. A key factor in the emergence of a more monolithic political structure among Turkish Kurds in Western Europe has been the consistent refusal of the PKK to tolerate the growth of rival political organizations. As befits an organization that has survived extensive repression in Turkey and has had to operate against a backdrop of logistical problems and political uncertainties, the PKK, like the PLO before it, has developed strong sinews. The PKK has also developed an apparently healthy financial base. The organization says that its financial success is a result of donations from businessmen and ordinary Kurds who share its political aims. Its opponents point to racketeering among Turkey's Kurdish community in Western Europe and involvement in the international drugs trade[22] as the main sources of these funds. British security sources indicate that while the charges of extortion, though hard to prove, do ring true, there is no evidence that the PKK is involved in illicit drugs in the UK.

TURKEY, THE KURDISH ISSUE AND THE STATES OF WESTERN EUROPE

Ankara's relations with the states of Western Europe can best be divided into two realms—relations with the smaller states of Europe and relations with those larger states whose extensive foreign interests prompt them to play a more active role in foreign relations. These smaller, predominantly northern states tend to have relatively little direct involvement with Turkey. Trade is nominal. Senior, bilateral contact is relatively infrequent. The absence of both broader interests and the projection of diplomacy and power tends to mean that single issues, notably human rights, rank higher on the list of foreign policy concerns for these states. These states have a more liberal refugee and asylum policy. Their traditions of open, liberal refugee government make them susceptible to influence by well organized political associations.

By contrast, the larger states have a more wide-ranging set of interests in their foreign relations. They have substantial trading relations with Turkey, are more likely to have made significant levels of direct investment there, and are generally cognizant of Turkey beyond the simple image of a state that routinely indulges in political repression. Moreover, strategic questions are also of greater importance. Regular visits at the senior level are paid, with frequent contact taking place at diplomatic, business and military levels. The notion of Turkey as an important ally, fostered by decades of close contact through the various branches of NATO, is embedded more deeply in the bureaucratic psyche than is the case with the smaller states. Furthermore, states such as the United Kingdom, France and Spain have all suffered from acts of terrorism in recent years and therefore were always likely to be sympathetically disposed toward Turkey's presentation of the PKK as an exclusively terrorist organization. Human rights is of course considered an important issue but only one issue among many. The lobbying efforts of émigré organizations and the local groups that befriend them are, in turn, countered by pressures from other more sympathetic constituencies, such as business and the military.

SMALL PLAYERS

The impact of the Kurdish issue on relations between these smaller states and Turkey tends to manifest itself in one of two ways. First, as will be seen later, it creates an indirect impact, through the institutions of the EU. The smaller states are a constant and vociferous lobby within the EU for human rights and democracy to be placed high up the agenda of the Community's foreign affairs. In the absence of a clear Community foreign policy, this is obtained through the harmonization of the positions of the members states. Community policy, pursued by the External Relations directorate of the Commission and the country that holds the presidency of the Council of Ministers, supported by the Troika,[23] is thus subject to a series of trade-offs that take into account the views and depth of feeling of the members. The second way in which the Kurdish issue impacts is through the direct bilateral relations of the smaller states with Turkey. Because of the minor importance of these states, contacts with Turkey tend to be spasmodic. Mindful of its EU membership aspirations, however, Ankara does tend to be periodically attentive to such states. For example, in December 1994, President Süleyman Demirel paid a visit to Portugal, even though the two countries have little contact and bilateral trade is worth less than $100 million annually. The aim of the visit was to ensure that relations were smooth as they approached an important period in EU-Turkish relations, namely the conclusion of a customs union.

With bilateral contacts fitful in nature, the spotlight usually only focuses on bilateral ties during periods of sudden and intense strain. Over the past five years the Kurdish issue has most frequently provoked such interludes. Two examples illustrate the point. When Turkey launched a major military operation in Iraqi Kurdistan in March 1995, the smaller states of the EU were the most critical. As a result, a number of the smaller states were willing to impose sanctions as a symbol of their disapproval. In the case of Denmark, these sanctions took the form of an arms embargo, which then, predictably, led to retaliation from Ankara in the form of putting such countries on a "red list," effectively reciprocating the arms embargo.

The second example relates to the establishment of the Kurdistan parliament in exile (KPE). In spite of its name, the assembly, which met for its inaugural session in The Hague on 12 April 1995, almost exclusively consisted of Kurds who had originated from Turkey. The assembly was heavily influenced by the PKK, thereby prompting one of the few Kurdish organizations abroad that exist independent of the PKK, the Kurdish Socialist Party (KSP) led by Kemal Burkay, to eschew involvement. The fact that Dutch authorities were unable or unwilling to stop the convening of the assembly placed an immediate strain on bilateral ties with Ankara. The Turkish government banned imports of Dutch arms in protest.[24] The Netherlands were heavily criticized in the Turkish media for what was considered "an unfriendly act."[25] Other accusations spilled easily from the pens of the Turkish press, including the charge that the Dutch and the Belgian[26] governments had "turned a blind eye" to the actions of the PKK on their territory, including the use of intimidation as a means to raise funds.[27] It should be noted, however, that once the deliberations of the assembly had finished and the initial anger had subsided, the foreign ministries of the two countries quietly set about trying to rehabilitate bilateral relations. As early as mid-May, Turkish foreign minister Erdal Inönü had met his Dutch counterpart, Hans van Mielo, with a view to stabilizing and improving ties.[28]

Greece too is clearly an example of a smaller state within the EU. Its relationship with Turkey is, not surprisingly, somewhat different from the others. As a close neighbor of Turkey's in a relationship of almost constant strain, relations are far less fitful than with the other smaller states of Western Europe. Moreover, there is clearly a long agenda of problem issues that preoccupy Ankara and Athens, from the Cyprus issue through the position of their respective minorities through a clutch of issues concentrated on the Aegean Sea and the potentially unstable situation in the Balkans. For Greece, the Kurdish issue pales in significance. However, the issue does periodically erupt, such as over Turkish concerns over the opening of a PKK office in Athens in February 1995 and accusations that the Greek government condones and even expedites the activities of the PKK.[29]

Within a multilateral European context, Greece has been forthright in drawing attention to Turkey's human rights abuses, which, as has already been observed, has tended to become synonymous with its handling of the Kurdish issue. For instance, when Greece formally sought the postponement of a key EU Association Council meeting, which was to lay the groundwork for a conclusion of the Customs Union, it did so on three grounds: the Turkish occupation of northern Cyprus; the bilateral problems that existed between the two states; and, of particular note, Turkey's human rights record.[30] Interestingly, and as a further example of the periodic bouts of small state antipathy toward Turkey, Athens was supported in this blocking maneuver by Luxembourg.

BIG PLAYERS

In contrast, bilateral relations between three of the EU's four major players—Britain, France and Italy—have remained remarkably unaffected by the Kurdish issue, in spite of the mounting intensity of the issue inside Turkey during the 1990s. Of the three, relations between Italy and Turkey have been the least subject to turbulence. Italy has sizeable commercial interests in Turkey. Fiat opened its first joint venture factory in Turkey as long ago as 1968; Italy topped the league for foreign direct investment in Turkey in 1993 with $419 million worth of capital;[31] in 1993 Italy exported nearly $2.6 billion worth of goods to Turkey. The Kurdish issue appears to have little resonance with the Italian public. The two countries have concluded an agreement to cooperate against drug trafficking, organized crime and terrorism. In March 1995 President Oscar Luigi Scalfaro visited Turkey on a trip that went smoothly. Though his visit virtually coincided with the Turkish army incursion into northern Iraq, President Scalfaro still felt able to give explicit support in its fight against terrorism, while appealing for respect for human rights.[32]

Relations between Turkey and both Britain and France have, by contrast, been subject to some strain in the recent past, although in neither case has this been as a result of the Kurdish issue. Ties between Britain and Turkey had few blemishes before 1993. This solid relationship was based on a common perception of security priorities, which laid a premium on the continued existence of a strong NATO and an Atlanticist orientation, and was skeptical of a more European approach to security. This similarity of views was complemented by a growing commercial relationship, which saw British exports top the $2 billion mark for the first time in 1993. More than two hundred British firms are active in Turkey in joint ventures.[33]

Political relations reflected these close links at the security and commercial levels. It was to the United Kingdom that Süleyman Demirel paid his first visit to Europe on becoming prime minister in November 1992.[34] British foreign secretary Douglas Hurd took a special and sympathetic interest in Turkey during his tenure in charge of British foreign policy. Hurd was a regular visitor to Ankara and formed a special relationship with his Turkish counterpart, Hikmet Çetin. On such occasions the human rights issue was raised but was not given a central prominence and was certainly not allowed to cloud relations. Hurd's public pronouncements on such matters during his visits to Turkey were of a low key, subtle nature, urging the Turks to introduce "quality democracy and human rights."[35] Indeed, during the British presidency Hurd set about giving substance to the promise of enhanced political cooperations between the EU and Turkey made during the Lisbon summit. This was to result in an Association Council meeting, under British auspices, which prescribed high-level bilateral meetings between the two sides, a status that hitherto was only enjoyed by Canada, Japan and the United States.

When Turkish officials expressed some misgivings over the Edinburgh summit, which occurred at the climax of the United Kingdom presidency, it was over the "insufficient" nature of the statements on Bosnia rather than any trace of criticism over the Kurdish issue. Indeed, Bosnia was then in the process of emerging as the issue that has partially blighted Anglo-Turkish relations over the succeeding two or three years. Only since the spring of 1995 and the successful application in London of a broadcasting license for MED-TV, which Ankara holds is nothing but a propaganda arm of the PKK, has the Kurdish issue emerged as a problematic issue in bilateral relations.

If Bosnia has been responsible for an uncharacteristic turbulence in Anglo-Turkish relations, it has been less of a problem between France and Turkey. However, relations between France and Turkey had been retarded since the 1970s by other factors, principally the Armenian issue—the three hundred thousand ethnic Armenian voters in France, it is claimed, acting as a powerful influence on policy-making in Paris. So cool were relations that when President François Mitterand visited Turkey in 1992 he was the first French head of state to do so since Charles de Gaulle in 1968.[36] After the Armenian issue, the Kurdish problem has been the second most important problem area since 1988,[37] especially in view of the pro-Kurdish activism displayed by President Mitterand's, admittedly estranged, wife, Danielle. So bad had ties been at one stage that formal relations had been downgraded to the level of chargé d'affaires.

France began to make a serious effort to placate Ankara over the Kurdish issue toward the beginning of 1992, paradoxically at a time when Turkish loss of life and a hard-line state security policy were both on the increase. The arrest of two members of the PKK, who were accused of using unacceptable methods to raise funds, was used to trumpet what was heralded as a "a new approach" in the French government's stance toward Turkey.[38] This tougher approach toward the PKK was further stiffened with the crackdown on the organization and its affiliated bodies led by the hard-line interior minister Charles Pasqua in November 1993. The French government banned two Kurdish groups that it claimed were front organizations for the PKK. Police raids were undertaken in Paris, Lyon, Marseilles, Strasbourg, Toulouse, Bordeaux, Rouen and in Brittany, and more than one hundred suspects were arrested.[39] It appears probable that the increasingly violent activities of militant Kurds in France the summer before, which had included the holding of six hostages at the Turkish Consulate in Marseilles, together with the seizure by the PKK of four French tourists in southeastern Turkey had helped to precipitate the backlash. Ankara duly expressed itself to be very happy with the French action.[40] On his next visit to the Turkish capital French foreign minister Alain Juppé appeared to tread carefully around the Kurdish issue, calling for Turkey to "carry out a dialogue" but without being drawn out who should be included in such a process.[41] Ankara's fondness for Juppé was to deepen during the French presidency of the EU Council of Ministers, when the final negotiations on the Customs Union were concluded. It was because of the close association with

Juppé that Ankara welcomed the election of Jacques Chirac as French president in May 1995.

The only one of Western Europe's four major players that found it hard to maintain relations with Turkey on an even keel during periods of heightened controversy surrounding the Kurdish issue was Germany. Instead, relations between the Federal Republic and Turkey have been subject to frequent periods of angry outbursts and recrimination, often directly as a consequence of the Kurdish issue. Granted, Germany has since the early 1990s formally labeled the PKK a terrorist organization. Bonn has, however, frequently been the subject of sniping from Ankara as to what it is prepared to do to give substance to this position.[42] While the PKK was "not visible" in Germany, it was claimed that it worked through organizations that were, such as the Patriotic Artists Association of Kurdistan and the Federation of Kurdistan Patriotic Workers Cultural Associations.[43]

From time to time this general uneasiness over the issue would decline precipitously. The use of German arms by the Turkish military against Kurdish targets proved to be a particularly sensitive subject. In March 1992 Germany halted all arms sales to Turkey[44] after it was asserted that armored personnel carriers sold to Turkey had been used in the anti-insurgency operations in the southeast.[45] The gravity of the issue was never in doubt. The subsequent bureaucratic error that resulted in fifteen Leopard tanks being delivered in spite of this ban was the cause of the German defense minister Gerhard Stotenberg's forced resignation. The affairs provoked tit for tat retaliation that saw Turkish education minister Köksal Toptan cancel a visit to Germany and call for a boycott of German goods,[46] while German labor minister Norbert Bluen canceled a visit in the opposite direction. An accompanying war of words included then prime minister Süleyman Demirel contrasting the position of Bonn with that of London, it being said that Britain had praised Turkey's "restraint" in its approach to its internal security problem. Turkish foreign minister Hikmet Çetin was later quoted as saying that at the time relations with Germany were at a "freezing point."[47] The bad atmosphere was relieved on that occasion by the resignation of the long-serving German foreign minister Hans Dietrich Genscher, who, it was argued, had been the root cause of difficulties in bilateral relations.[48] The Bundestag Commission for Foreign Affairs rescinded the embargo just over one month later.

Tension flared up again in October of the same year, during the Turkish military's extended ground and air operations in northern Iraq. Reports that a PKK fighter had died after being hitched to the back of a German-made armored car appalled opposition politicians. The Social Democratic Party (SPD) subsequently put the Bonn government under "increasing pressure," in the course of which they demanded a severing of relations with Turkish police and intelligence bodies and the substitution of economic for bilateral military aid.[49] German military aid for the next three years was subsequently halved to $86 million, while German chancellor Helmut Kohl apparently found it prudent to delay a planned visit to Turkey.[50]

Though ties warmed up once again during 1993, the nervousness of the German government in the face of accusations of the improper use of German weaponry by the Turkish military resurfaced again in the spring of 1994. Bonn actually halted shipments of German arms merely on the suggestion that German tanks had been used against Kurdish insurgents in southeastern Turkey,[51] a move that resulted in a predictably angry response from the Turkish foreign ministry.[52] These charges, it was subsequently admitted, were false, and the embargo was consequently lifted.[53] What was particularly revealing was that Bonn so readily believed the initial accusation and that the overriding need was for the federal government to protect itself against domestic criticism rather than trying to evade Turkish anger.

German government opprobrium was again provoked by the second extended intervention by the Turkish military in northern Iraq in March 1995. Bonn's first reaction was, as in the past, to restrict sales of military hardware; in this case the withholding of grants promised to help in the purchase of two frigates. With President Demirel implying in a piece of loose talk that the Turkish military might remain on Iraqi soil for up to one year, German foreign minister Klaus Kinkel threatened a total halt in military aid if Turkey did not withdraw quickly.[54] Against a backdrop of renewed calls from the SPD to cease military sales to Turkey,[55] a shipment of military hardware, provided for according to a 1990 agreement made under the Cascading Initiative,[56] was suspended.[57] The fact that the extended nature of the Turkish intervention in northern Iraq resulted in growing public protests by Germany's Kurdish population, notably a twenty-thousand-strong demonstration in Düsseldorf on 1 April,[58] brought home to the Bonn government the growing domestic cost that such behavior by the Turkish state could bring about.

Though there is still no such thing as a European Union foreign policy, the EU does have foreign relations with nonmember states such as Turkey. A number of institutions have a role in helping to mould these foreign relations. The discussion here will be limited to those institutions that have political responsibility for conducting and developing such relations. The Presidency of the Council of Ministers and the Troika, which is an extension of the presidency, will be considered as the leading institution at the heart of government. The European Parliament, which now has formal responsibilities with respect to foreign relations, will then be viewed as an example of an EU institution that has a peripheral relationship with the political center.

AT THE CENTER: THE PRESIDENCY

The Presidency of the Council of Ministers is occupied by each member of the EU in turn for a six-month period. The state that holds the presidency is the lead country in terms of the formulation and implementation of policy, with the plenary session of the Council of Ministers holding ultimate power. The presidency has responsibilities in many different areas, including trade policy, the deepening of community institutions, the expansion of the EU to include new members and relations with nonmember states. The presidency is assisted by the Troika, which gives added ballast to the presidency, especially if it is held by a small state with limited bureaucratic resources, narrower interests and less gravitas in the international system.

In the main, relations have been viewed in a strictly bilateral way between the EU and Ankara. Turkey does not figure prominently in statements on the widening of EU membership, especially compared to the EFTA and Visegrad countries. However, Turkey is routinely mentioned in the six-month summit declarations, though more as a reflection of the "almost paranoid" concerns of Ankara[59] than any evolution in the substance of the relationship. The emphasis on the bilateral aspects of relations means that Turkey rarely features prominently as an EU matter, other than in areas of direct importance. In the 1990s these areas were: the strategic issue of anchoring Turkey to the West; the economic relationship, most frequently expressed through negotiations over the establishment of a customs union; and the conduct of the Turkish government, with human rights and Turkey's extra territorial actions giving the greatest cause for concern.

The nature of successive presidencies toward Turkey has shown a remarkable consistency. This has owed much to the convergence of thinking among the big players on Turkey and the relatively pliant nature of smaller states during their presidency terms. For instance, it was during the Portuguese presidency that Britain, which was by this time a member of the Troika, began to develop the idea of a special relationship between Turkey and the EU, akin to that which prevailed with the United States and Japan.[60] Douglas Hurd then pushed this idea at the EU foreign ministers meeting, resulting in the Portuguese foreign minister asking Hurd to "draw up a framework for relations between Turkey and the Community." The goal was pursued without any linkage, or apparent reference, to human rights or the Kurdish issue. This vision was given substance at the Lisbon summit of June 1992, which prescribed an enhanced political dialogue. With the ideas and the framework developed during the Portuguese presidency, nothing further was required from the British presidency that followed, other than to implement it.

A second example of the role played by the big players came during the Greek presidency. Leading states, such as Britain, France and Germany, were concerned that Athens might seek to exploit its presidency to spoil EU relations with Turkey. The best that Ankara could hope for was that relations would not be disrupted during this period, an objective that was realized due to the activities of the big players. In order to ensure that this was indeed the case and to draw attention to the close ties with Turkey, Britain and Germany undertook a preventive maneuver just prior to the start of the Greek presidency.[61] It was announced that regular trilateral meetings would be held at a senior level between government figures from the three states. These high-level meetings were subsequently opened up to France. Again, the human rights situation and the Kurdish problem did not prevent the implementation of such an initiative; Britain and Germany instead used the occasion as an opportunity to talk about such subjects. While meetings in such a form have since lapsed, the mechanism was successful when judged against its own objective of taking responsibility for political relations with Turkey out of the hands of Athens during the Greek presidency.

As well as maintaining the focus on bilateral relations with Turkey during their own and the smaller states' presidencies, the big players have also been instrumental in seeking to limit the damage caused by individual events on Turkey's relations with the EU. In doing so, the big players have had to pursue a well judged line. On the one hand, they have sought to take a firm attitude toward Ankara. Pressure from opposition politicians (in the case of Germany) and special interests groups (in the case of Britain, for instance), together with pressure from the smaller states has obliged such a stance. In the case of the Kurdish issue, this attitude has been amplified by a general sense of uneasiness as to whether the security policies being pursued by the Turkish state are really in the long term interests of stability in Turkey. On the other hand, the big players have sought to ensure that any one issue does not come to dominate bilateral relations and that issues such as human rights and the Kurds are balanced against other interests.

An excellent example of such factors in play came with the Turkish intervention in northern Iraq in March 1995, in the middle of the French presidency. The first reaction of the French presidency was a statement by the then French foreign minister Alain Juppé in which he attempted to give a balanced though clear reaction. He stated squarely that the EU viewed the PKK as a terror organization but said that Ankara had to abide by principles of legality and human rights as an associate member of the EU.[62] He further stated that the EU supports "in Turkey, as elsewhere, the principle of territorial integrity and sovereignty," but that, in the case of "the current incursion," Turkey had "violated basic principles of international law."[63] While the French attempted to manage the situation through a balanced approach, the overall EU stance appeared to be tougher because of the altogether milder language used by the U.S. government at the time.[64]

As if to confirm the centrality of the big players in driving EU policy in this matter, a diplomatic offensive by Ankara to explain the nature and causes of the intervention in northern Iraq targeted London, Paris and Bonn. While Foreign Minister Erdal İnönü traveled to the German and French capitals, deputy prime minister Hikmet Çetin flew to Britain. With the diplomatic offensive also taking in the United States, neither man visited any of the other European capitals.

ON THE PERIPHERY: THE EUROPEAN PARLIAMENT

The European Parliament (EP) has long been an institution without a role. In an effort to make itself more important and to give itself some function, the EP increasingly sought to be active on the issue of human rights. Moreover, until the signing of the Maastricht Treaty in 1992, the European Parliament was an "outsider" body, both devoid of power and short on influence with those institutions that wielded real power. The Maastricht Treaty was a threshold in the development of the EP. Concerned at the so-called "democratic deficit" at the heart of the EU, Maastricht sought to bring the EP in from the outside, yielding to it certain responsibilities. Chief among these was to ascribe to the EP responsibility for passing the EU budgets and endorsing treaties with external parties. Consequently, it was widely agreed within Western Europe that the EP has to endorse the Customs Union with Turkey in order for it to be formally adopted by the EU.[65]

The EP has long been interested in and critical of the human rights situation in Turkey, especially as it applies to the Kurdish issue. For instance, after the widespread clashes and loss of life during the Nevroz (New Year) festival in March 1992, the EP was highly critical of Ankara in expressing its overwhelming condemnation at the excessive use of force by the Turkish military. Not only was its language much more directly critical than the coded phrases used by member states, but the EP proposed a raft of measures to penalize Turkey for its actions. These included demands for an international investigation of the Nevroz events; the Commission and the Council of Ministers to take the initiative to find a solution to the Kurdish issue through the UN; and the EU-Turkish joint parliamentary commission to monitor the human rights situation inside Turkey. The EP resolution was certainly not without balance: it condemned the PKK's use of violence; it also stopped short of requesting a general arms embargo to be implemented by member states.[66] This attempt at balance cut no ice in Ankara, which was particularly angered by the EP's references to Turkey's Kurds as a minority, implying that they should have the political rights of a minority.[67] The Turkish government simply dismissed the report on the grounds of bias, an important step in the development of a somewhat disdainful attitude that the Turkish establishment has routinely displayed toward the EP.

A second example of the uneasy relationship that has prevailed between Turkey and the EP was the case of the Kurdish MPs, who had their parliamentary immunity lifted and were subsequently tried, found guilty and sentenced in Turkey in 1994. Members of the EP, who were in any case sensitive to the treatment of fellow elected representatives, were livid to discover that some of the charges brought against the MPs related to statements that they had made during a visit to the EP.[68] Increasingly concerned at the prosecutions, the EP Political Affairs Committee decided not to convene a meeting of the joint EU-Turkish Parliamentary Committee while the case was still in progress.[69] When the guilty verdict was returned and the sentencing took place, the EP passed a strongly worded resolution recommending that work on the Customs Union should be suspended and a meeting of the Association Council, scheduled for 19 December, should be postponed.[70] This prompted a predictably tough retort from the Turkish side, with Tunç Bilget, co-chairman of the joint committee, saying that there was no difference between the postponement of the Customs Union and an unconditional no. He further observed that the EP had never passed a favorable resolution on Turkey.[71] In a public exposure of the limited importance of the EP, the Commission and the Council of Ministers ignored both the parliament's recommendations.

The tendency displayed by the insider institutions of the EU and the Turkish government to brush aside the pronouncements of the EP ended once the final negotiations at the conclusion of a Customs Union were completed in March 1995. The matter then formally passed to the EP for ratification. From the beginning of 1995 the EP started to come under tremendous pressure from the Commission and member states to adopt the Customs Union.[72] Euro MPs were subject to an intensive campaign, which carried both personal inducements and the threat of institutional penalties. The former included an invitation to visit Turkey on a "study tour" paid for by Ankara.[73] The latter involved the implicit threat of a diminution of the EP's standing through the use of the 1996 Inter-Governmental Conference, which will re-examine the powers of the EP. The Commission also initiated a vigorous media campaign in the EU in support of the CU, as an indirect method of influence.[74] Throughout, the arguments used to win over MEPs in support of the CU were that the Customs Union was in the EU's best material interests, and the EU's leverage over Ankara in the area of human rights could only be sustained if there was a successful conclusion to the Customs Union.[75]

In the end, following much uncertainty and an approximately nine-month delay on voting, the EP endorsed the Customs Union. The initial deferment was made due to Turkey's incursion into northern Iraq, which the EP condemned in language significantly stronger than that used by the Troika.[76] As a result, meetings of the joint parliamentary commission were frozen. After the withdrawal of Turkish forces in May, the EP waited for Ankara to take substantive action over the issues of democratization and human rights. The Turkish government, now taking the EP significantly more seriously than it did in 1992, realized that it had no choice but to act if the CU was to come into force on time. In a display of considerable political will, the Çiller-led coalition managed to take substantive, though limited, action in three areas. It steered a democratization package through its parliament, gained amendments to the notorious Article 8 of the Anti-terror Law, and, through a process of judicial appeal, secured the release of two of the six Kurdish MPs still in prison. This laid the base for what ended up as a deceptively easy endorsement of the CU by 343 votes to 149 (with 36 abstentions),[77] with a record turnout of MEPs.[78] In spite of the Turkish establishment's antipathy, the EP had enjoyed some success in gaining concessions from Ankara over the human rights and Kurdish issues during the short period when its powers were of a decisive importance to the interests of Turkey.

The Kurdish issue has clearly emerged as a visible and controversial factor in relations between the EU and Turkey in the 1990s. For the smaller states of the EP and a marginal institution such as the EP, it has also emerged as an issue of substance. For such actors, the Kurdish issue has increasingly been perceived as being synonymous with the issue of human rights. Both the smaller states and the EP have repeatedly criticized the Turkish state for its actions toward the country's Kurds. In doing so, they have acted largely unfettered by wider interests and considerations. Ankara in turn has been largely dismissive of such criticisms, choosing instead to rely upon the larger states backed up by the Commission to determine the substance of EU policy toward Turkey.

These tempestuous moments, therefore, have had only a limited effect on both relations between the larger states of the EU and Turkey and Ankara's dealings with central institutions, such as the presidency and the Troika. The larger states, with their more extensive and complex relations with Turkey, have not allowed the Kurdish issue to dominate bilateral ties; official statements have always been balanced and the language used has been measured. Indeed, with the exception of Germany, the bigger players of the EU have largely been able to cocoon the Kurdish issue from the process of policy-making. At the level of EU institutions, the big players have had a moderating effect on the smaller states.

Only over the ratification of the Customs Union by the European Parliament has the balance between the center and the periphery of power within the EU been disturbed. In 1995 the Turkish government was forced to take seriously an institution that it had come to revile. Though the EP came somewhat reluctantly to approve the CU, it did not do so before having obliged the Turkish state to make three sets of compromises in the direction of greater liberalization. In one of these cases, that of the imprisoned MPs, the Kurdish issue was an explicit factor; in the other two, which involved matters of democratization and human rights, the Kurdish issue was an implicit factor. For the first time the impact of the Kurdish issue on Euro-Turkish relations may be said to have been as real as it was apparent.

NOTES

1. I am grateful to the Leverhulme Foundation, whose generous financial assistance has enabled the work on which this article is based to take place. I am also grateful to Angela Gillon and William Hale, both of whom read earlier drafts of the chapter, for their valuable comments.
2. In addition to Professor Gönensay, the delegation consisted of two members of the Foreign Ministry of ambassadorial rank and two who were not officials: the Social Democrat Populist Party deputy Professor Mümtaz Soysal, who was to have a short tenure as foreign minister later on in the year, and a Turkish journalist.
3. The author was the chairman of the meeting in question.
4. Over the preceding seven years the Institute had led the way in the study of Turkey in the UK with, for example, three bilateral roundtable meetings with the Ankara-based Foreign Policy Institute, two research projects on different aspects of Turkish foreign policy and a one-day conference on Turkey, convened in February 1993.

5. Throughout, the acronym *EU* will be used, even though the name of the collective has periodically changed, being, for instance, the *European Community* prior to late 1993.

6. Such concerns on the part of the Turkish government were entirely justified. In 1987 Turkey had dealt with an earlier, smaller influx of Iraqi Kurds by allowing them to find refuge on Turkish soil and mounting an appropriate relief operation. This won the Turkish government plaudits among officials in the West. However, this humanitarian assistance soon turned into an open-ended commitment, as the Iraq Kurds refused to return home, while other states were chary of assisting in their settlement.

7. For a history of the PKK, see Ismet Imset, *The PKK* (Ankara, 1992).

8. Casualty figures have to be treated with some skepticism, as they are issued by the state, while the complete news blackout on the southeast of the country make verifications extremely difficult. It may be assumed that casualty figures for the rebels are greatly exaggerated, while those for the security forces are underestimated.

9. Report in *Turkish Daily News* (henceforth *TDN*), 1 May 1995.

10. The most obvious examples of this phenomenon were the extended raids that began in October 1992 and March 1995; this period was, however, punctuated by more limited bombing and commando raids.

11. Examples include the 1992 Nevroz celebrations, during which, according to the Turkish Human Rights Foundation, ninety-two people were killed, and the onslaught against the town of Şırnak in August 1992

12. Though such figures are difficult to verify, by the beginning of 1995 more than 2 million people in the southeast had been displaced due to village burnings and evacuation; *TDN*, 3 Jan. 1995. A report in the same newspaper a little over five months earlier (*TDN*, 28 July 1994) quoted the Turkish Human Rights Association as stating that more than 1,360 Kurdish villages had been destroyed. By 1996 Amnesty International reported that some twenty-three hundred villages had been destroyed.

13. The emergence of the death squads came toward the end of 1991 and led to conduct by the Turkish state described by one Western human rights activist as being South American in form.

14. Recently we have witnessed the somewhat curious case of police being accused of having tortured policemen who themselves were suspected of involvement in the death in custody of the journalist Mete Göktepe. See *Independent*, 1 Feb. 1996.

15. Mehmet Ali Birand in *Sabah*, 20 March 1995, reprinted in *TDN*, 21 March 1995.

16. Peri Pamir, "Turkey in its Regional Environment in the Post-Bipolar Era: Opportunities and Constraints." Unpublished paper presented to IPRA Commission on Peace-Building in the Middle East, Fourteenth IPRA Conference, 27-31 July 1992, Kyoto, Japan.

17. *Independent*, 1 Dec. 1993.

18. *International Herald Tribune* (henceforth *IHT*), 6-7 Nov. 1993.

19. Ibid.

20. *Independent*, 1 Dec. 1993.

21. The Turkish Constitutional Court formally closed the HEP in mid-July 1993; the DEP was closed in the spring of 1994.

22. This is an accusation persistently leveled against the PKK by the Turkish state. As one European intelligence source was quoted as saying: "It suits the Turks to blame the [drugs] trade on terrorists." It seems widely agreed, however, among knowledgeable

neutral sources, that the PKK is involved in drugs smuggling, though the scale of this involvement if difficult to estimate. See *Guardian*, 5 Jan. 1994.

23. The Troika consists of the three countries that have the current, immediate past and immediate future presidencies of the Council of Ministers.

24. *TND*, 4 May 1995.

25. Editorial by Ilnur Çevik in *TND*, 14 April 1995.

26. The reason the Belgian government was included in such accusations was because of the operations of the DEP Solidarity Office in Brussels, the nerve center of the political activities of the former DEP MPs.

27. Çevik ed. in *TDN*, 14 April 1995.

28. *TDN*, 16 May 1995.

29. For example, in an interview with the Italian newspaper *La Repubblica*, emergency rule regional governor Ünal Erkan was quoted as saying that Greece condones the activities of the PKK and that the Greek government allows the PKK to organize pro-Kurdish gatherings and press conferences. See *TDN*, 23 July 1993.

30. *TND*, 17 Dec. 1994.

31. *Turkish Probe*, no. 148, 13 Oct. 1993.

32. For more details of the visit see *Turkish Probe*, no. 121, 24 March 1995.

33. British ambassador to Ankara, John Goulden, in an interview with the *TDN*, 7 Jan. 1994.

34. *Times*, 23 Nov. 1992.

35. *TDN*, 21 Jan. 1994.

36. *TDN*, 13 April 1992.

37. Madame Mitterand did not accompany her husband on his visit to Turkey in 1992.

38. *TDN*, 14 April 1992.

39. *TDN*, 19 Nov. 1993.

40. *TDN*, 16 March 1994.

41. *TDN*, 18 March 1994.

42. For example, in early 1992 Turkish interior minister Ismet Sezgin openly challenged the German government to implement its rhetorical position and oust the PKK. See *TDN*, 18 Feb. 1992.

43. *TDN*, 24 March 1992.

44. The importance of this issue may be seen in the fact that in the thirty years after 1964 Germany supplied Turkey with $3.9 billion worth of arms. See *IHT*, 21 May 1993.

45. *TDN*, 28 March 1992.

46. *TDN*, 28 March 1992.

47. Reference contained in report of visit to Ankara by Helmut Kohl. See *TDN*, 22 May 1993.

48. It was claimed that this bad feeling had begun in 1987, when Genscher had a heated argument with Mesut Yılmaz, who later became Turkish foreign minister and prime minister, before he lost the election to Demirel in October 1991. See *TDN*, 14 July 1992. This perception was not confined to Turks. One senior Western diplomat speaking on condition of anonymity, said that Genscher had "a phobia" about Turkey. Interview, 28 June 1992.

49. *TDN*, 23 Oct. 1992.

50. Mehmet Ali Birand writing in *Sabah* and reprinted in *TDN*, 9 Dec. 1992.

51. *TDN*, 8 April 1994.

52. *TDN*, 9 April 1994.

53. *Turkish Probe*, vol. 5, no. 77, 13 May 1994.

54. *TDN*, 29 March 1995.

55. The SPD actually said that it held the German government partly to blame for the incursion because the supply of German weaponry had been instrumental in giving the Turkish armed forces the "capacity to invade." See *TDN*, 4 April 1995.

56. Whereby military hardware surplus needed in the central European theater in the wake of the end of the cold war would be transferred to countries on the NATO flank.

57. *TDN*, 30 March 1995.

58. *TDN*, 3 April 1995.

59. To quote the view of one senior member of the Commission in a letter to the author dated 5 January 1996.

60. Hurd spoke specifically in such terms during a visit to Ankara in April 1992. See *TDN*, 23 April 1992.

61. *Turkish Probe*, vol. 4, no. 54, 2 Dec. 1993.

62. *TDN*, 22 March 1995.

63. Ibid.

64. The U.S. government, for instance, said that it understood what Turkey had done, though it did not condone it.

65. While this is the consensual view within the EU, Ankara believes otherwise, based on the fact that the EU and Turkey agreed in 1963 to conclude a Customs Union— that is, before the adoption of the Maastricht Agreement.

66. *TDN*, 10 April 1992.

67. *TDN*, 11 April 1992.

68. *TDN*, 13 July 1994.

69. TRT TV, 18 Sept., in BBC Summary of World Broadcasts. Eastern Europe, 20 Sept. 1994.

70. Mehmet Ali Birand in *Sabah*, 15 Dec. 1994, reprinted in *TDN*, 16 Dec. 1994.

71. *TDN*, 17 Dec. 1994.

72. With 626 MEPs drawn from some fifty political parties and containing many political mavericks and elder statesmen, the protracted and intensive campaign was probably required.

73. Up to seventy MEPs availed themselves of this opportunity in the six months up to the EP vote.

74. The Commission office in Ankara estimates that during 1995 it briefed and entertained around seventy visiting journalists from Europe and the United States on the issue of the CU.

75. Interview with leading Commission official, 7 Feb. 1995.

76. *TDN*, 7 April 1995.

77. For instance, Pauline Green, the leader of the largest single grouping inside the EP, the Socialists, in a speech during the debate prior to the vote said that many were voting "with sorrow, with heavy hearts and without enthusiasm." Quoted in *Reuters*, 13 Dec. 1995.

78. *Financial Times*, 27-28 Jan. 1996.

Part 3

THE KURDISH NATIONALIST MOVEMENT AND ITS IMPACT ON TURKEY'S DOMESTIC POLITICS AND HUMAN RIGHTS POLICIES

7

POLITICAL CRISIS AND THE KURDISH ISSUE IN TURKEY

Hamit Bozarslan

This chapter analyzes the link between the Kurdish issue and the crisis of the political system in Turkey. The connection can only be understood if we take a long-term period as our research framework. Such an approach will enable us to observe that, due to its pluralist future, its pressure groups and a complex mechanism of clientelism, the Turkish political system distinguishes itself from other Middle Eastern political systems. But we will also notice that the autonomy of the "civilians" in Turkey is rather restricted by the army and by the bureaucratic and judicial establishment. These institutions constitute a suprapolitical power. The doctrinal "normativity" of this power is formulated in a quasi-metaphysical manner in the successive constitutions, namely in that of 1982, and poses the ultimate limits of autonomy of civil actors.[1] We will also observe that, as far as sensitive questions, such as the Kurdish issue, are concerned, the consequences of the restriction of civilian politicians are very grave.

Despite the predominance of the army in the management of this question and despite the imprisonment of the Democracy Party (DEP) deputies in 1994, I will argue that the Kurdish political actors are not passive agents of a system imposed by Ankara. Various mechanisms of subordination, clientelism and participation link them to the center of Turkey-wide political formations. Those links imply negotiation and a constant game of legitimization between them and the center as well as the political parties. The terms of these negotiations and the legitimization game are determined, among other elements, by army pressure, Kurdish radicalism and ongoing guerrilla warfare since 1984, evolution of clientelists groups and the transborder nature of the Kurdish issue. Through these processes, the Kurdish dynamic imposes itself as a constituent element of the Turkish political system. More than in Iraq, Iran and Syria, the evolution of this issue itself depends on the balances and tensions determining the Turkish political space. Other elements have an obvious impact on the evolution of the Kurdish issue, including the internal contradictions of the political system, splits among the political parties, the relationship between civilians and the armed forces and the integration or the exclusion of other minority groups.

The study of the articulation of the political system and the Kurdish issue cannot be linear or reduced to only one dimension. Such a study will be undermined if it emphasizes only the impact of the army on political life or only the conflictual relations between Kurdish political actors and the Turkish parties. Without underestimating the elements of exclusion, we must also question the existing channels of integration, or the channels that had worked for a long period before becoming anachronistic. Bearing in mind this necessity, I will analyze a few aspects related to my subject. First, I will question the official doctrine, which is supposed to establish the borders of political life and determine the border of licit and illicit activity in this field. Second, I will try to elucidate the processes of fragmentation within the Turkish political space, namely its two traditional poles: conservatism and social-democracy. Consequently, I will analyze the reasons behind the success of the Welfare Party (WP) in the Kurdish regions. Third, I will concentrate on the evolution of the independent Kurdish actors and their impact in the political arena. Finally, I will evaluate the impact of the constraints of the Kurdish issue on the state and particularly on its political space. I will then provide some prognostications for the future.

Doctrinal Imperative and Political Participation

According to the Turkish constitution, Kemalism is the official doctrine, and it is protected by a series of juridical and coercive instruments. The political parties are obliged to adhere to it or to accept banishment by the Constitutional Court. Given this context as well as the sanctions against its opponents,[2] one could conclude that Kemalism constitutes the common doctrinal and juridical basis of the entire political space. However, this conclusion would not entirely reflect reality. A political doctrine is juridically never delineated sufficiently to have precision. Moreover, the definition of Kemalism remains highly problematic.[3] In fact, if we take Kemalism as it is imposed by the Turkish constitution, i.e. as an almost religious doctrine, it can be used in order to legitimize virtually every kind of political practice—pluralism and democracy, military dictatorship, communism, fascism, even a theocratic system. The reason for this is quite evident: the constantly republished Kemalist mantras are contradictory. They do not build a corpus of abstract recommendations because they are products of particular historical contexts. Not surprisingly, almost every politician uses them. Turgut Özal, whose political program was to bury Kemalism as an official doctrine could describe himself as Kemalist. A political party quite remote from the Kemalist discourse, the *Refah* or Welfare Party (WP) can also find some useful material in it ("Atatürk would have been a member of our party if he were still alive"). Even some Kurdish actors use the abundant correspondence of Mustafa Kemal in order to give, not without a certain malignity, a legality to their claim of "equality between the Kurds and Turks." This places constitutional court judges, bearing other phrases in mind, in a particularly difficult situation. In other words, it is obviously impossible to transform Kemalism into a research subject, and, even less, into a viable judicial system. The researcher can, at most, try to understand the surviving cult of Mustafa Kemal and/or his place in the popular and bureaucratic imagination.

However, if we adopt a methodology that consists of historicizing Kemalism as a doctrine and a practice of political power as well as a juridical system as it was elaborated during the 1930s—secular reforms as well as instrumentalization of religion, six principles (arrows) of the single party, fusion of party and state, anthropological nationalism, the cult of "Eternal Chief," and rejection of the Ottoman past—we would naturally conclude that Kemalism did exist. But, in such a perspective, we will almost admit that, as most single-party experiences of the interwar period, it was already dead in 1945.[4] It is true that some of Atatürk's reforms, which prolonged the secularization movement of the late Ottoman Empire, have survived. Nevertheless, nobody in Turkey can imagine a future political system in which "only the head of human society is worthy of being sanctifying."[5] In a similar way, no politician can make an apology of political and economic *étatisme*, measure the skeletons to prove the racial superiority of the Turks, propose the fusion of the state with a party, nominate deputies or force the professors of history to recognize, over a table covered with alcoholic drinks, that they are "ignorant." The strict application of Kemalism (and of the constitution) would bring a *de jure* banishment of all political formations, with the exception of the MHP or Nationalist Action Party (NAP).

We can then conclude that Kemalism is either nonexistent or anachronistic. However, this does not mean that Turkey has no official doctrine: it does, but it is not Kemalism. It is rather the vague system elaborated from the 1910 through the 1920s by Ziya Gökalp. In the 1970s, a club of right-wight intellectuals (Home of Intellectuals—Aydınlar Ocağı) resurrected this doctrine as "The Turkish-Islamic Synthesis." This synthesis has been consequently adopted by the generals of the 1980 coup.[6]

As it was elaborated by Gökalp, this doctrine had three aims: to eradicate the claims of the Ottoman liberalism of Prince Sabaheddin (Ottomanism, private initiatives and decentralization); to arrive at a synthesis between the Westernizers, Islamists and Turkish nationalists; and finally to homogenize the unionist program and discourse. This system, which enabled the Unionist regime to obtain an alliance of different intellectual groups, had three slogans. The first one, "Turkification," was the *raison d'être* and the main aim of the Turkish nation; the suffix *tion* proved that it was a process rather than a given fact. This aim was to remain unchanged through the years, independent of other social, cultural or political variables. The second aim was "contemporanization," which signified "Westernization." It was supposed to enable the Turks to enter into the most developed stage of civilization. It necessitated a radical program and the leadership of an elite. Finally, "Islamization," also a process rather than a given fact, emphasized that religion was the soul of any society. It should be Turkified and cease to be understood as unity of the *'umma*. It was expected to enable the populace (*avam*) to combat the unavoidable but necessary harms that civilization would bring. Just as the program of "civilization" was to be determined and applied by the elite, the "nationalized" religion was a domain reserved for the populace.

In spite of certain hesitations, such an aggressive anti-religious policy, or, during the 1930s, a sliding from cultural nationalism to a racial interpretation of the nation, Kemalism perpetuated the Gökalpian synthesis but sacrificed the prestigious name of its founding father. As it was re-elaborated by the Home of Intellectuals, the synthesis neither excluded Westernization nor put a particular emphasis on it. The new version included some eclectic references from the pre-Ottoman, Ottoman, Unionist and Kemalist periods. It still possessed contradictory aims, however. Its goals were to bring maximum legitimacy to the state by assuring the alliance of the Turkish and Sunni populations and to persist with the leadership of the Westernized bourgeoisie and elites. Thanks to this transmogrification, Kemalism could be bequeathed a metaphysical position in the constitution and become, more than before, a taboo, while the synthesis was offered the place of the official doctrine. In turn, it enabled President Kenan Evren (1980-88) to use interchangeably the Quran and the *Speeches and Discourses,* a compendium of Mustafa Kemal's political ideas.

One can hardly deny that the Turkish-Islamic synthesis legitimized the military regime. Later, civilian governments also used it to legitimize themselves simultaneously, by Turkishness, their Ottoman past, Kemalist symbolism and Westernization. However, as far as the evolution of political space is concerned, the success of the synthesis seems to be limited. The first obstacle to its realization is that its different terms do not accept the place offered to them by Ziya Gökalp and by the Home of Intellectuals in their nomenclature of values. (Turkishness is not the main objective of all Turkish groups; Westernization and Islamization fight each other to have the leading place.) And, if each term is able to obtain the support of one section of the population, it provokes, at the same time, the exclusion of others and reduces political participation. Turkification excludes the Kurds and does not offer them any solution other than assimilation. It is obvious that this policy did not succeed in convincing the Kurds that Turkification should be their main aim. This failure obliged all the political parties, with the exception of the NAP, to introduce a small dose of "Kurdishness" into their discourse. Islamization is based on the postulate that the Alevis, both Kurdish and Turkish, are Muslims. This is not only seriously ignorant, it is, moreover, inefficient. Obviously, the Alevis do not adhere to the constraints of Islamization that are imposed on them, and even the WP is obliged to develop locally a specific discourse to earn their trust. Finally, the Westernization imposed from above provokes marginalization as well as strong reactions from the Turkish-Sunni population of the Anatolian provinces and the inhabitants of the shanty towns in the big cities. The ban during the late 1980s on the so-called Islamic veil in the schools has given ample evidence that a section of the university youth either did not accept the Westernization coming from above or, at least, did not understand it as Mustafa Kemal did. It is true that the Westernization of Turkey seems to be an irreversible process, and even the WP adheres to it by its practice if not its discourse. But the Kemalist practice of Westernization reinforces the weight of Islam as political opposition in a way that Ziya Gökalp could not, of course, foresee.

THE TURKISH POLITICAL SYSTEM FROM BIPOLARITY TO FRAGMENTATION

We can conclude that the Gökalpian doctrine that delineates the borders of the political space has evaporated with the emergence of new segments of the Anatolian population as political actors. It is true that the newcomers share elements of political culture with the old actors—the mechanisms of clientelism, the game of negotiating and bargaining and the defection of members and deputies from one party to another—but they do not accept the terms of the official doctrine or, at least, not all of them. But their emergence, which inevitably enlarges political participation, also changes the other datum of the system, condemning it to a fragmentation or to a painful and long period of recomposition.

As Idris Küçükömer noticed in the late 1960s, since 1908, the political system has been characterized by a bipolarity that did not conform to the ideological criteria (revolutionaries versus reactionaries) of the Unionist and Kemalist elite. The CUP (Committee Union and Progress), dominated by the army and the bureaucrats, later gave birth to the Republican Peoples' Party (RPP) of Atatürk and Inönü.[7] The liberal tradition, on the other hand, emanated from society. Since the days of its founding father, Prince Sabahaddin, it had given birth to the conservative formations of the Democratic Party (DP) and the Justice Party (JP). The "ideal-type" of Küçükömer, which explained a long period of Turkish political history, could, however, not be confirmed during the next decades because the genealogy ceased to be at that point linear. The 1960s and 1970s were dominated by an extraparliamentary opposition, which had a strong capacity for mobilization. Moreover, independent of their durability, the emergence of other formations, such as the YTP or the Party of New Turkey (PNY), the Turkish Workers Party (TWP), and the Union Party of Turkey (UPT), changed the facts of the political space and threatened the monopoly of the RPP and JP. Finally, the two poles, that I will name "traditional," because of their places as references in the left and right wings, were weakened during these decades by internal tensions and schisms. This process of fragmentation became more serious after the 1980 coup. The military regime wanted to create a narrow political space that it could easily control. The banishment of the old politicians was expected to transform the political field into a "Rosary." However, this measure did not have sociological viability. The old politicians, depositors of political legitimacy, returned as powerful as they had been before the military coup. Nevertheless, thanks to this measure, other organizational structures and clientelist networks emerged and offered a real autonomy to new actors and to the old dissidents of the former political parties. This result accelerated the processes of fragmentation.

Several factors have deeply transformed the political system:

- The RPP-CHP has considerably weakened. It no longer represents a bureaucratic power. Under the pressure of the students' and workers' movements and also because of the contacts of the Kemalist intellectuals with Marxism during the 1960s and 1970s, the RPP tried to formulate a synthesis between Kemalism and social-democracy. The historical mission of this effort suggests the impossibility of such a synthesis. This failure deprived the RPP of the support of the armed forces and of the population, condemning it to a fragmentation, including two or three parties such as the Social Democratic Party (SDP), the RPP, currently fused with the SDP, and the Democratic Left Party (DLP).
- The army and the bureaucracy were, during long decades, organically liked with the CUP or the RPP, or they were subordinated to them. Subsequently, they were able to earn real autonomy and were able to become suprapolitical arbiters of the political arena. The position of the army in political life was reinforced by legitimization of the "patriotic" and "progressive" missions of the army by the political actors' role of the "guardian of internal stability" offered to it by the constitution, the impact of the 1960 military coup, which was supported by the intellectuals, and the blandishment of the threat of the military intervention by the civilians in their internal conflicts. It is true that it in many fields the army can no longer impose (or even express) its opinions and is obliged to admit the supremacy of the civilians. Moreover, as it is a bad manager, it does not want to occupy a visible position in the political arena. Nevertheless, this does not signify that it has also renounced its role as arbiter. It played this role with great energy during the 1980s and 1990s by accepting confrontation with almost every political leader.[8]
- Adopting a defensive position toward the army and frightened by the social movements of the 1960s and 1970s, the liberal movement in Turkey passed through a rapid transformation and become clearly conservative. In spite of reformist figures such as Turgut Özal, it seeks the status quo, if not government, as a mode of survival. In its opposition to the left during the 1970s it instrumentalized the extreme right. This enabled it to have the support of some officers and bureaucrats, but, in turn, this has reduced its autonomy and credibility. Nowadays, the attraction of power makes possible similar alliances. Finally, since the 1960s this camp has passed through an accelerated fragmentation including the emergence of the Motherland Party (MP), the True Path Party (TPP) and half a dozen minor formations. This fragmentation can partly be explained by the coup

d'etat, which favored the MP, and by the difficult sharing of the inheritance of Turgut Özal, who died in 1993. But it seems also to be a result of different contradictory imperatives (*status quo* versus reform, rural Anatolia versus the bourgeoisie of Istanbul etc.).

- Political Islam emerged as a parliamentary force. Political Islam is not a new phenomena in Turkish history. As an organized force, it has existed since 1908. It was a powerless spectator of the conflict between Unionism and Ottoman liberalism, to which it was close. It reemerged during the Independence War but was later condemned to an illegal, intellectual and marginal opposition. It survived in a diffuse and disorganized way. Over the last two decades it has passed through a vertiginous transformation to become a mass movement. Oscillating between contradictory messages and imperatives, it has shown nevertheless its ability to develop pragmatic policies enabling it to profit from the fragmentation of other movements. Its later avatar, the WP, constitutes its only unified current in Turkish political life.
- The pan-Turanist tradition survived as a racial nationalism during the 1940s and as the Nationalist Action Party (NAP) since the 1960s. It gave birth to the radical right during the 1970s. It has some affiliations with Kemalism, but at least on two points it distinguishes itself: explicitly in the past and implicitly nowadays, it is affiliated to the Sunni populations and it interprets Turkish nationalism clearly as a doctrine of civil war. This is its force and its weakness—its force because it can obtain a solid clientele group between the Sunnis, namely in the mixed Sunni-Alevi regions, and its weakness because elsewhere it has very little credibility. However, one should note that its radical opposition to Kurdish nationalism can assure it a new electorate outside the mixed provinces.

THE KURDISH PROBLEM AND THE TWO TRADITIONAL POLES

One can conclude from the above that the Kurdish issue evolves in a political space that suffers from two processes of "disintegration" of the official doctrine and of the political system. Together with political Islam and Alevism, it also participates fully in both processes. In fact, as early as the 1946 election, the political parties tried to obtain a Kurdish clientele group and abandoned the theory of national sovereignty that should have been incarnated, according to both Ziya Gökalp and Mustafa Kemal, by the elites and the Kurdish chiefs. The integration of the traditional Kurdish actors, namely in the case of the family of Sheikh Said, symbolizing two banned ideologies from the republic—Kurdish nationalism and religious opposition—signified a real enlargement of the political space. Later, with the notable exception of the NAP, all the formations have obtained Kurdish representation implicitly recognized as such, even if no deputy could legally describe himself or herself as Kurdish. Even the NAP tried to find Kurdish religious clients and, in the mixed Alevi-Sunni regions, took advantage of a Kurdish Sunni electorate.

The political system was in fact competent and elastic enough to integrate traditional Kurdish actors. In turn, those actors played a key role in the legitimization of the system. For decades, participation in the elections was higher in Kurdistan than in the rest of the country. Access to local and national power has become a key in the Kurdish regions, giving birth, in some cases, to vendettas or to shifts of entire villages from one party to another.

The military's claim to stop what Kemalist terminology calls feudalism and to eradicate traditional Kurdish representation, according to them incompatible with national sovereignty, succeeded only during the coups d'etat periods. At other times, the Kurdish actors imposed themselves as valued electoral factors. Moreover, the political formations succeeded in finding a *juste milieu* between two imperatives: to have some Kurdish representation and to manage the susceptibilities of the army and the establishment. However, from the 1970s to today, the political game has become more complex. The terms of negotiation, which before included largely clientelism have changed under the pressure of two simultaneous evaluations.

First, the pressure of Kurdish radicalism is a durable fact in the Kurdish political arena. This pressure was obvious during the 1977 municipal elections. It gave birth later to the guerrilla movement of the PKK (Kurdistan Workers Party) and to the organizations such as HEP (Peoples Labor Party) and DEP (Democracy Party). As I will explain later, it would be groundless to confuse these two organizations. However, they are products of the same radical response to a system that failed in integrating genuine Kurdish representation.

Second, the Kurdish actors who were traditionally well integrated into the system could not remain indifferent to this radicalism. Their desire to remain integrated and to gain access to the resources it ensured was still dominant. Nevertheless, under threat of extinction, they had to accept the minimum nationalist demands—to end the state of emergency, to stop the destruction of the Kurdish countryside, to respect human rights and to recognize cultural rights. The implicit recognition of their Kurdishness, as in the past, was no longer enough to enable them to preserve their own clientele groups, especially their impact in the urban centers. We observe this transformation in the composition of HEP and the DEP political parties. Some of their key members, such as Ahmet Türk, were affiliated before with the JP or the RPP. But this was also true in the cases of Kurdish deputies such as Abdülmelik Fırat, Azimet Köylüoğlu and even Kamran Inan, who belonged until recently or still belong to the traditional Turkish formations. All the Kurdish political actors did not desert the Turkish political arena, but the traditional formations, perceived as responsible for the Kurdish policy of Ankara, have been largely boycotted in the Kurdish regions. This situation obliged the Kurdish members of those formations to distinguish themselves from the leaders.

In short, the terms of negotiation between the Kurdish actors and the center, but also between them and the parties, have changed since the late 1970s. The *sine qua non* condition of policy-making in Kurdistan was then to enlarge the political space and redefine it, by inclusion of the Kurdish actors *qua* Kurdish and by recognizing their claims. Their inability to understand this transformation and the pressure of the army and the Kurdish guerrillas condemned the social democratic and conservative poles to certain immobility and to an unmanageable series of paradoxes.

Quite independently from their doctrinal affiliations, both the conservative and social-democratic parties faced or face such paradoxes. The conservative camp, for instance, is often described as Turkish nationalist as well as politically *étatiste*. The declarations of main conservative leaders (Yılmaz, Çiller, Demirel) might have led us to accept this assumption. In fact, as I have already mentioned, this camp has become, against its own will, the defender of the Kemalist inheritance, which it dislikes,[9] and of the *status quo* with the army and the establishment that enabled it to gain access to power. It has been a target of the army over the last forty years and at the same time, due to its position, it has had to apply and assume responsibility of the politics decided by the armed forces, to outbid them in defending law and order, and to give more and more guarantees to the armed forces to convince them of its good faith. Meanwhile, it still shares some of the aspirations of late Ottoman and Turkish liberalism, such as decentralization and less state control. It draws its sources from an ethnically pluralist society. Finally, its principle of balance of power with the armed forces remains the same: the double legitimization of the army, champion of civilization and patriotism, can be counterbalanced only by a superior legitimization—i.e. popular legitimization. The leader of one of the minor liberal parties, Cem Boyner, explains this as "having a government which is stronger than the state."[10] This imperative necessitates the enlargement of political participation and representation.

Given those paradoxes, one can easily understand why this camp so strongly defends a unitary Turkey and is so suspicious toward Kurdish nationalism while at the same time so willing to have a Kurdish clientele or even to integrate the Kurds into the system. The cases of Adnan Menderes (prime minister, 1950-60, executed in 1961) and Turgut Özal, two historical figures of Turkish liberalism, as well as Aydın Menderes (son of Adnan Menderes), Yusuf Bozkurt Özal (brother of Turgut) and Cem Boyner (radical liberal leader of the New Democracy Movement) show that the conservative camp is not monolithic and that some of its members desire a Kurdish representation *qua* Kurdish, a rather positive condition according to them, consolidating ties between this minority and the center. One should also add that some members of this camp (namely Özal and Boyner) proposed or propose to found a Second Republic and bury Kemalist symbolism, to introduce a large administrative autonomy and largely autonomous regions, as well as to legalize the banished Kurdish parties.

At the same time, the attachment to the status quo, the fear of the army and the fragmentation that implies an exaggerated emphasis on the nationalist discourse has immobilized this camp, reducing it, at most, to a position of manager of the crises. Since 1984, the temptation of neutralizing the armed forces by containing them in a civil war and by offering any required financial means has been a strategy that Özal until 1990, and Demirel and Çiller since 1991, have assumed. In a similar way, the competition between its leaders also includes the instrumentalization of the military threat and an preemption of in the Kurdish issue, as far as political Islam is concerned. This means that every step toward a political solution taken by a conservative leader is stopped by the opposition of another conservative leader. If Mesut Yılmaz, the leader of the MP, makes what is interpreted to be an anti-Kemalist proposition, Çiller will become a champion of Kemalism and vice versa. Even Hüsamettin Cindoruk, former speaker of the Parliament, who is one of the most open-minded liberal politicians, has played this game. Finally, political survival pushes this camp to alliances with nationalist leaders, as we observed through the rapprochement of Çiller to Alparslan Türkes, leader of the NAP, and Bülent Ecevit, leader of the DLP, during the formation of the minority government in the fall 1995, through the inclusion of figures of the extreme right (namely Baki Tuğ and Ayvaz Gökdemir) or those close to the army (Coşkun Kırca) in this government. It is worthy to note that all this happened shortly after the report prepared by Doğu Ergil was published in the spring of 1995.[11]

The social-democratic parties also face similar paradoxes. On one hand, they are the organic heirs of the RPP of Mustafa Kemal and still keep its six principles. On the other hand, they attempt to integrate the claims of a largely non-Kemalist left as well as the Kurdish left. When they are in government, the social-democrats give guarantees to the army that open them to claims of being too far to the left, but they are also obliged to have a Kurdish electorate. In the 1970s, Bülent Ecevit, who espoused nationalist positions, qualified as "racist" the claim of recognition of Kurdish ethnicity. He was, however, obliged to integrate Kurdish nationalists (namely Ahmet Türk and Nurettin Yılmaz) both locally and nationally. That was also the case of the SDP, the social-democratic party of the 1980s, which was led by Erdal İnönü, son of Ismet İnönü, the very Kemalist second president of the Republic. This party has made concessions to the establishment and the army and has supported the banning of the Kurdish deputies who participated in the 1989 International Conference on the Kurds, held in Paris. This exclusion had a very heavy price: the SDP was eradicated from the Kurdish towns where it was the main political formation. However, during the 1991 elections, it was obliged to accept Peoples Labor Party (PLP) or HEP members on its list once again and, in 1994, while in government, it was obliged to oppose the lifting of the parliamentary immunity of the Democracy Party (DP) or DEP deputies. In a similar way, it has published several reports on the Kurdish issue. All of this, however, did not prevent it from joining the coalition government and sharing the responsibly of its Kurdish policy, which was the worst since 1938. It withdrew from the government in the fall 1995, but the reason was not the Kurdish issue or its minimal program of democratization but, simply, a question of survival.

WHY THE WELFARE PARTY SUCCEEDS WHILE OTHERS FAIL

The Welfare Party (WP), which has existed as an organized movement since 1971, also faces these paradoxes. It faces Kurdish radicalism, and it is the only political formation that is clearly designated as an enemy by the army. It is then obliged, more than other political parties, to manage the susceptibilities of the armed forces. Moreover, this party did not have a linear trajectory in Kurdistan. Its ancestor, the National Salvation Party (NSP), entered the Parliament in 1973. However, it found "its real identity only when it increased its votes" in the Kurdish towns in 1977.[12] It obtained 7.8 percent of the vote during the municipal elections of 1987. Its score was 20 percent in Kurdish towns such as Diyarbakır, Bingöl, Bitlis, Elazığ, Siirt, Muş, Van, Adıyaman, Urfa, Ağrı. In the beginning of the 1990s it faced a dramatic decline: its alliance of 1991 with the NAP of Türkeş ended its impact in Kurdistan. And, finally, during the 1994 municipal elections, it earned an overwhelming victory by obtaining almost the totality of the Kurdish towns.

How can we explain such a victory only three years after such a defeat? The well known pragmatism of the WP has surely played a role in this success but is not the sole reason. Moreover, despite a Kurdish nationalist discourse, locally the WP did not become a "state-party" and even less an antipode of Kurdish radicalism, even if it profited from the banishment of the DEP. Quite the contrary, it did succeed because it espoused some aspirations of the banished Kurdish formations. Moreover, it succeeded in putting those aspirations in a wider, more universal register, that of the Muslim brotherhood of the two peoples, a theme that Mustafa Kemal developed in 1919 and 1920. In a similar way, it has used its organic ties with the Kurdish nationalist movement. We need detailed studies to understand exactly the nature of these ties, but we can, nevertheless, add that the Kurdish revolts in the 1920s and 1930s were largely dominated by religious orders (*tarikats*). Nowadays, despite many internal conflicts, those transethnic orders link Kurdishness to larger political entities. Finally, one should add that locally the WP is a Kurdified party. It is not implemented by Ankara but is composed of Kurdish members and in many cases Kurdish nationalists.

A second feature can also explain the success of the WP: It is the only formation that is perceived, concerning the Kurdish issue and many others, as autonomous from the state. It is the only formation that does not present itself as Kemalist, even if for legal reasons it cannot adopt a clearly anti-Kemalist position.

The elaboration of such an image is facilitated by the fact that this party does not assume any governmental responsibility—in other words, it has free and "clean" hands. This enables it to develop a radical discourse on the Kurdish issue, as we observe it in the report prepared by Tayyip Erdoğan (current mayor of Istanbul) in 1992. This report, the most brilliant document of political pragmatism ever seen in Turkey, allowed the WP to change its position after its very pragmatic but disastrous alliance of 1991 with Turkish extreme right. This report suggested "to publicly question the official ideology which is based on negation and assimilation, to defend the necessity to abrogate all the laws that obstruct the recognition and development of Kurdish culture, to develop a more sensitive program than the other political parties on the human rights issue, to send high-level missions to the region to evaluate rapidly the evolution, to condemn state terror as much as that of the PKK and to oppose, in an identical way, the Kurdish and Turkish racism."[13]

One should add to this capacity of navigating between different poles, combining locally both Turkish and Kurdish nationalism, one last advantage that the WP possesses: It presents itself as an opposition group that nevertheless has succeeded in integrating into the system without violence. One can legitimately think that for some Kurdish political actors, this constitutes a "legalist" alibi and offers the possibility of policy-making without risk. All these elements explain that the WP discourse—maybe because it has no real effect and it is not a discourse of political practice—can be welcomed in the Kurdish regions and at the same time can be tolerated by the state as long as it remains an opposition party.

KURDISH RADICALISM AND INTEGRATION INTO THE POLITICAL SYSTEM

The WP, however, is in no way a substitution for the Kurdish nationalism that expressed itself in the 1990s by the formation of the Peoples Labor Party (HEP) and, later, of the Democracy Party (DEP). Locally, the WP is one of the expressions of Kurdish radicalism or coexists with it. The current situation forbidding any Kurdish legal representation[14] should not lead us to erroneous interpretations: Kurdism was and is a given fact since the 1960s in the Turkish political arena. Without necessarily representing themselves as radicals, Kurdish nationalists participated, for long decades, in the political game. Their actions were determined by a double character: on one hand, nationalism or at least some degree of Kurdishness constituted their common ground and allowed them to act collectively in some situations.[15] On the other hand, they were differentiated according to the political cleavages that concerned Turkey as a whole and acted as Turkish political actors. Even when they passed from one party to another, they acted in conformity with a common pattern of Turkish culture. This explained their internal divisions and political affiliations. At least three political formations, the NSP, the JP and the RPP, had their nationalist Kurdish politicians known as such or even condemned by tribunals for separatism.

The formation of the HEP and, subsequently, the ban of the DEP, signified that Kurdish nationalism, already obvious during the popular meetings of the 1960s and on a municipal level in the 1970s, strove to have an organized and legal form. This also allowed urban radicalism to create a junction with Kurdish political actors who were already well integrated into the system, for those actors were affiliated by past relationships to other political formations. Kurdishness became a sufficient and solid ground to envisage the creation of a separate organization. That was also a necessary condition for their own survival. HEP persisted and, supported by the urban mobilization of 1989-92 and reinforced by this junction, easily became the major political force especially in the provinces of Mardin and Diyarbakır and the old Batman province.

However, this radicalism emerged under peculiar conditions in which a guerrilla movement, the PKK, and not a political opposition, was the reference of the Kurdish movement. The HEP and later the DEP have suffered from at least three handicaps. First, they failed in their attempt to invent an identity of their own. Instead of targeting the position of credible interlocutors of the Kurdish issue in the Parliament, they proposed only to become a mediator between Ankara and the guerrillas. This has naturally degraded their image without offering them the mobilizational capacity of the PKK and a recognition from one of the protagonists of the war. Until 1993, at least, the PKK was the most active element in Kurdistan, both militarily and in the urban centers. This situation reduced the field of action of the HEP and the DEP, forbidding them to develop independent policies. The legal structures of the HEP and the DEP coexisted with that of the PKK and were hoped, at most, to be able to play a political role one day in the future. These structures are not to be confused with those of the PKK, neither ideologically nor organically. They distinguished themselves from the PKK in many cases by their attempts to condemn violence, but they could not prevent being presented as a legal branch of the PKK. Secondly, the HEP and later the DEP regrouped different generations and types of political actors. Some of them were already integrated in the system while some others were brought to the political arena by urban radicalism. Those generations proposed different patterns of action.

Finally, and more important than everything else, as the HEP before it, the DEP was the main target of the army, the establishment and the media that could not tolerate an independent Kurdish representation. Dozens of its members and one of its deputies have been killed. The DYP, in search of popularity[16] just before the municipal elections of 1994, did not hesitate to sacrifice it for political reasons. At the same time, the DEP was finally finding international support and could now more easily present itself as the interlocutor for the Kurdish issue in Turkey. This process would inevitably lead to the politicization and internationalization of the debate, which could not be tolerated by the state.

Kurdish radicalism is now largely reduced to a extraparliamentary presence. But it can easily regroup if a political process to resolve the Kurdish issue were decided. It has its social base, namely in the provinces of Diyarbakır and Mardin and, more generally, among the Kurdish intelligentsia. However, its unity seems to be difficult to perpetuate because of its non-nationalist affiliations (adherence to conservatism or social-democracy, Islamism and Alevism) will become more important in the future. Moreover, in the perspective of the legalization of the Kurdish formations, namely of the PKK and the PSK, its electorate or even cadres will polarize according to those affiliations rather than maintain distinct partisan structures. The division of the nonarrested members of the DEP between a few organized formations and initiatives is, from this point of view, rather significant. If we adopt the hypothesis of a political process of resolution of the Kurdish issue, we can foresee that those formations, affiliated with other political parties or not, will seek to negotiate new alliances with Turkish political parties.

Partisan Pawns and the Future of the Kurdish Issue in Turkey

Finally, it seems necessary to insist on the constraints imposed by the Kurdish issue on the state and the political system in Turkey. The analysis of these constraints necessitates two remarks. First, in the current situation, the Kurdish issue does not threaten the survival of the Turkish state. This survival is assured by the existence of the army and a suprapolitical establishment, commanding the bureaucracy and almost entirely dominating urban Kurdistan. Moreover, by combining protection and coercion as well as redistribution, the state disposes of a legitimacy that goes far beyond partisan division and that covers a large part of the Turkish-Sunni population, including the electorate of the WP. The management of the legislative domain is then not so difficult. Only a victory of WP (and in the perspective that this party challenges openly and concretely Kemalist symbolism) would seem to be able to change the situation and provoke a direct intervention of the army.

Nevertheless, it is no longer possible to discuss the Kurdish issue in Turkey only in the terms of the survival of the state. We have also to take into consideration other factors: the legitimization mechanisms and constraints that assure the durability of the state are not given once and for all. The legitimization depends more than ever on the enlargement of redistribution whose failure provokes large social protest. It also depends on the credibility of the so-called military solution. If the Kurdish war enabled the army to have military experience, the absence of a notable victory in one decade has created a problem of credibility, including the military field *stricto sensu*, pushing some high-ranking officials to evoke the inefficacy of the military solution. Moreover, in Turkey as elsewhere, the state is not a monolithic bloc. The army, which is probably the most homogenous corps of the state is not sheltered from internal contradictions and the dynamics of centrifugal groups. The last years of Turkish military history are marked by mysterious deaths, such as those of Eşref Bitlis and Cem Ersever, and mini-coups that provoked open polemics and insults between the armed forces in the press. The war against the Kurds has aggravated these conflicts.

One should also remember that the Kurdish dynamic is not the only one that can bring violent protest. Political Islam and Alevism also proved that, when excluded, they are able to act in a similar way and weaken the immunity of the center.[17] The current management of the Kurdish crisis and, in a more discrete way, of the Alevi question, by the transfer of the "protection" from the state to the local communities over large militarized regions has allowed the state to enlarge its support but has provoked, in many places, dynamics that it cannot control. Moreover, the repercussions of the Kurdish war enlarged the Kurdish "political periphery" and implemented it in the big cities of the country. This can, according to a very traditional pattern, also reduce the immunity of the center, give birth to violent protest or, at least, weaken social democratic and conservative poles.

Without giving a dichotomic explanation to the state and the political system, one should admit that they are not exactly the same thing. The long history of pluralism in Turkey shows that the political system can assure its own durability against the state, with three conditions. First, it must be able to create a favorable power balance with the army and the establishment. Second, in order to do this, it must integrate the forces that are excluded from the system and transform them into electorates. Third, the durability of the system depends on the creation of a strong partisan structure, namely, Islamist, leftist and conservative. The current fragmentation of the system in Turkey can then be interpreted as the prelude of new recompositions. But these recompositions necessitate, once again, an enlargement of the electoral bases, among them the Kurdish base.

Finally, the impossibility of facing a multiplicity of protest (Kurdish, Alevi and Islamist) and the complex interplay that is the result of this multiplicity engenders an imperative for the political system: to integrate all of them on the basis of a new social and political contract. The above-mentioned elements (weakening of the immunity of the center and the internal contradiction of the state) can be particularly dangerous for the political system. In the end, it is not the army but the civilians who pay for such a crisis. It is a peculiar logic that it is the armed forces who during crisis evict civilians, who are the only ones able to proffer to opponents the haven that is necessary to reimpose state authority via the armed forces.

Other constraints can be easily managed by the army, but not by the civilians. Among those constraints one should first of all mention the economic ones. Obviously, the state, in Turkey as elsewhere in the Middle East,[18] is able to manage a certain level of economic crisis. But this management might be difficult if a country wants, at the same time, to maintain a pluralist political system. The Kurdish war now costs on average some $10 billion dollars annually to Turkey; this figure is almost equal to that of annual deficit of external commerce. The continuation of the war will only be possible at the price of the militarization of the economy. Economic structures and redistribution networks of countries like Iraq and Syria can allow such a militarization, but that is not the case of Turkey, which has a strong private sector that the state does not control. For the private sector such a militarization implies making a larger contribution to the war and participating in the process of resource allocation. However, in Turkey as elsewhere, the "patriotism" of the bourgeoisie has its limits. The continuation of the war has already provoked important reactions and explains the hostile declarations of the TÜSIAD, the leading businessmen's association of Turkey, as well as the report of the Chamber of Commerce. Shortly after this report asking for a political solution, Sakıp Sabancı, representing the second most prominent family in Turkish economic life, presented his report containing the same conclusion.[19] The most prominent individual in economic circles, Rahmi Koç, explained that he, too, supported the initiative of Sabancı. The pressure of the IMF has the same orientation and demands that Turkey reduce its public expenses, namely military spending. Finally, the difficult strikes of September and October 1995 have demonstrated that civilians cannot avoid enlarging the redistribution without considering the risk of the mobilization of the working class. It is obvious that a civilian government does not have the capacity to easily ban the strikes and to impose the heavy bill of economic restructuring as the military regimes of 1971 and 1980 were able to do.

One must also mention the importance of Western pressure, which can be explained more by the impact of the Kurdish issue in Germany than by the supposed pro-Kurdish attitude of Western countries. The growing American pressure can of course not be explained by the presence of a Turkish diaspora but is based, paradoxically, on a pro-Turkish policy (the necessity of having a stable Turkey). These pressures could remain manageable for a military regime that is not accountable before an electorate but not for civilian politicians. The reason for this is quite simple: since 1946, Western support and the external credibility of the country have always been an element of legitimization of civil governments inside Turkey. It is true that Western pressures can give birth to nationalist and populist campaigns in Turkey, but these campaigns support the big political parties and only reinforce the impact of the extreme right, such as the NAP.

The above-mentioned paradoxes and constraints permit us to conclude that the future of the Kurdish issue depends on the evolution of the political system. In a similar way, we can postulate that the three processes of integration—those of the Kurdish movement, political Islam and Alevism—go hand in hand. The triple integration is problematic, but the political system has, in principle, enough resources to realize it and its survival depends on it. Beyond this conclusion, however, the future of the Kurdish issue and that of Turkish political life remains unpredictable. The above-mentioned constraints, the multiple attempts to start a political process that we observed during the early 1990s, the limits of the military solution, which, with the departure of the general staff Doğan Güreş, its architect and main defender, become obvious, and the latest initiatives of the businessmen are the signals of a change of course.

One should also notice that the Kurdish issue per se did not allow the armed forces to contest the legitimacy of the pluralist political system. It is true that the nonshared responsibility that they had in the management of the Kurdish issue would delegitimize a more heavy presence of the armed forces on the political arena. However, one cannot exclude such a possibility in the future. The presence of two other formations claiming integration, Alevism and political Islam, as well as the reinforcement of the NAP, which enables us to foresee a period of violence as in the 1970s, are important elements that we have to take into consideration. These elements can naturally change the data of the Kurdish issue.

Turkey faces, once again in its history, a crossroads between two options. The election of 1995 can determine the choice that it will make. Nevertheless, one point can already be given as guaranteed: This choice will also determine the trajectories of Turkey in the year 2000.

EPILOGUE

This chapter was written at the end of October 1995. Less than two months later, on 24 December 1995, parliamentary elections were held in Turkey. Their results confirmed the analysis put forth in this chapter, namely the continuing fragmentation of the conservative and social-democratic poles.[20] The WP continued its ascension but without being able to form a majority in the Turkish National Assembly.

The elections demonstrated a continued momentum for political mobilization in Kurdistan. Kurdish radicalism showed a remarkable capacity to overcome the judicial restrictions imposed upon it by the state and a certain psychological moroseness. The main Kurdish formations formed a bloc behind the PDP (HADEP). This bloc, which was supported by the extraparliamentary Turkish leftist organizations, obtained 4.1 percent of the total vote.[21] In some provinces the PDP obtained a very high vote: 46.7 percent in Diyarbakır; 22 percent in Mardin; 26 percent in Şırnak and Siirt; 27.7 percent in Van; 37.4 percent in Batman; and 54.3 percent in Hakkari.[22]

These results can be interpreted as proof of the continuing mobilizational capacity of Kurdish nationalism; they also indicate its limits in the obtaining conditions. In fact, the PDP (HADEP) succeeded well in some Kurmanji-Sunni homogenous regions.[23] Elsewhere its impact seems to be limited or even quite poor. For example, it obtained 18 percent in Ağrı; 7 percent in Bingöl; 10 percent in Bitlis; 4 percent in Elazığ; 1 percent Erzincan; 6 percent in Erzurum; 6.7 percent in Kars: 2.8 percent in Malatya; 2.7 percent in Maraş; 17 percent in Muş and Tunceli; and 13.6 percent in Urfa. In most of these towns the WP also received quite high number of votes: 30 percent in Ağrı; 51.6 percent in Bingöl; 28.8 percent in Bitlis; 42 percent in Elazığ; 32 percent in Erzincan; 38 percent in Erzurum; 37 percent in Malatya; 27.8 percent in Siirt; and 26 percent in Urfa. The other political parties had rather poor showings in the Kurdish provinces.

Finally, one should add that the PDP (HADEP) had little impact in the Turkish towns where large Kurdish communities reside. It received only 6.7 percent of the vote in Adana; less than 3 percent in Ankara; and less than 4 percent in Istanbul and Izmir. This poor showing seems to indicate that the metropolitan cities continue to have an important integrative function that give birth to new political formations. This does not, however, mean the end of Kurdish radicalism in the big cities of Turkey. It means, rather, that in spite of emotional, cultural and, in some case, economic mobilization, the politics of these towns are shaped by other socio-political determinants.

NOTES

1. Taha Parla, *Türkiye'de Anayasalar* (Istanbul, 1989), 23.
2. For instance, the parliamentary immunity of Hasan Mezarcı was lifted when he asked for the rehabilitation of the opponents executed by the Kemalist regime in 1926. A press campaign and meetings had been organized by the government and the armed forces.
3. Ernest Gellner, *Encounters with Nationalism* (Oxford, 1994).
4. Mete Tunçay, "Atatürk'e Nasıl Bakmak?" *Toplum ve Bilim*, no. 4, 90-95.
5. Taha Parla, *Türkiye'de Siyasal Kültürün Resmî Kaynakları*, vol. 3, *Kemalist Tek-Parti İdeolojisi ve CHP'nin Altı Oku* (Istanbul, 1992).
6. For the documentation on this synthesis, cf. Bozkurt Güvenç and G. Seylan, Ilhan Tekeli, Türk-İslam Sentezi (Istanbul, 1991) 1991.
7. Idris Küçükömer, *Düzenin Yabancılaşması* (Istanbul, 1969).
8. President of the Constitutional Court Güngör Yekda Özden and his close friend chief of the general staff (1991-94) Doğan Güreş opposed publicly and on many occasions civilian leaders such as Turgut Özal, Süleyman Demirel, Hüsamettin Cindoruk and even Tansu Çiller.
9. Tanju Cilizoğlu, *Zincirbozan'dan Bugüne Demokrasi Mücadelesinde Demirel*, (Istanbul, 1988), 9. Demirel explained on more than one occasion the horror he felt concerning the anti-Kurdish military campaigns of the 1920s and 1930s.
10. *Milliyet*, 11 Nov. 1995.
11. Ergil, 1994. This report has been financed by Turkey's Chamber of Commerce, whose president, Yalım Erez, is himself an ethnic Kurd and very close to Tansu Çiller.
12. Ruşen Çakır, *Ayet ve Slogan, Türkiye'de İslamî oluşumlar* (Istanbul, 1990), 219.
13. *Cumhuriyet*, 27 Dec. 1991.
14. The HADEP (Peoples Democracy Party), which will probably also be forbidden by the Constitutional Court, does not have the same social base and prestigious figures as the HEP and DEP did.
15. For instance, in 1975, the collective initiative of the Kurdish deputies prevented the proclamation of the state of emergency in Kurdistan.
16. One of the DYP deputies, Coşkun Kırca, chaired the parliamentary commission asking for the lifting of the immunity of the Kurdish deputies. According to him, Kurdish deputies were guilty of not recognizing Atatürk's dictum: "Happy is he who can say he is a Turk," see the minutes of the Turkish Parliament (sessions presided over by M. Kalemli), 2 and 3 March 1994.
17. During the so-called "terror period" in Turkey in the 1970s, the state was paralyzed and its agents expelled from many towns.
18. Ghassan Salamé, editor *Democraties sans démocrates. Politiques d'ouverture dans le monde arabe et islamique* (Paris, 1994).

19. This refers to *The Southeast Report*, published in August 1995, sponsored by Turkey's Chamber of Commerce and supported by the Çiller government. The report advocates the acceptance of the Kurdish reality in Turkey and proffers some solutions; of note 11.

20.

Party	% vote	no. deputies
WP (RP)	21.32	158
MP (ANAP)	19.66	133
TPP (DYP)	19.21	35
DLP (DSP)	14.65	75
RPP (CHP)	10.71	49
NAP (MHP)	8.18	
PDP (HADEP)	4.17	

21. According to the Turkish consitution, parties obtaining less than 10 percent of the total vote cannot become members of the Assembly. This very high barrier has prevented the HADEP as well as the MHP from representing their electoral constituency.

22. The PDP (HADEP) obtained 27,792 votes in this province. It owes this success both to its mobilization and to its tribal alliances. In fact, it obtained the support of two major tribal leaders, Macit Pirüzbeyoğlu from the Pinyanis tribe and Hamit Geylani of the Geylani tribe. See A. Harmancı, "Hakkari'de Dengeler HADEP'ten Yana," *Özgür Politika*, 19 Dec. 1995.

23. On the impact of the intra-Kurdish ethnicities in this region see Martin van Bruinessen, "Natinalisme kurde et ethnicitiés intra-kurde," *Peuples Méditerranéens*, no. 68-69 (1994): 10-37.

8

The New Democracy Movement in Turkey: A Response to Liberal Capitalism and Kurdish Ethnonationalism

Robert Olson and Yücel Bozdağlıoğlu

The Turkish Republic, created in the aftermath of World War I when the international economic order was dominated by Keynesian economics, established the Turkish economy on a Keynesian foundation.[1] Lacking sufficient capital accumulation for industrial investment, Keynesian economic policies encouraged the emergence of a national bourgeoisie. Statist economic policies also affected political life. Established by Kemal Mustafa Atatürk, the leader of the Turkish nationalist forces in the War of Independence, the Republican People's Party (RPP) dominated Turkish political life up to the late 1940s. The RPP allocated the country's resources to create a national economy.[2] In the 1940s, under Ismet Inönü, Ataürk's successor, who was the leader of the RPP and the president of Turkey until 1950, Turkey experienced a civil revolution that witnessed the emergence of party politics despite these seeming changes. In the 1950 election, the Democrat Party (DP), led by Adnan Menderes, won a majority in parliament and came to power. During the DP period, the bourgeoisie continued to be protected by government regulations. After DP rule was ended in 1960 by a coup d'etat, Turkey experienced two more military coups—in 1971 and 1980—which the bourgeoisie applauded because the 1960 constitution, as far as they were concerned, had granted too many rights to workers and unions. These rights were thought to be the causes for the anarchy and terror that plagued Turkey in the 1970s, justifying the 1980 coup. The 1980 coup became the cornerstone of subsequent Turkish economic and political life. In the 1983 elections, new actors appeared on the Turkish political scene. Supported by the generals, Turgut Özal, leader of the Motherland Party (MP), came to power and dominated Turkish political life for seven years. In many ways this was the most interesting period in Turkish political and economic life since DP rule in the 1950s, when Turkey experienced substantial transformation in its economy. Under Özal, Turkey strove to change from an import-substitution to a market-based economy. These efforts to liberalize the economy created huge challenges. Since it did not have enough capital accumulation and knowledge to build a market-based economy, income distribution was so distorted as to create egregious imbalances. During this period the bourgeoisie maintained a low profile, a role they had taken historically in the political arena, preferring instead to let their representatives influence politicians.

In the 1970s changes emerged in both the domestic and global arenas causing transformations in Turkey similar to those in European countries such as Italy and even in the United States. In these countries, the bourgeoisie began to participate increasingly in politics from the 1980s onward. Ross Perot in the United States, Silvio Berlusconi in Italy and Cem Boyner in Turkey are examples of these trends. First, they represent the bourgeoisie and, second, their economic policies are similar. They defend the principles of neo-liberalism and globalism, whose principles were extolled by Ronald Reagan in the United States and Margaret Thatcher in England. Their movements appeared as these countries' economies began to experience difficulties. Neo-liberalism flourished as it coincided with the collapse of communism.

The generals who brought a halt to party politics in Turkey with their 12 September 1980 coup probably lacked a firm notion of the policies they wanted to implement. When they put an end to the activities of the rightists and leftists, whom they accused of terrorism prior to the coup, they also put an end to those parties that represented deeply rooted leftist and rightist mainstreams in Turkish political life. Two respected Turkish journalists have commented that the generals "thought they were creating a new political arena in Turkey. And even though new parties, which were continuations of the old ones, were established and even won in elections and formed governments, Turkish political life would be very different from what it had been prior to 12 September."[3]

However, the generals did not count on the rambunctiousness of Turkish political life. In less that a decade a coterie of different political parties would take charge of the government. Fourteen years after that interval and eleven years after the return to democracy under terms that the new constitution specified, the existing parties have been unable to determine their functions and roles. Political parties in Turkey are desperately trying to find a new role for themselves. The major parties in the ruling coalition since 1991—the True Path Party (TPP) and the Social Democrat People's Party (SDP) and the major opposition MP—have still not found their balance. However, after several elections, parties such as the Motherland Party (MP), the True Path Party (TPP), the Social Democratic Party (SDP), the Welfare Party (WP) and National Action Party (NAP) have emerged as major players.[4]

THE EMERGENCE OF THE NEW DEMOCRACY MOVEMENT

The NDM, which officially became a party in December 1994, is the twenty-third political party to participate in current political life. Although it is a new party in the political arena, it has attracted considerable media and public attention. Its radical program stressed the importance of privatization and a smaller state and the necessity of closing of the State Economic Enterprises (SEEs). The MP attempted to include as many compatible political tendencies as possible into a single party. In this process, Turgut Özal also attempted to tackle major economic challenges and, as a corollary, to demolish the differences among ideologies. This platform appealed to many voters and the party won a majority in the 1983 elections. But its popularity depended on other factors as well. After the 1980 coup d'etat, all political parties were banned and several others were created artificially. This gave the MP a great advantage vis-à-vis the other parties. It succeeded in its aim to include diverse tendencies in a single party since there was no other party or parties for politicians to join. However, this attempt to bridge differences created tensions within the MP when radical Islamists joined the party. This was to be the main handicap of the MP. By 1994, two other parties, similar to the NDM, began to appeal to these same groups. Like the MP of Turgut Özal, the NDM advocates privatization, closing and selling of SEEs and a smaller central government.

In the political arena, as distinct from the economic arena, the NDM's focus on the Kurdish problem accounts for both its current popularity and the strong opposition it has generated. Its accusations that the state is responsible for the Kurdish problem has brought strong opposition from right wing nationalist parties, parties with which Boyner once sympathized. On occasion Boyner has been interrogated by the State Security Court, the watchdog on any alleged seditious activities against the state, especially any activities that seem to support the Kurdish nationalist movement.[5]

The difference between the NDM and the MP is most notable in the structure of its party membership. In spite of its aim to include all political persuasions, the NDM has been unable to attract the Islamists, but it does include Kurds, which the MP did not, at least, up to late 1995. According to Ismet Giritli, "As was the case in the establishment of the MP, it is evident that the NDM's goal is to put the rightists, leftists, nationalists, traditionalists and, in addition to all of these, the Kurdish nationalists in the same pot."[6] Furthermore, there are some people called "Second Republicans" in the movement who are known for their strong opposition to the current structure of the state, arguing that it is not based on a "civilian" constitution. They maintain that because the current republic was founded by commanders of the War of Independence, it does not represent the real will of the Turkish people; furthermore the state was formed according to the principles of state ideology defined as Kemalism. Because of this, Kemalism must be demolished and replaced with a new ideology in a second republic. Boyner stressed that, "We are neither communists, fascists nor Kemalists."[7] The Second Republic's leaders and theoreticians advocate the necessity of a new constitution and a new state based on principles determined by the Turkish people not Kemalist ideology.

There are many interesting names in the party, some of them worth noting. Cem Boyner is a businessman and a former president of TÜSIAD, the leading organization of Turkish businessmen; Asaf Savaş Akat, an economics professor known as an advocate of the Second Republic; Cengiz Çandar, a journalist and former sympathizer of the leftist Turkish Workers' Party (TWP); Memduh Hacioğlu, a businessman and former president of the Istanbul Chamber of Industry (ISO); Şerif Mardin, a political scientist and currently chair of the religious studies department at American University in Washington, D.C.; Zülfü Dicleli, a theoretician of the NDM and a former member of the Turkish communist party (TCP); Etyen Mahçupyan, a former member of the TWP and a Turkish citizen of Armenian origin; Canan Balkır, an economics professor; Ümit Fırat, a Kurdish intellectual and publisher; Sedat Ilhan, a retired brigadier general who is known for his opposition to former President Kenan Evren (1983-91); Mehmet Emin Sever, a member of parliament from the province of Muş and a former member of the Democracy Party (DP), a Kurdish party; Hülagü Balcılar, a former president of an office of the NMP in Adana; Mustafa Paçal, a unionist and the president of Hak-Iş Union; and Mehmet Altan, a well known journalist and an advocate of the Second Republic. Altan recently left the NDM, accusing it of being a leader-dominated party.[8]

It is evident from the list of the founders that the NDM is an elite movement, even though it professes equality among all supporters including those with questionable legal status. There are no delegates and no veto mechanism. Although it advocates a democratic resolution to the Kurdish problem, only 7 percent of its votes are from the Southeast; 5 percent from the Black Sea region; 9 percent from the Aegean Sea region; 6 percent from the Mediterranean Sea region: and 11 percent from Central Anatolia.[9]

The NDM has been successful in attracting people from different ideologies except for the Islamists, Kemalists and, some argue, workers or representatives of workers. There are several reasons why few Islamists join the NDM, the most important being the manner in which Cem Boyner characterized the prophet Muhammad. He reportedly said, "We must exceed both Muhammad and Atatürk."[10] After this rankling remark, Cengiz Candar, a journalist and a former member of the Turkish Workers' Party (TWP), was delegated to smooth relations with the Islamists. Candar visited some religious figures and stressed that Boyner was very willing to speak with them.

Islamist politicians hesitate to join the NDM, whose future is uncertain, when the WP is increasing in popularity. In addition, there is a belief among the Islamists that the NDM has been formed to prevent the growth of the WP. Furthermore, there are not many Islamist politicians who believe in the economic liberalism that is the backbone of the NDM's program. The belief that the NDM is supported by the media, whom the Islamists do not trust, diminishes the support from this group. Other Islamist groups known as "liberal-Islamists" also want little to do with the NDM and prefer to join other parties such as the Democrat Party (DP) of Aydın Menderes, the New Party (NP), and the Reborn Party (RP). In fact, these groups were actually sympathetic to the NDM as they viewed it as a second MP. But Boyner's derogatory words about the prophet Muhammad were exploited by a wide range of Islamists and they distanced themselves from the movement. Another reason the Islamists look warily at the NDM is its liberal economic agenda.

The NDM's program regarding religion is not entirely opposed to the ideas advocated by the Islamists. The NDM emphasizes separation of religion and state. Cem Boyner proposes that any member of parliament who wants to take an oath on the Quran should be allowed to do so and advocates that state control over religion should be lifted and left to the religious societies (*cemaats*). While he asserts that secularism is a fundamental principle of modern and democratic Turkey, he qualifies this by saying that "under the present conditions, secularism should be redefined: all religious education should be in the hands of the public."[11] Cem Boyner does not appear to perceive the religious-based WP as a danger to Turkish democracy. He thinks religious movements are increasing in the world because people are seeking spiritual sustenance in the wake of the collapse of the bi-polar world system. He stresses that in Turkey religious movements are largely reactions to the collapse and corruption of the current political system, and he views the popularity of the WP as an answer to this corruption. Such ideas frighten secularists, who sympathized with Boyner in the beginning, but now fear his ideas and his attempts to gather Muslims under the NDM umbrella.

Businessmen seem to be divided into two groups concerning the NDM. While the Sabancı family, which is one of the leading business families, supports the NDM, other businessmen are disturbed by its economic agenda. In a widely circulated interview, Sakıp Sabancı said, "We support Cem Boyner."[12] Another indicator of the Sabancıs' support is the membership in the NDM of Aziz Köylüoğlü, who is the president of one of the Sabancıs' companies and very close to the family. Güler Sabancı, the daughter of Sakıp, has also expressed enthusiasm for the NDM. The Koç family's position, however, is different. One newspaper account attributes the silence of the Koç family to the fact that they do not like the NDM's antiprotectionist policies; many of the Koç family enterprises benefit from those policies. It must be noted, however, that the Sabancı and Koç empires do cooperate in certain undertakings. But Boyner has declared, "I am part of this order and I gained a lot from this order, but now I oppose it. This order must be changed and we are ready to change it. Businessmen who are opposed to the Customs Union with Europe and against liberalism are those who are fed by the current order."[13] Such remarks are sure to send shivers through businessmen and industrialists still prospering from protectionist tariffs and taxes. It seems that many businessmen who support the NDM are also against wasting resources to solve the Kurdish problem, especially Ankara's war against the PKK, by military means. They want the resources spent on the war, estimated to amount to some 6 to 7 billion dollars a year since the end of the Gulf war, to be devoted to economic development.[14]

From the view point of the Kemalists, the NDM is not an attractive movement to join. They do not like Boyner's criticism of the deficiencies of the Kemalist legacy; indeed, Kemal is so revered that insulting him is a crime under current Turkish law. Boyner, however, aims to substitute Kemalism and its emphasis on statism with the ideology of Western liberalism: "If you look at the six principles of Kemalism, you notice one word is missing—democracy."[15] Asaf Savaş Akat, an economist and strong advocate of the Second Republic and who is on the NDM's board of advisors, adds that the lack of the democracy principle is at the heart of Turkey's dilemma.[16] Celal Boratav supports Akat's analysis, adding that "the NDM says that it is the continuation of all movements in the past that provided Turkey with important services. While they are content with everybody else, their main enemies are the Kemalists and the socialists who recognize the Turkish Revolution."[17]

In the foreign press and in diplomatic circles, the NDM attracts wide attention. It is evident that European and American media and those close to government circles and members of governments themselves are interested in and support the new movement. *Time* magazine mentioned Cem Boyner as one of the world's one hundred youngest leaders. Comparing Boyner with Silvio Berlusconi of Italy, it declared that "Cem Boyner changed has changed the political agenda in Turkey."[18] *The Los Angeles Times* suggested that Cem Boyer might fill the gap in Turkish politics after the death of Özal in 1993 and that Boyner was trying to wake up the Turkish people before the ethnic and religious conflicts in regions near Turkey inundate the country.[19] Boyner has spoken to the European Parliament as well as the foreign minister of Germany and other leaders of European governments. These meetings increased dramatically in the three months prior to 24 December 1995 general elections in Turkey.

What are the reasons that Europeans are so interested in the NDM? It seems European leaders perceive the NDM as a new element in a changing Turkish political structure. According to Hadi Uluengin, a journalist for the daily *Hürriyet*, the NDM leader speaks the same language as Europe, frequently punctuating his speeches with the words *freedom, democracy* and *liberal economy*.[20] Second, Europe did not want to make things too difficult for Turkey on the eve of its admission to the European Customs Union (ECU): a policy that paid off when Turkey was admitted to the ECU by an overwhelming vote on 13 December 1995.[21] Turkey even received support from former radicals such an Daniel Cohn-Bendit, who noted, "Secularization of Europe took 200 hundred to 250 years. By the time stability had come, Europe had paid a heavy price. Now Europe does not want to experience the same problems because of Islam. This frightens Europe.

For all of these reasons, Europe sees the NDM as a new formation that will allow smoother relations with Europe." According to a senior official with the U.S. administration, Boyner "appears to have the charisma and willpower, but he still needs time. Officials in Washington who follow Turkey closely believe that someone like Boyner, under current conditions in Turkey, could think of success only after some five to seven years of organizing and campaigning."[22]

It is clear, despite the diverse reactions, the NDM has attracted attention. What are the reasons for its appeal vis-à-vis other political parties? Some claim the NDM is protected by the government to prevent the further rise of the WP. Others claim that it is supported by certain government circles to enable safe discussion of the Kurdish problem in the public arena.

There are two major academic theories regarding the emergence of the NDM as a political force in Turkey, one that is domestic and one that is international. In order to discuss these two theories it is necessary to examine the NDM program.

THE NDM's PROGRAM

The NDM's chief objective in the newly emerging world order is to align Turkey with the league of Western industrial and capitalist democracies. The NDP advocates ending human rights abuses, especially against the Kurds, allowing more cultural freedom to the Kurds and lifting state control over religion and the economy. These radical ideas made the NDM more attractive to the intelligentsia in spite of strong opposition from nationalist right wing circles, and some armed forces commanders and the former Joint Chiefs of Staff.

The NDM thinks Turkey can develop faster if its political structure is based on three fundamental freedoms: speech, religion and enterprise.[23] What the NDM means by the freedom of enterprise is a reduced role for the state in the economy.

The NDM's economic program reflects a pure liberalism. It emphasizes the necessity of a reduced state. According to its theoreticians, the state must not engage in any economic enterprises. Its fundamental job must be to organize economic activities and economic life in general. It must transfer this responsibility to the private sector. In order to do this, the SEEs must be closed or sold; privatization is the most urgent task. The NDM thinks the market economy is the only way to increase productivity. Boyner says, "We must remove political subventions, customs, immunities and protectionist regulations. We have to privatize immediately and the state's role in the economy must be reduced. It must leave all economic activities to citizens and private enterprises. On the other hand, the state must be a big state in terms of justice, education and social security."[24]

According to the NDM's program, when the world stepped into a new epoch in the 1980s, Turkey had serious problems. Democratic institutions could not produce solutions. On the contrary, all institutions were corrupt: "Under these conditions, our country went into an extraordinary era. In this era, some radical decisions were taken. Even though it had no democratic base, it has been successful. It has been noted that Turkey could compete with European countries in a free market economy, but that the democratic institutions to encourage these developments were unable to be formed."[25] These positions make it clear that the NDM does not think of itself as simply a movement for a refurbished democracy; rather, it is a new movement for a new democracy. It is the first mainstream political movement in Turkish politics to advocate the dismantling of Kemalism. Unlike other political parties, at least in 1994, the NDM also stresses the connection between the political economy and the Kurdish problem, a problem to which the NDM proffers a solution.

The NDM's approach to the Kurdish problem is the most significant reason that the NDM has attracted attention from all groups in Turkey. As two respected journalists have noted, "Neither Boyner nor any of his closest circle are of Kurdish origin, but the argument is that once this problem is solved other solutions will follow. No one should preach to another on motherland, nation, flag or religion. . . . A solution to the Kurdish problem can only be found in Parliament."[26]

The NDM views the Kurdish problem as Turkey's most serious challenge, and Boyner has promised to solve it peacefully. The NDM states emphatically that the Kurdish problem is largely a matter of identity.[27] In the view of its theoreticians, the ongoing Kurdish problem and, especially, the war against the PKK is not just a Kurdish problem but a Turkish problem: "Today, Turks cannot solve the Kurdish problem, nor can Kurds. This problem can only be solved by both Turks and Kurds together. Indeed, there is not a Kurdish problem in Turkey. The Kurds only want to speak and write in their own language, that is, they want what they have now."[28] The NDM proposes several ways to deal with the Kurdish problem. First, the Kurdish-Turkish and the Sunni-Alevi splits must be bridged; second, Turks must accept the Kurdish reality and Kurdish culture; third, all players must engage in dialogue; and, four, the "terrorist" PKK must be separated from the Kurdish problem. The NDM is not opposed to the establishment of a Kurdish political party. Boyner "believes that the Kurdish reality should be accepted, but that Kurds must recognize that Turkey is a country shared by everyone and that it is indivisible." If that is acknowledged, then the Kurdish language, culture and education should be developed. Boyner accepts the Democracy Party (DP) as playing a crucial role in fulfilling a historical role in creating a dialogue between Turks and Kurds: "I cannot think of Parliament without the DP. It is not because I agree with them. Even though they say the exact opposite of what I say, I do fight for their right of free speech."[29] According to Boyner, there is no problem in giving rights to the Kurds individually, but there is a problem in recognizing them as a national identity. In his view, Turkey can solve this problem by granting all democratic rights to the Kurds and by recognizing the Kurdish reality.

Boyner emphasizes that Turkey has reached a point of no return with regard to the Kurdish problem. He compares the Palestine-Israel, South African and Britain-Ireland problems with the Kurdish problem. He sees the autonomy agreement signed by the PLO and Israel and Mandela's success in South Africa as references for Turkey. He emphasizes that these developments demonstrate that even the most difficult problems can be resolved with good will and dialogue.[30] In one of his interviews, the NDM spokesman stated that he would meet anyone, including Abdullah Öcalan, leader of the PKK, if the PKK would stop its "terrorism." "When I give the example of the PLO and Israel," said Boyner, "I mean the circumstances in the world can change. The PLO was established in 1964 and recognized by the United Nations in 1974. Now the PLO is not what it was in the past; neither is Israel. They changed and they decided to solve their problems peacefully, i.e. condition change. Today the PKK is a terrorist organization, but I don't know what is going to happen in the future.[31]

This implies that the NDM is ready to make an agreement with the PKK as long as it does not resort to force. The NDM currently describes the PKK as a terrorist and fascist organization: "The PKK is a fascist movement, and you cannot evaluate this organization in the context of the right of speech or any other right. Any organization which uses terrorism to reach its goal is dirty."[32] The NDM's ideas regarding the Kurdish problem brought strong reactions. Its radical thoughts about the Kurdish problem (which as time passes seem increasingly less radical in Turkey, as even mainstream political parties advocate the necessity of solving and recognizing the challenge of Kurdish nationalism) brought harsh criticism from the nationalist right wing parties and some military commanders, who accused the NDM of being a Kurdish party. The NDM rejects all such charges. It denies being a Kurdish party, describing itself as a party that believes in free and public expression.[33] On the other hand, the PKK and Kurdish nationalists characterize the NDM as an instrument of the bourgeoisie class. Abdullah Öcalan has stated that "The Turkish business class created a new party to solve the Kurdish problem. It is interesting that the Turkish people cannot find any solutions, but that Turkish businessman can. They see a solution in which we can be in association with Turkey and that is proper for us. Because they are the class in production and know very well what they are doing."[34]

The NDM theoreticians think there are many reasons for the party to proffer solutions to the Kurdish problem. The question is: Why is the NDM so radical about the Kurdish problem when its position may cause it to lose support? As mentioned above, the NDM sees the Kurdish problem as a matter of identity. But why does it concentrate on the identity problem and ignore the socioeconomic disequilibrium that fosters the growth of Kurdish nationalism? The NDM program asserts that the new Turkish republic was founded on the ashes of the Ottoman Empire, which was multicultural and multi-ethnic. Due to the fear that the newborn republic could not be protected if the new government were to recognize all languages and cultures, a new official ideology was developed. Except for the minorities recognized by the Lausanne Treaty, signed in 1923, the ruling class aimed to melt all cultures in the majority Turkish culture. However, this effort, the NDM stresses, has not been successful. Today the Kurdish problem endangers the democratic life in Turkey. The NDM manifesto states that the Kurdish problem can only be solved by Turks and Kurds themselves. It also declares that the Turkish government must grant rights to Kurds and allow them to establish a Kurdish party to improve their cultural and societal conditions.[35]

The NDM stresses three approaches to the Kurdish problem: a solution must be reached democratically, prejudices must be eradicated and both Turkish and Kurdish extremist nationalism must be curtailed. It is important to prevent increased Kurdish support for the PKK. The problem of identity plays an important role in the NDM's program. Etyen Mahçupyan, one of the theoreticians of the NDM and, interestingly, a Turkish citizen of Armenian ethnicity, points out that the NDM brought the question of culture to the fore when it was established. According to Mahçupyan, the Kurdish problem rose from the concept of citizenship specified in the constitution: "We must find a new citizenship concept. We have to define it again to include all identities in Turkey. These problems, in fact, are not only that region's [here he refers to the southeastern region of Turkey, which is predominately Kurdish and where war between the government and the PKK has raged for the past decade] problem, but all of Turkey's. These problems are the consequences of certain conditions. When these consequences meet, conflict of identity results. Problems going on in the East and Northeast have also emerged."[36]

THEORETICAL FRAMEWORK

Since its establishment the NDM has appealed to different political groups. In order to understand the emergence of the NDM, one must also look at the domestic and international variables that impelled the NDM to emerge on the Turkish political scene. Internally, the NDM should be evaluated in terms of the structures and roles of the current parties. But it should also be studied in terms of the changing structure of the Turkish economy and the increase in the rise of Kurdish nationalism since the Gulf war in 1991.[37] The emergence of the NDM must also be evaluated in terms of international economic and political theories that influence the NDM's program.

After the coup d'état in 1980, Turkey witnessed fundamental transformations in its economy and political life that created problems at the macro level. Efforts to transform Turkey from an import-substitution to a market-based economy created many problems in social and political life. Distorted income distribution and corrupt political life increased support for Islamist movements and parties, especially the WP. Heightened Kurdish nationalism gave rise to heightened Turkish nationalism and chauvinism. As a result, Islamist movements in general have gained momentum during the last decade. The fear that current political parties lack balance and were increasingly unable to keep pace with the changing world order brought businessmen into political life. According to Boyner, "Political parties in Turkey do not reflect social opposition. This is obvious from the votes they obtain in the elections. The party that got most of the votes still only received 20 percent of the total vote. This means that 80 percent of the people do not support that party. Since people are not satisfied with current parties, they indicate their unhappiness by giving support to the Islamist parties like the WP. The NDM has been representing the social opposition since its establishment. This is the main strength of the NDM."[38]

There is nothing new in the fact that businessmen influence political life in Turkey and the Parliament; this is increasingly evident since 1950. While the owners of small and middle-scale firms and provincial businessmen have always been represented in Parliament, now in the 1990s industrialist and businessmen seek election to Parliament. Unlike in the past, when they influenced the decisions of Parliament via their representatives, nowadays they want to influence the decisions of Parliament directly. The daughter of Vehbi Koç, who is perhaps the most well known businessman in Turkey, became a member of the MP. Another businessman, Besim Tibuk, established the Liberal Party (LP).[39] The former president of TÜSIAD, Erdal Kabatepe, is trying to organize a new movement called the Liberal Movement (LM). Why do all of these wealthy men want to participate in political life as members of Parliament? The answer seems to be that "they do not trust their representatives anymore. They realize that politicians are very slow in making decisions, especially when circumstances demand that they move fast. They now want to take control of political life and determine the direction of politics."[40]

As noted above, the theoreticians of the NDM and some other observers opine that the NDM phenomenon occurred in Turkish politics as a result of the changing structure of Turkey and of the world; the changes heightened doubts among wealthy businessmen that existing parties and politicians were capable of managing these changes. We argue that the NDM's ideas and program reflect the consequences of these changes. When writing about the NDM, one must take three determinants into account: the Turkish economy, the structure of the state and the Kurdish problem. It is obvious that these variables should be evaluated in terms of international political economic theory.

As an economic variable, the first determinant is the rules of the new world order that caused the NDM to emerge in Turkish political life. In the 1920s, there was only one economic rightist ideology representing the business class, namely, liberalism, the classic economic theory that advocates no state intervention in the economy, or at least as little as possible. However, the appearance in the 1920s and 1930s of nazism in Germany and fascism in Italy, both of which advocated state intervention in the economy, resulted in new challenges to liberalism. World War II, in a sense, was the conflict between nazism-fascism and liberalism.

But, paradoxically, it was Keynesianism, the antithesis of liberalism, that emerged as the dominant economic theory and practice, after the war. Keynesianism advocated that the state play a role in the economy, especially in providing the means for embarking on new economic "take-off." Keynesianism stood for more equal distribution of wealth. Keynesianism was not, however, anticapital. The period after 1945 was a golden one for Keynesian economics. But beginning with the 1970s, capitalism underwent a serious crisis. As long as the Keynesian policies were continued, the economic crisis became worse. Conditions were ripe for the emergence of a new liberalism with a new theoretical base. By the end of the 1970s, a world economic system emerged according to this new liberal-right ideology. This new neo-classical economic theory stresses that the state should play little or no role in the economy. Unlike Keynesian economics, neo-liberalism stresses the capacity of enterprising individuals to affect economic change. Neo-liberalism began to dominate first in the Northern Hemisphere and subsequently in the Southern Hemisphere and the non-Western world via the IMF and the World Bank.

Turkey encountered economic neo-liberalism and the accompanying new right political ideas in the early 1980s during Turgut Özal's stint as prime minister. In the 1990s, the NDM and other political formations with more radical liberal ideas than those of Özal and his MP party are emerging into the political area. The NDM synthesizes two tendencies strengthened in the 1980s. One is the "New Right," whose principles were carried out by the Reagan and Thatcher governments in the United States and Great Britain and that of the military dictatorships of Latin America, which was brought to Turkey by Özal and the MP. The other tendency is a post-Marxism, postmodernism, which was adapted by radical intellectuals affected by the failure of the social movements in Europe in 1968-73 and assimilated by academic environments and the media. In the view of Ergin Yıldızoğlu, "These two trends believe that all ideologies are death and that they themselves are the expression of the era in which there is no other ideology. What they have in common are ideological hypotheses which are as old as the capitalist production system itself; society is not the organic sum of individuals, but the mathematical sum of individuals. Due to this belief, the starting point is the individual, not society; the free market is the source of democracy and individual freedoms. People can only overcome the conflicts among themselves based on humanitarian values and historical common ethics."[41]

In Yıldızoğlu's view, two groups are playing important roles in the ideological thrust of the NDM. The liberal "new-rightist" wing and the "democratic liberal-leftist" wing. Boyner and his businessmen supporters are the advocates of the liberal new-rightist wing. It is clear that the ideas of this wing center on economic issues. As mentioned above, this group wants to implement the economic ideas of neo-liberalism in the Turkish economy. According to them, Turkey is experiencing a very serious economic crisis. It does no good to approach this crisis with traditional projects and resolutions; instead they want to transform Turkey so as to prevent future crises. In order to do this, they want to remove all barriers that prevent the market from operating freely. Again according to Yıldızoğlu, "Cem Boyner sees state intervention as the reason for economic crisis. In order to overcome or manage the crisis, the state should have no influence in the economy."[42] This new right wing hypothesizes that the world is made up of individuals independent from each other and who seek only their own advantages.

Another group affecting the NDM's program is the "liberal leftists." This group consists of some scientists and journalists. While the new right wing focuses mostly on economic issues, the liberal leftist or post-Marxist wing concentrates heavily on the structure of the state, society and Kurdish issues. They think that politics should not simply be a struggle for power. Zülfü Dicleli characterizes the ideas of the liberal leftists in the following manner: "In the past, as was the case in other countries, people could be divided into two camps in Turkey and politics was a struggle for power. However, we have come to the end of this kind of politics. It is impossible for societies to be divided into two camps: socio-economic, cultural, geographical, ethnic and religious differences are increasing. Furthermore, there is a propensity for people to act and think individually and relations with the outside world are being diversified. This brings a process to the fore in which societies become atomized. Every identity and interest, in order for them to be accepted by someone else, exaggerated their own interests and identities which causes tribalism and micro-nationalism."[43]

Many scholars introduce differences of civilizations, religions, cultures and identities to describe the current and future evolution of civil society and international relations. This post-Marxist, postmodernist wing seems to agree with the ideas of the inevitable "clash of civilizations" as first expressed by Samuel Huntington in the United States, who wrote that "the fundamental source of conflict in this new world will not be primarily ideological or primarily economic. The great divisions among humankind and the dominating sources of conflict will be cultural. Nation states will remain the most powerful actors in world affairs, but the principal conflicts of global politics will occur between nations and groups of different civilizations. The clash of civilizations will dominate global politics."[44]

The theoreticians of the NDM seem to be heavily affected by the clash of civilizations theory. Their ideas regarding the Kurdish problem and the religious issues confirm this. They believe that "to obtain power through the support of one or several entities in the country increases conflicts and wastes the energy of other groups which are not in power. Under these circumstances, to insist on the traditional operation of politics invites threats that may result in the division of the country. This is what makes the NDM approach new and different. It does not oppose the multiplicity of the nation. What it wants to prevent is multiplicity turning into polarization and the mushrooming of conflict. It aims to create a synthesis of different groups within the nation. The NDM's main goal is to establish a new movement that will gather the representatives of these different groups under a single roof."[45] The democratic liberal leftist wing also recommends that religion be entirely separate from the state. In one of his interviews Cem Boyner stated that "people can establish ethnic or religious parties."[46]

The NDM stresses that Turkey, whose population is 99 percent Muslim, is experiencing a religious conflict. The developments that occurred in the province of Sıvas in July 1993 in which some thirty-eight people, most of them Alevi writers, authors and intellectuals died as a result of Sunni arson of a hotel, must be prevented. The conditions that gave rise to riots by Alevis and Kurds as a result of Sunni provocations in the Gaziosmanpasa suburb of Istanbul in March 1995 must be addressed. The NDM argues that these events occurred because religion, under the control of the state, is interpreted solely as Sunnism. In so doing, the state ignores peoples who adhere to other sects of Islam, such as the Alevis. The Alevis, called Alawiyya in Arabic or Nusayriah, are Muslims who comprise approximately 15 to 20 percent of the total population of Turkey of about 63 million. Further, around 15 to 20 percent of the Kurdish population of 10 to 12 million is Alevi. Alevis or Alawiyya/Alawites also comprise about 10 to 11 percent of the population of Syria. The Alawites are a powerful group in Syria who have controled the highest echelons of power in Syria since 1970. Hafiz al-Asad, the president of Syria, is an Alawite/Alevi.[47]

It is not coincidental that the liberal leftist group believes in the demise of ideologies and advocates neo-liberalism. This is clear from their ideas regarding the structure of the state and economy. Boyner explains, "When saying ideology, if one means liberalism, capitalism, fascism and socialism that have been dominant since the 1800s, we think these ideas have lost their validity. Today the world is going into a new epoch. Knowledge and communications are shaking up the world as much as the invention of the machine. We have to form a new viewpoint that can embrace this new world in a wholeness. We have this kind of ideology. In this ideology, there is democracy, freedom, a competitive and productive market economy and the idea of social equality and justice."[48] The main goal of this wing of the NDM is democracy, even radical democracy. Given that socialism collapsed and all ideologies are death, there is only one thing left to fight for: democracy. The liberal leftists seem to be influenced by the ideas of Francis Fukuyama, especially on the issue of ideologies. In "The End of History?" Fukuyama asserts that "the passing of Marxism-Leninism first from China and then from the Soviet Union will mean its death as a living ideology of world historical significance . . . And the death of this ideology means the growing 'Common Marketization' of international relations, and the diminution of the likelihood of large-scale conflicts between states."[49]

Ergin Yıldızoğlu, however, is not altogether convinced by Fukuyama's theory. Marxism, he points out, expresses a relation between the idea of democracy and equality and the struggle for democracy is ensconced in the "grand narrative" of socialism. Given that socialism has collapsed, the struggle for democracy cannot be sustained on the hypotheses of Marxism.[50] A second theoretical position of the NDM is the "Post Modernist Situation." This idea was articulated by the "nouveaux philosophes" in the 1960s based on the rejection of the ideas of the Enlightenment. The starting point of this new philosophy was the assertion that the world is understandable and changeable and that mind and reality are indeed illusions, a view contrary to the 18th century's Enlightenment tradition.

Jacques Derrida has opined that there is no place for concrete reality. Language is always a barrier between humans, preventing an empirically based understanding of reality. Post-Marxism and postmodernism complete the economic perspective: the post-industrial society envisaged by Daniel Bell, who was one of the philosophers of the "New Right" during the 1970s. According to this hypothesis, "In the new era, the production of knowledge gains in importance compared to materialism. These two philosophical and economic perspectives constitute the Post Modernist Situation of François Lyotard, who supports the end-of-history thesis. The postmodernist thesis spawned the political trend of post-Marxism."[51]

Post-Marxism developed as a result of the political and moral failure of the 1968 social movements in Europe. Post-Marxism advocates the basic tenets that postmodernism rejects, i.e. that the basic determinants of societal and political identities are objective class structures that can be described historically; that production relations and economic bases have primary explanatory functions while politics and ideology are secondary; that the proletariat has objective interests other than socialism; that only objective interests of classes can be entertained; and, finally, that capitalism can be transformed into socialism. In this process the proletariat has a different and more privileged position than others.

The NDM's post-Marxist wing seems to be affected by these postmodernist and post-Marxist ideas, which seem to affect their ideas concerning the challenge of Kurdish nationalism in Turkey, what they refer to as the Kurdish problem, and their ideas about the role of ideologies in society.

The NDM is a synthesis of two ideologies: neo-liberalism and post-Marxism. While neo-liberal principles are dominant factors in economic issues, liberal leftist or post-Marxist ideas are evident in their views of the structure of the state and the Kurdish problem. The NDM aims to include both rightist and leftist principles. If this is the case, where do we place the NDM in the Turkish political spectrum? Is it on the left or the right of center? Or is it in the center? In order to answer these questions, we must look at the current Turkish political line-up.

The TPP-RPP government (prior to the 24 December 1995 election) was a coalition of center-right and center-left, which grew weaker throughout 1994 and 1995. This became clear in the elections of 27 March 1994, when neither the center-right nor center-left but rather the more extremist right parties, such as the nationalist NAP and the Islamist WP, strengthened their power. While the TPP and the MP received around 40 percent of the vote, the RPP-DLP (Democratic Left Party) alignment received 27 percent of the vote. Extremist nationalist and religious parties such as the NAP and the WP got nearly 30 percent. As a result, the unification of the TPP and the MP came to the fore in the center-right agenda. The big bourgeoisie especially want an end to this division. Powerful businessmen would also like to pull the right-wing NAP more to the center. On the left side, the DLP, led by Bülent Ecevit, seems to have an advantage and is seen by many observers as the only party that can stop the rise of the WP. It is not surprising that in late November 1995 former members of the RPP, which at that time was led by Deniz Baykal, abandoned the party and migrated to Ecevit's DLP. One of the migrating members was Mümtaz Soysal, an ardent nationalist and respected constitutional specialist who served as foreign minister of the TPP-RPP government in 1994. On the left side, the DLP is seen by many observers as the only party that can stop the rise of the WP.

In this context the NDM finds its place in the center-right wing. But the leaders of the NDM do not want to be classified as rightist or leftist. They stress that politics must be removed from the quagmire of artificial definitions.[52] The NDM's targeted groups are those that experienced disappointments and failures with the center right and left parties, namely the Alevis and Kurds.

The NDM is a movement of the center-right that is trying to gather support from diverse groups. Its primary aim is to harmonize the ideas of neo-liberalism and of the democratic liberal left in its structure. While neo-liberalism principles are dominant factors in its economic program, post-Marxism thought is dominant in its social and cultural agenda, especially with regard to the Kurdish problem. What worries the theoreticians of the NDM concerning Turkish political life is the fear that the world is entering a new epoch and that the current crop of politicians is incapable of meeting the challenges of the new world order. It is obvious that the NDM movement is a continuation of the Özal era. Although it has new and radical ideas about the state, economy and the Kurdish problem, the NDM also has some handicaps.

The main factor that makes the NDM a new and radical political party is its approach to the Kurdish problem. Its advocacy of a peaceful and political solution to the Kurdish problem was/is appreciated by many observers. But the NDM sees the problem as a struggle of establishing identity, i.e. as a clash of identities (rather than of civilizations) between Turks and Kurds. It seems unlikely, however, that the struggle between Turkish and Kurdish nationalism will abate without a reallocation of economic resources.

The NDM's analysis of the state also does not fit the facts of Turkey. Second Republicans in the movement assert that the current state was established by the generals of the War of Independence and that the Kemalist ideology it spawned no longer reflects the will of the Turkish people. The NDM's assertion that the state is under the complete control of the civil-military bureaucracy has not been true since at least the 1950s. During the establishment of the Turkish Republic, the civil-military bureaucracy took its place in power along with the big bourgeoisie and landlords. This was the situation up to 1946, which marks the beginning of multiparty politics. After 1946, those who directed the state were big bourgeoisie-industrialists and the large land owners. The balance of power among these factions changed in the 1970s, and the big bourgeoisie represented in TÜSIAD gained control of the state.[53] The NDM sees the coup d'ètats of 1960, 1971 and 1980 as efforts by the civil-military bureaucracy to strengthen its control of the state, but the NDM theoreticians cannot explain why the bourgeoisie applauded and even invited all of these coups.

It is clear that the NDM leadership's perception of democracy is based on individualism. As Korkut Boratav points out, "The perception of democracy based on individuals and leaving them alone with their rights and responsibilities is primitive. The main mechanism of democracy is organized society, i. e. the organization of productive people, unions, cooperatives and voluntary associations."[54] Korkut Boratav is of the opinion that the NDM wants to accomplish what Özal tried to do with the aim of obtaining 45 percent of the vote in a general election. But, he states, the NDM does not understand the glaring contradiction: While Özal was engaged in these politics he not only allowed the poor villagers migrating from the countryside and villages to build *gecekondus* or shanty houses on the outskirts of the big cities, he granted them subventions to do so. In a biting critique of the NDM's economic program, Boratav says, "People supported Özal in order to receive these benefits; if you take them away, why do people want democracy?"[55]

This is the dilemma facing the neo-liberal, post-Marxist, post-modernist approach (one dare not call it an ideology) of the NDM as it has emerged on the Turkish political scene. If the people do not want democracy on the terms proffered by the NDM it seems unlikely that the NDM will be able to implement an economic strategy that will satisfy the economic needs or hopes of ordinary Turks and the bulk of Kurds. The NDM program to foster economic development of Turkey and its strategy to contain Kurdish ethnonationalism seem fundamentally contradictory.

These contradictions were borne out by the parliamentary elections of 24 December 1995, in which the NDM received a total of 135,250 votes; less than 1 percent of the total. In the heavily populated Kurdish provinces in the east and southeast, the NDM received 4.41 percent of the vote in Şırnak and 2.67 in Van. It obtained more than 1 percent of the vote only in Bitlis, 1.83; Bingöl, 1.06; Ağrı. 1.05; Diyarbakır, 1.59; Muş, 1.12; and in Siirt, 1.30 percent. Such a poor showing may well place the future of the NDM itself in jeopardy as well and the neo-liberal economic program it put forward to coopt the challenge of Kurdish nationalism.

Notes

1. The republic was declared on 29 October 1923.
2. The RPP, founded on 6 December 1923, was first called the People's Party (*Halk Fırkası*). In 1935 the word *republic* was added.
3. Gül Demir and Niki Gamm, *Turkish Daily News,* 4 Aug. 1994.
4. Ibid.

5. For more on Boyner's and the NDM's position on the identity problem see Robert Olson, "The Kurdish Question and Turkey's Foreign Policy, 1991-1995: From the Gulf War to the Incursion into Iraq," *Journal of South Asian and Middle Eastern Studies* 19, no. 1 (fall 1995): 1-30. Boyner was interrogated for allegedly making the statement, "The army is a threat to democracy (*ordu demokrasiyi tehdit ediyor*)."

6. Ismet Giritli, *Türkiye*, 31 Dec. 1994.

7. *Cumhuriyet*, 17 Jan. 1994.

8. *Sabah*, 21 Dec. 1994.

9. *Sabah*, 21 Dec. 1994.

10. *Milliyet*, 23 Dec. 1994.

11. *Cumhuriyet*, 11 Sept. 1993.

12. *Sabah*, 13 Jan. 1995.

13. *Sabah*, 13 Jan. 1995.

14. For more on the conjectured costs of the war see Olson, "Kurdish Question," 23-25.

15. *Turkish Daily News*, 30 Sept. 1994.

16. Ibid.

17. *Cumhuriyet*, 30 Aug. 1994.

18. *Hürriyet*, 29 Nov. 1994.

19. *Sabah*, 8 Aug. 1994.

20. Hadi Uluengin, *Hürriyet*, 16 Feb. 1995.

21. The vote was 343 in favor, 149 opposed and 36 abstentions.

22. Gül Demir and Ismet Imset, *Turkish Daily News*, 10 Sept. 1994.

23. NDM's program.

24. Ibid.

25. Ibid.

26. Gül Demir and Ismet Imset, *Turkish Daily News*, 30 Sept. 1994.

27. For the treatment of identity, nationalism and ethnonationalism relevant to the challenge of Kurdish nationalism in Turkey, see Anthony D. Smith, *National Identity* (Reno, 1991); Donald L. Horowitz, *Ethnic Groups in Conflict* (Berkeley, 1985); and Robert Ted Gurr, *Minorities at Risk: A Global View of Ethnonational Conflicts* (Washington, D.C., 1993).

28. Cem Boyner, *Sabah*, 30 Aug. 1994.

29. *Sabah*, 8 Nov. 1993. By November 1995, even Mesut Yılmaz, the leader of the MP seemed to realize the significance of recognizing the Kurdish problem and the increasing challenge of Kurdish nationalism to the current configuration of the Turkish state. On 17 November he visited Yaşar Kemal, the noted Turkish author of Kurdish ethnicity who was at that time under indictment for publishing an article in the German weekly, *Der Spiegel*, that the State Security Court prosecutors termed "treasonous." The incident has continued to be at the center of major brouhaha. After their meeting Yılmaz said that "If you do not solve the Kurdish problem, we will not be able to bring democracy to Turkey (*Bu sorunu çözmezsek, Türkiye'ye demokrasiye getiremeyiz*)." In late November, Boyner and Yılmaz even held discussions regarding a possible coalition between the NDP and the MP in the run-up to the 24 December election.

30. *Demokrasi Haberleri*, 15-31 July 1994.

31. Ibid.

32. *Cumhuriyet*, 27 Nov. 1994.

33. *Sabah*, 16 April 1995.

34. *Milliyet*, 8 Feb. 1995.

35. *New World, New Turkey, New Democracy*, a manifesto published by the NDM.

36. *Milliyet*, 3 Jan. 1995. Here Mahcupyan is referring to clashes between Sunnis and Alevis as well as Kurds and Turks.

37. In this regard see Olson, "Kurdish Question," 26-30.

38. Cem Boyner, *Demokrasi Haberleri*, 15-31 July 1994.

39. The LP is similar to the NDM on economic issues but differs with regard to the Kurdish question.

40. Hilmi Köfteoğlu, *Iktisat*, Sept. 1994.

41. *Iktisat*, Sept. 1994.

42. Ibid.

43. Zülfü Dicleli, *Demokrasi Haberleri*, 15-31 July 1994.

44. Samuel Huntington, "The Clash of Civilization," *Foreign Affairs* 72 (summer 1993), 22.

45. Zülfü Dicleli, *Demokrasi Haberleri*, 15-31 July 1994.

46. Cem Boyner, *Sabah*, 8 Nov. 1993.

47. The fundamental article of the Alevi belief system is the absolute oneness of God, though it does not attempt to define his existence or attributes either philosophically or theologically. The Alevis believe, among other things, that Ali, the son-in-law of the prophet Muhammad, is the last manifestation of the deity and consummate reality. God appeared on earth seven times in different forms and has three personalities, corresponding to a trinity comprised of Ali, Muhammad and Salman al-Farisi or Salman al-Pak, a man of Iranian origin and one of the first adherents to Islam. This God, Ali, also created Muhammad and charged him to preach the message of the Quran. Muhammad then occupies an inferior position in the trinity to Ali. Alevis worship light, symbolized by the sun, which in turn represents the mysteries of God. For more on the Alevis' religious beliefs and history see "Alawiyah," in *The Oxford Encyclopedia of the Modern Islamic World*, ed. John L. Esposito (Cambridge, 1995), 63-64.

48. Cem Boyner, *Demokrasi Haberleri*, 15-31 July 1994.

49. Francis Fukuyama, "The End of History?" *National Interest* (summer 1989): 17.

50. Ergin Yıldızoğlu, *Iktisat*, Sept. 1994.

51. Ibid.

52. Mustafa Sönmez, *Iktisat*, Sept. 1994.

53. Mustafa Sönmez, *Iktisat*, Sept. 1994.

54. Korkut Boratav, *Iktisat*, Sept. 1994.

55. Ibid.

9

NATIONALISM AND THE RULE OF LAW IN TURKEY: THE ELIMINATION OF KURDISH REPRESENTATION DURING THE 1990S

Mark Muller

The aim of this chapter is to focus on Turkey's domestic policy[1] toward its Kurdish intelligentsia since the Gulf war and consider the long-term implications of that policy for the rule of law within Turkey. I provide a brief historical account of the establishment of the rule of law and how it has been undermined by an official state policy of repression toward minorities and examine how the ideological imperatives that underpin such a policy have fundamentally affected the Turkish legal and political structure. I document how this policy has led to the virtual elimination of Kurdish representation within the press, Parliament and the courts throughout the 1990s and conclude with an assessment of the long-term impact of this policy for the rule of law, Turkey's body politic, and its future relationship with Europe.

THE ESTABLISHMENT OF THE RULE OF LAW

There can be little doubt that the Turkish political revolution of the 1920s had a profound effect on the rule of law within the central territories of the Ottoman Empire. The creation of a modern republican constitution in 1924[2] symbolized Turkey's desire to transform itself into a progressive, Western-orientated, secular nation state. The constitution also provided a useful legal mechanism to entrench political and cultural reform. Thus, although forged in war, the secular character of the republic was secured by the prudent deployment of Western legal reforms.

Mustafa Kemal Atatürk, the architect of the new state, understood the fundamental role that legal reform could play in affecting such political and social transformation within society. In a speech in 1924 he commented, "Changing the rules of life in accordance with the times is an absolute necessity. . . . Nations cannot maintain their existence by age-old mentalities. . . . Superstitions and nonsense have to be thrown out of our heads."[3]

By 1925, legislative measures had secured the abolition of the Caliphate and religious courts[4] and brought public education and religious institutions under the control of the executive.[5] Legal reform was also used in the dissolution of religious sects, the banning of the fez, the introduction of the Gregorian Calendar and the adoption of the Latin script. The principle of secularism was enshrined in the Turkish constitution by amendment in 1937.

The enactment of the civil law code of 1926 deepened the secularization of Turkish civil society and further entrenched the Western concept of the rule of law. It created a unified system of law in which all citizens became equal before the law, irrespective of their religious or ethnic disposition. The special status reserved for Muslims and principal non-Muslim communities—Greek, Armenian and Jewish—were abolished. It established familiar Western secular principles of equality, freedom of contract, private property and enforceable individual rights and drew heavily on the Swiss and German civil codes and the Italian penal code.[6]

The 1926 code represented Turkey's final break with its Ottoman and Islamic past and crystallized the Kemalist commitment to the rule of law. Its preamble began: "There is no fundamental difference in the needs of nations belonging to the modern family of civilizations. Perpetual social and economic contacts have . . . been transforming a large civilized body of mankind into a family. . . . We must never forget that the Turkish nation has decided to accept modern civilization and its living principles without any condition or reservation. . . . The aim of law is not to maintain religious regulations, nor to maintain any other habitual customs, but to ensure political, social, economic and national activity at all costs."[7]

The widespread use of such legal measures not only entrenched political revolution, it established the notion of equality before the law and created an appreciation of the civilizing qualities of law. In this respect, the Kemalist principles of republicanism, secularism and modernism contributed significantly to the establishment of the rule of law within Turkey.

However, in other important respects, the development of Kemalist ideology had a fundamentally negative effect on the establishment of the rule of law. In particular, its consistent obsession with national unity undermined much of the progress achieved through legal reform. This obsession was borne out of the experiences of the War of Independence, which followed in the wake of World War I and the dismemberment of the Ottoman Empire. By 1917 the Great Powers of Europe had already secretly agreed to the division of the Middle East and were not in any way predisposed to the creation of an independent state for Turks.[8] Mustafa Kemal used the energizing power of nationalism to win the War of Independence.

He therefore based the legitimacy of the fledgling republic upon the principle of a national homeland for Turks.

Throughout the next two decades, Kemal reinforced the policy of ethnic nationalism in an attempt to foster within the Turkish people a deeper allegiance to the new republic. In a speech at the opening of a faculty of law in Ankara in 1925 he remarked: "The Turkish Revolution . . . means replacing an age-old political unity based on religion with one based on another tie, that of nationality."[9] According to Mustafa Kemal, the central weakness of the Ottoman Empire emanated from its acceptance of its own multicultural nature. This had led to the search for independence and autonomy by minority groups, such as the Armenians and the Kurds, which had resulted in self-mutilation. This experience helps explain the regime's deep-seated fear of minorities and its consistent oppression of them.

Thus, the 1930s saw a series of cultural measures designed to emphasize the cultural homogeneity of the Turkish people. History books were rewritten to exalt the achievements of Turkish culture as distinct from Ottoman or Islamic culture. Institutions, such as the Turkish Historical Society in 1931 and the Turkish Language Association in 1932, were established to assert the superiority of Turkish culture over other indigenous cultures.

The tendency to herald the achievements of Turkish culture to the exclusion of all other minority cultures led to the glorification and idolization of the greatest living exponent of that culture. Over the next thirty years Mustafa Kemal's nationalistic teachings enveloped all state institutions and created a rigid state ideology. By adopting the title *Atatürk,* Mustafa Kemal made "Turkishness" synonymous with the state that he had founded. As a result, ethnic-nationalism came to underpin the whole raison d' etre of the Turkish State.

The principle of ethnic-nationalism received international credence in the Treaty of Lausanne in 1924,[10] which overturned previous international recognition of the right to autonomy for other minorities in the region such as the Kurds.[11] The Treaty of Lausanne failed to recognize ethnically based minorities. As Lord Curzon noted: "The Turkish delegation insisted that these minorities [Kurds, Circassians and Arabs] required no protection and were quite satisfied with their lot under Turkish rule."[12] In one stroke the Kurdish people lost their right to exist as a recognizable and distinct people and became incorporated into the Turkish nation by virtue of their Muslim heritage.

Since then, this treaty has been used by the Turkish authorities to justify the absence of special status or provisions for the Kurds of Turkey. In a BBC interview on 24 March 1992, minister of the interior Ismet Sezgin invoked the treaty to assert that the Kurds were not a minority but actually "first-class citizens of the Turkish state." The historical reality could not have been more different. The failure to recognize Kurdish interests led to a rebellion in February 1925 by Kurdish nationalist and religious leader Sheikh Said of Piran. Two further revolts occurred in 1930 and between 1936-38. For the Turkish authorities these rebellions established the Kurds as the preeminent separatist threat. Since then, Ankara has pursued an iron-fist policy toward Kurdish dissent.

The international legitimization of Turkish nationalism had a profoundly corrosive effect on the Kemalist commitment to the rule of law and recognition of minority rights. The abolition of special status for non-Muslim communities had been accepted on the basis that henceforth all citizens could invoke constitutional rights that guarantied cultural freedom. The Treaty of Lausanne (1923) fundamentally undermined that enterprise and effectively disenfranchised Muslim and non-Muslim minorities.

Yet it was the not nationalism per se but the adoption of ethnic-nationalism that resulted in the denial of minority rights. More particularly, it was the attempt to create allegiance to the new republican state through membership or adherence to an ethnic culture rather than through the idea of national citizenship. As a result, the nature, character and boundaries of the Turkish state became inextricably linked to the idea of ethnic-nationalism.

This authoritarian drive for ethnic national unity led to the destruction of the fundamental principle of equality before the law. Turkish citizens of Kurdish origin are no longer able to invoke fundamental rights in the constitution pertaining to freedom of association, movement and expression unless they accept and act upon the precept "Happy is he who is a Turk." Any expression of their own cultural identity precludes them from invoking such rights.

Since 1924 all other principles and constitutional rights guaranteed under the Turkish constitution have been made subject to the "Supreme Principle of Ethnic-Nationalism." In order to assert and/or enforce any right a citizen must ensure that he or she does not contravene this supreme principle. Any expression of minority identity is interpreted as an attack on the character and indivisibility of the Turkish state, since indivisibility is defined by the official ideology of "Turkishness." This leads to the effective disenfranchisement of minorities within Turkey. An example of this can be found in the basic principles of the constitution of 1982 which are laid down in Article 2: "The Republic of Turkey is a democratic, secular and social state ruled by law, respecting human rights in the spirit of social peace, of national solidarity and of justice, bound to the nationalism of Atatürk and founded on the principles pronounced by the preamble."

Nationalism is also entrenched in Article 26, paragraph 3, and Article 28, paragraph 2, of the 1982 constitution, which give the legislature the powers to adopt laws that prohibit the use of certain languages.[13] These provisions find further concrete expression in the several provisions concerning the National Security Council and its powers, in the provisions on limitations of human rights and in the spirit of the provisions of the emergency law.[14]

Yet the denial of minority existence has created an inherent and dynamic tension within the Turkish body politic resulting in constant political conflict between the state and those elements in society opposed to its official ideology. Any expression of cultural and/or ethnic dissent is, by ideological necessity, classified as a threat to national security, regardless of whether such activity is violent or nonviolent in nature. This continual source of conflict can only be resolved by fundamental reform to Kemalist ideology or by the adoption of an iron-fist policy toward dissent. To date Turkey has chosen the latter alternative. This has led to the militarization of the entire legal and political structure which has not only undermined the exercise of individual rights but also compromised any effective separation of powers and threatened the independence of the entire judiciary.

THE EFFECT OF ETHNIC NATIONALISM ON THE LEGAL STRUCTURE OF TURKEY

Throughout its seventy-three-year history, the Turkish military has consistently intervened in politics to preserve the Kemalist character of the Turkish state. One such example was in 1960, when General Cemal Gürsel removed the civilian government and declared himself president. There can be little doubt about his attitude toward the rights of a quarter of the republic's citizenry when he stood on an American tank in the southeast city of Diyarbakır and declared, "There are no Kurds in this country. Whoever says he is a Kurd, I will spit in his face."[15] In June 1960, 485 Kurdish notables were arrested and detained and some 55 were exiled.[16]

The military interventions of 1961, 1971 and 1981 established the military's profound influence over all state institutions as "supreme protector of the nation." The Kurdish issue, together with the growth of radical politics, was sufficiently serious to require a coup d'etat in 1980, which resulted in further oppressive measures against the Kurds during the next three years of military rule. The military-inspired approach continued under the civilian administration of Turgut Özal, who in 1985 introduced a system of civilian militia known as the village guard system to supplement gendarme operations.[17]

Since 1980, political stability has largely been achieved by integration of the military within the Turkish executive. This has led to the creation of the National Security Council but also to the development of a separate court structure in relation to matters purportedly concerning national security. As a result, Turkey has a complex interrelated court structure of inferior and superior courts. Broadly speaking, the system is made up of judicial, military, administrative and security courts. These courts are of first instance and are subject to appeal to a plethora of interrelated superior courts. The superior courts consist of the Constitutional Court, the Court of Appeals, the Council of State, the Military Tribunal of Appeals, the Supreme Military Administrative Court, the Court of Jurisdictional Dispute, the Court of Accounts, and the Supreme Council of Judges and Public Prosecutors. The distinctive feature of this court structure is the role played by military and security tribunals. Theoretically, the jurisdiction of these tribunals concerns national security. However, since national security is equated with national unity, and national unity with Kemalist ideology, all political opposition to this ideology, in practice, falls within the ambit of this jurisdiction. As a result, these military and security courts have become the arbiters of what constitutes legitimate political dissent.

Thus, while the Kemalist commitment to republicanism and secularism has strengthened the Turkish legal system, its adherence to the supreme principle of ethnic-nationalism has led to the development of a number of military and security courts, which have fundamentally hampered any effective separation of powers and threatened both the independence of the judiciary and the rule of law.

The State Security Tribunal is a nonjudicial court that exclusively deals with all political and terrorist offenses. Its practical jurisdiction is now so pervasive that it has the power to determine the parameters of all political and civil rights, such as the right to freedom of expression, movement and association. To a very great extent it has usurped the traditional functions of the judicial courts and is a significant threat to the concept of judicial justice.

The Tribunal's composition consists of one military judge appointed by the minister of justice or the minister of national defense and two civilian judges appointed by other government ministries. However, the exact status of this arrangement remains uncertain. Article 143 of the 1982 constitution states: "Courts of the Security of the State shall be established to deal with offenses against the indivisible integrity of the State with its territory and nation, the free democratic order, or against the public whose characteristics are defined in the constitution, and offenses directly involving the internal and external security of the State."

Thus, although the Turkish constitution provides for the establishment of such tribunals to hear such cases, the composition and competence of these tribunals may well be contrary to other provisions of the constitution. Clearly, tribunals that do not use the duly established procedures of the legal process should not be created to displace the jurisdiction belonging to the ordinary judicial courts.

What is certain is that the composition of the State Security Tribunal breaches the principle concerning judicial independence. A court should be independent from the executive branch; the executive should not interfere in a court's proceedings and a court should not act as an agent for the executive against an individual citizen. The composition of the Tribunal breaches Article 6 of the European Convention, which guarantees the right to a fair trial and states "everyone is entitled to a fair and public hearing by an independent and impartial tribunal established by law."

Just as the Turkish constitution loosely provides for the establishment of security tribunals to deal with political offenses concerning national security, it also provides for the enactment of legislation that defines which type of activities shall be come within the jurisdiction of such tribunals. Thus, although the 1982 Turkish constitution states that everyone possesses inalienable fundamental rights and freedoms[18] and that "the press is free,"[19] such rights and freedoms may be restricted by law to safeguard the integrity of the state.[20]

The constitution further provides under Article 14 that those who abuse these freedoms "with the aim of violating the indivisible integrity of the State with its territory and nation, of endangering the existence of the Turkish State and Republic" and "who incite and provoke others to do the same shall be subject to punishments determined by law." The law is contained in the various provisions of the Turkish penal code and the 1991 Anti-Terror Law.

The Anti-Terror Law was introduced in 1991 to replace the much discredited articles of the Turkish penal code, namely 140, 141, 142 and 163, which legitimated prosecutions against writers and journalists accused of advocating "separatism." However, as Article 19 has noted, instead of introducing greater rights of freedom of expression it "defines terrorism so broadly and vaguely that almost anyone can be convicted of it: no violent act is required."[21] As such, it is the decision to prosecute that effectively determines guilt.

Article 1 of the Anti-Terror Law states that "terrorism is any kind of action conducted by one or several persons belonging to an organization with the aim of changing the characteristics of the republic as defined by the constitution, its political, legal, social, secular and economic system, damaging the indivisible unity of the State with its territory and nation, endangering the existence of the Turkish State and Republic, weakening or destroying or seizing the authority of the State, eliminating fundamental rights and freedoms, or damaging the internal or external security of the state, public order or general health by any one method of pressure, force and violence, terror, intimidation, oppression or threat."

Under Article 6, methods of "pressure" are defined to include writing and reporting ideas. It states that "those who print or publish leaflets and declarations of terrorist organizations" are to be punished by heavy fines between 50 and 100 million TL. While Article 7 renders liable "those who assist members of organizations constituted in the manner described above or make propaganda in connection with the organization . . . to sentence by imprisonment of between one and five years and a fine of between 50 and 100 million TL even if their offense constitutes another crime." As a result, many actions that had been banned by the repealed provisions of the Turkish penal code are now banned by the new Anti-Terror Law. It is Article 8 that is most commonly deployed for this purpose. It states that "written and oral propaganda and assemblies, meetings and demonstrations aimed at damaging the indivisible unity of the State of the Turkish Republic with its territory and nation are forbidden, regardless of method, intention, and ideas behind them. Those conducting such activity are to be punished by a sentence of between two and five years' imprisonment and a fine of between 50 and 100 million TL." This provision has been used against journalists, members of Parliament and lawyers alike.

These security measures are strengthened by Articles 119 through 122 of the 1982 constitution, which provide for a state of emergency in four specific situations. Emergency civil administration is advocated in the event of natural disaster, dangerous epidemic or an economic crisis, emergency civil administration, or upon serious indications of widespread acts of violence aimed at the destruction of the free democratic order or a serious deterioration of the public order. A dual system of civil and military administration is proscribed in the event of very serious political disorder threatening the security of the nation or in the event that the country enters a state of war.

The civil state of emergency is regulated by the State Emergency Act of 1983 and provides special powers for local governors.[22] The military state of emergency is regulated by the Military State of Emergency Act of 1971 as a amended between 1980 and 1983.[23] The state of war is regulated by the State of War Act of 1983.[24] A declaration of a state of emergency needs parliamentary approval and cannot be issued for more than six months, after which it can be extended for consecutive periods of four months. In normal circumstances Article 91 of the constitution provides that statutory orders can only have force of law if they issue from a statute passed by Parliament and are capable of review by both Parliament and the Constitutional Court. These requirements are not in effect when Articles 119 to 122 are invoked.

These articles were invoked in 1987, when, under Turgut Özal's premiership, the government introduced a state of emergency in ten provinces in the southeast of the country.[25] However, it is the civil state of emergency that has been in force in the ten provinces of the southeast region since 1987. Extraordinary powers were vested in the regional governors. These powers were radically extended by a statutory order with force of law, which concentrated the whole of civil power in their hands[26] and in April 1990, through the adoption of *Kararname* (decree) 413, subsequently revised as *Kararname* 424.[27]

As Philip Robins has noted, the main thrust of this package of measures was to increase the punitive effect of measures that could be applied to the region and to restrict the flow of information by imposing increased restrictions on the media.[28] Likewise, the constitutionality of measures deployed by the Motherland Party (ANAP) governments have also created great concern, including the extensive use of state of emergency powers without respect for fundamental rights or the right to judicial review of any act issued by state authorities. As Christian Rumpf has remarked: "Under this legislation, enjoyment of individual rights has been reduced to a very low level; in violation of the constitution, judicial review of any act of the administration or responsibility of public servants in the field of emergency issues have been excluded."[29]

The conduct of the Turkish authorities is, however, subject to international legal scrutiny. Although the Turkish State has not ratified the International Covenant on Civil and Political Rights and is therefore not bound by its specific provisions, it has pledged to meet human rights standards set by the Paris Charter of the CSCE. More important, it is a party to the European Convention of Human Rights. Indeed, the 1954 Act not only ratified the convention but incorporated it and its jurisprudence into Turkish domestic law so as to become enforceable within Turkish courts as a species of national law.

Thus, in 1963 the then–Constitutional Court declared that the fundamental rights set forth in the 1961 constitution corresponded to the rights contained in the European Convention and thereafter began to interpret fundamental rights in the light of the Convention.[30] However, the presently constituted Constitutional Court has so far declined to invoke the Convention in interpreting the constitution. Nevertheless, it is clear that Turkey remains bound by its provisions. In fact, the Turkish government further strengthened its Convention obligations in 1987, when it recognized the right of individual petition to the European Commission with limiting reservations. Those reservations were subsequently declared ineffective by the Commission.[31]

Moreover, by a derogation notice of 1992, communicated by the permanent representative of Turkey to the Council of Europe, Turkey withdrew its original notice of derogations from articles 5, 6, 8, 10, 11 and 13, as permitted under Article 15, and accepted the binding nature of all of the above substantive articles, save Article 5.[32] As a result of this derogation withdrawal notice, Turkey is subject to the substantive Convention articles establishing the rights to freedom of expression, freedom from racial or ethnic discrimination, and the right to a fair trial. The conduct of its institutions can therefore be subjected to review.

THE ELIMINATION OF KURDISH REPRESENTATION

Since the Gulf war, little attention has been paid to Turkey's adherence to international obligations. Despite periodic promises of democratic and legal reform, the Turkish government has systematically and methodically destroyed all legitimate forms of expression of dissent by Kurds. It has deployed the security measures outlined above to crush all forms of nonviolent political opposition and has allowed its security forces to operate with impunity throughout the emergency regions and beyond.

On 20 October 1991 the new coalition government of President Süleyman Demirel published its *Principles of Democratization,* in which it conceded that Turkey had failed to meet its human rights obligations under the CSCE process and the Paris Charter. It promised root and branch reform and, in particular, reform of the constitution and the legal system in accordance with contemporary democratic values; adoption of legislation to ensure media freedom; and recognition of the right of every individual to speak in his or her mother tongue and to develop his or her culture.

Unhappily, none of these promises have been met.[33] The 1991 Anti-Terror Law, which was designed to deal with violent opposition, has been used to silence nonviolent dissent. None of the cultural freedoms for Kurds has been granted. Even the two widely publicized initiatives, the Parliamentary Human Rights

Commission and new minister for human rights, have been disappointing in their impact. As Article 19 noted in its 1992 report on Turkey: "the majority of reforms affecting freedom of expression have not been introduced and it appears that the Government lacks the political will to implement these much needed changes."

Instead, since 1991, the Turkish state has consistently restricted Kurdish rights to freedom of expression, association and movement. The hopes of a return to liberal democracy all but faded as the intensification of the conflict continued between the state and the PKK. In 1991, the Motherland Party (ANAP) government for the first time in decades allowed the celebration of Nevroz, the Kurdish New Year festival. By 1992 the spirit of reconciliation had disappeared. Kurdish colors, songs and slogans were banned. That year's Nevroz festivities left at least ninety-one people dead in just three towns of the southeast, Cizre, Şırnak and Nusaybin.[34]

The polarization of the Kurdish situation led to the militarization of the entire southeast region by the security forces. By late 1992 the war against the PKK had virtually destroyed the entire civic and judicial structure of the southeast region. Allegations abounded of systematic torture, extrajudicial killings and wholesale destruction of Kurdish villages. Amnesty International reported that security forces appeared to be operating with impunity and with little regard for the constitution.[35]

Over two thousand villages were alleged to have been destroyed and over two million Kurds exiled to western Turkey during this period.[36] These reports were later confirmed by regional governor Ünal Erkan, who, on 13 July 1995, stated that 2,667 villages had been depopulated and over 311,000 people displaced since 1994. The terrorization of the populace intensified with the emergence of *Hizbollah*, a shadowy contraguerrilla organization reputedly controlled by the security forces, who carried out indiscriminate executions, arson attacks and assaults.[37]

Having traumatized the local populace into submission, the Turkish authorities now turned their attention toward the Kurdish and liberal press in an attempt to silence dissent over the government's iron-fist policy toward the Kurdish issue. The onslaught on the liberal media was comprehensive and systematic. Restrictions were placed on the press, foreign journalists,[38] political speeches,[39] assemblies,[40] demonstrations, academic publications,[41] television and radio[42] and the arts.[43]

The authorities used a multitude of legal provisions in order to affect comprehensive censorship. Apart from the all-encompassing provisions of the Anti-terror Law much use was made of several articles of the Turkish penal code. Article 158 makes illegal any "insult" or "aggressive language" expressly or by implication, including "by allusion or hint" of or toward the president of Turkey; Article 159 applies the same criteria to any insult directed toward "the Turkish nation, the Republic, the Grand National Assembly, or the moral responsibility of the Government or the military or security forces of the State or the moral responsibility of the judicial authorities." Articles 311 and 312 prohibit "others to commit crime" and "praising crime," respectively. These general articles are supported by more specific laws directed toward particular forms of expression, such as Law 5680, the Press Law; Law 1117, the Law to Protect Minors from Harmful Publications; Law 3257, the Act on the Works of Cinema, Video and Music; Law 5816, the Law on Crimes Against Atatürk; Law 2911, the Demonstration Act;[44] and Law 2908, the Association Act.[45]

These provisions have been enacted and deployed to devastating effect solely to preserve the ideological imperatives created by Atatürk's conception of ethnic-nationalism. They continue the tradition of using legal measures to affect social and political transformation, albeit of a profoundly oppressive character. The success of this policy depends upon the complete obliteration of any form of cultural dissent. Since this is not possible without the wholesale physical elimination of the Kurdish and liberal intelligentsia, a war of attrition has began with no end in sight.

The greatest example of this war of attrition was, throughout 1993 and beyond, the systematic persecution of Kurdish-owned national newspapers, such as *Özgür Gündem* (Free Agenda), the most consistent and outspoken critic of the Turkish regime.[46] The persecution meted out was twofold in nature—first, the use of oppressive legal measures including confiscations, raids and the institution of legal proceedings, and, second, the use of extra legal measures from psychological harassment to arson and murder.

The combined effect of the legal measures led to the closure of the paper on 15 January 1993, with an attendant loss of over 300 million TL. The financial problems occurred when the paper's distribution company, Erganı, was induced to break its contract. The paper's subsequent attempt to organize distribution by volunteers largely failed due to intimidation. A total of at least fourteen distributors, newsvendors and paper boys/girls were murdered.[47]

The paper started publication again on 26 April 1993, when it merged with another radical Kurdish newspaper, *Yeni Ülke* (New Nation). In the following sixty-eight days, forty-one issues of *Özgür Gündem* were confiscated. Between the date of relaunch and 11 November 1993 a further 134 out of 198 issues were confiscated. A press release by the editorial board announced on 3 July 1993 that the publishers and editors of the newspaper had been charged with total fines of 8.6 billion TL ($736,5000) and sentenced to prison terms totaling from 155 years and 9 months to 493 years and 4 months.[48]

These terms were variously imposed for offenses under the Anti-Terror provisions relating to separatist propaganda and membership in a proscribed organization. Many of the indictments were based upon the simple reference by the newspaper to the words *Kurds* and *Kurdistan*. The institution of a further 170 legal proceedings against the newspaper occurred in 1993. By the end of the year, Yaşar Kaya, the newspaper's proprietor, faced a total of 16 trillion lira in fines and between three hundred and nine hundred ninety years imprisonment.[49]

The newspaper was also subjected to widespread intimidation and physical attack. Six of the newspaper's journalists were killed in 1993, adding to the ten other journalists killed since January 1992.[50] Other journalists were routinely arrested, detained and subjected to various degrees of ill treatment and torture. Newsvendors continued to be subjected to harassment and assault throughout 1993. Staff bureaus became the target of arson attacks. The year culminated in a series of simultaneous raids on the newspaper's premises across the country on 10 December 1993, International Human Rights Day, in which equipment was seized and over one hundred employees were arrested, detained and variously prosecuted[51]

The paper was eventually closed by the Supreme Court on 14 April 1994. Its successor, *Özgür Ülke* (Free Nation), fared no better, being subjected to the same forms of legal and extralegal measures. On 3 December 1994 its offices in Istanbul and Ankara were bombed, leaving one dead and twenty injured. The paper was subsequently closed on 3 February 1995, when it was held that it was subject to the same ban as *Özgür Gündem*.[52] There can be little doubt, however, that the events of 1993 substantially reduced the ability of Kurdish intelligentsia to express and communicate its concerns over the Kurdish issue and its possible resolution.

What is clear, however, is that the law in relation to censorship reflects the state of freedom of expression in Turkey today. By embedding ideological requirements into law, the Turkish authorities have allowed civil rights activists the opportunity to highlight breaches of its international obligations concerning the right to freedom of expression without reference to the circumstances of particular cases. This has led to numerous challenges to these provisions in both the domestic and international courts.

Article 6 of the Convention sets out in clear terms internationally recognized legal norms governing the establishment of a fair trial. Article 14 sets out the right of nondiscrimination on grounds of race, ethnic identity and culture. Article 10 establishes the right to freedom of expression and states that "Everyone has the right to freedom of expression. This right shall include the freedom to hold opinions and to receive and impart information and ideas without reference by public authority and regardless of frontiers."[53] But this right is not absolute. Paragraph 2 of the Convention goes on to limit the extent of the right in that the exercise of these freedoms "may be subject to such formalities, conditions, restrictions or penalties as are prescribed by law and are necessary in a democratic society" and goes on to list the various permissible restrictions, including "in the interests of national security, territorial integrity of public health or morals, for the protection of disorder or a crime, for the protection of the reputation or rights of others, for preventing the disclosure of information received in confidence, or for maintaining the authority and impartiality of the judiciary." However, in order to invoke the use of paragraph 2, contracting states must abide by the judgments of the European Court of Human Rights and the decisions and recommendations of the Committee of Ministers, which have established that the respondent state is obliged to show that any restriction is "prescribed by law"; "has a legitimate aim" (i.e. paragraph. 2); and is [3] "necessary in a democratic society" to promote that aim.[54]

In devising this tripartite test, the court has emphasized that, in evaluating a particular restriction, it is faced "not with a choice between two conflicting principles but with a principle of freedom of expression that is subject to a number of exceptions which must be narrowly interpreted." Thus, the court has ruled that to be "prescribed by law" a restriction must be "adequately accessible" and foreseeable, that is, "formulated with sufficient precision to enable a citizen to regulate his conduct." The restriction, however, does not have to be codified; it is sufficient if it is "reasonably foreseeable" from the case law.[55] A restriction must also be in furtherance of, and genuinely aimed at, protecting one of the permissible grounds listed in Article 10(2) in order for it to be classified as having a legitimate aim. The court further ruled that the list contained in Article 10(2) is exhaustive. "Necessary" should not be equated with "indispensable," though any restriction must be more than merely "reasonable" or "desirable." A "pressing social need" must be demonstrated, the restriction must be proportionate to the legitimate aim pursued, and the reasons given to justify the restriction must be relevant and sufficient.[56]

In considering whether any particular interference is justified, that is, "sufficient," the court will have regard to any public aspect of the case, the breadth of the particular restriction and the appropriate margin that contracting states may legitimately have in determining the necessity of the restriction.[57] As regards the breadth of a restriction, the court has made it quite clear that an absolute restriction is unacceptable. Instead, the court will treat each case on its particular merits but, in doing so, will have regard to the practice of other contracting states in assessing a restriction's necessity.

Turkey is in clear breach of its international obligations under the treaty. First, the all-embracing nature of the Anti-Terror Law is in conflict with the general spirit of the rights establishing freedom of expression. Second, its subsequent application by the authorities is at odds with its original purpose. The law was not designed to restrict nonviolent dissent. Third, even if it were designed for such a purpose, it could not be said that its subsequent application was "necessary," "sufficient" or "proportionate to its legitimate aim," as required by the tripartite test. As Article 19 has noted, it does not conform to analogous provisions legitimately restricting the freedom of the press in other member states.

As regards the case of *Özgür Gündem*,[58] it should be noted that the European Court has repeatedly declared that "freedom of political debate is at the very core of the concept of a democratic society."[59] In particular, it has ruled in favor of special protection of political expression in relation to a government's failure to investigate and prosecute murders of people involved in a separatist movement.[60] The use of Article 13 of the 1982 constitution and the Anti-Terror Law to restrict such debate is clearly contrary to international law. On a broader level, the Turkish government has failed to protect what the European Court has described as the "pre-eminent role of the press in a state governed by the rule of law."[61] In a number of recent judgments the court has consistently stated that penalties against the press for publishing information and opinions concerning matters of public interest are intolerable.[62]

Turkey is legally obliged to honor its obligations under the European Convention. It has a duty to ensure that its domestic legislation and jurisprudence thereunder does not conflict with or inhibit any of the rights set out and guaranteed by the Convention. It is also under a positive duty to abide by the Convention provisions and case law in relation to freedom of expression.

In fact, defense lawyers who operate in the state security tribunals have increasingly used the 1982 constitution and the European Convention on Human Rights to challenge the legitimacy and authority of such laws as the 1991 Anti-Terror Law. The deployment of such submissions, together with the tactical use of the procedures of the tribunals, has led to a number of adjournments, additional hearings and appeals to the higher courts. This has delayed and frustrated the ability of the authorities to clamp down swiftly on nonviolent dissent.[63]

As a result, 1994 saw a change of emphasis on the part of the Turkish authorities. Instead of harassing journalists and broadcasters, the focus shifted to those that supported and represented them in the domestic courts. In effect, the war of attrition moved from the media and into the courts. Thus, 1994 witnessed increasing allegations of institutional and anonymous harassment of Turkish lawyers involved in sensitive political cases before state security tribunals. This policy of harassment culminated in the "unknown perpetrator" killing Medet Serhat, a prominent liberal Istanbul lawyer. For many it represented the full-scale start of the "terrorization" of the Kurdish legal intelligentsia in Istanbul.[64]

In fact, the process had began earlier in the year in the state security tribunals in Diyarbakır, southeast Turkey, when sixteen Diyarbakır defense lawyers were arrested and detained in November and December 1993.[65] On 17 February 1994 they, together with six other lawyers, appeared before the Diyarbakır state security tribunal, charged with a multitude of political offenses under articles 168/2, 31, 33, and 40 of the Turkish penal code and Article 5 of the Anti-Terror Law. The particulars of the indictment alleged participation in terrorist activity, including the passing of material to PKK prisoners; membership in a proscribed terrorist organization, namely the PKK; and the sending of communications to European human rights organizations. This was later clarified to mean "the making of false and unwarranted applications to the European Convention."[66]

The evidence called in support of these charges rested largely upon the oral testimony of one prosecution witness, Mr. Abdulhakim Güven, himself a convicted murderer, and upon confessions obtained during pretrial detention. The lawyers claimed that they had been subjected to harassment, ill treatment and in some cases torture.[67] They rejected the allegations in their entirety and claimed the confessions had been obtained through force. They further prayed in aid of Turkey's acceptance of the right of individual petition to the European Commission. Despite a series of hearings on 28 April, 23 June, 15 September, and 22 November 1994, no such prosecution witness came forward. The case remains pending to this day.

The importance of the lawyers' case is twofold. First, it casts light on the current plight of Turkey's system of justice. It highlights the authorities' failure to investigate, detain and initiate prosecutions in accordance with the law; to investigate allegations of torture and mistreatment during pretrial detention; to provide access to legal advice and representation when available; and to provide an effective mechanism whereby these failures can be reviewed and their consequences assessed in relation to the fairness of proceedings.

Second, and more important, the lawyers' case amounts to a sustained attack on those lawyers within the Diyarbakır bar still willing to undertake defense work in political cases. At present the Diyarbakır bar, which is the main bar association in the southeast region, consists of 211 practicing advocates, of whom under 40 practice in the state security tribunals.[68] In essence, the prosecutions form part of a wider attack on the right to legal representation hitherto protected and guaranteed by the constitution to all citizens.

During the course of 1994 the Turkish authorities broadened this attack to include rights to Kurdish representation within Parliament. This process had been set in motion on 14 July 1993, when the Constitutional Court banned the pro-Kurdish Peoples' Labor Party (HEP) on the grounds that the party had violated the constitution[69] and the Law on Political Parties, which states that "political parties are prohibited from stating that on the territory of the Republic of Turkey there exist minorities of differing nationality, religion, culture or confession, race or language. They are not permitted to have the aim of destroying national unity by creating minorities by means of the protection, development or dissemination of languages or cultures other than the Turkish language and culture, and they are not permitted to develop any activity whatsoever of this sort." Up until this ruling at least forty-eight of the party's officials had been murdered by death squads.[70]

This ruling effectively put paid to the promises of a move to genuine democracy and a recognition of Kurdish rights by the True Path Party (TPP) and the Social Democratic Party (SDP), following Tansu Çiller's election as prime minister on 13 June 1993. The Coalition Protocol of June 24 1993 undertook to abolish the state of emergency, eliminate the village guard system and remove "the legal and other obstacles that hinder the free expression of our people's ethnic cultural and language rights."

However, the Democracy Party (DP), which had been formed to replace HEP, became subject to the same form of attacks. On 4 September 1993, Mehmet Sincar MP and Metin Özdemir, chairman of Batman DEP, were shot dead in Batman. Six days later the house of Sincar's father was also bombed, injuring six others.[71] On December 1993, Ankara state security prosecutor Nusret Demiral instituted proceedings to ban the Democracy Party.

In that hearing Demiral submitted that Yaşar Kaya, chair of the DEP, had by implication incited a struggle for "an independent and unified Kurdish state" by demanding a "political solution . . . in which Kurdish identity is recognized" and by stating that the Kurdish question should be resolved according to the CSCE process and the Paris Charter. According to Demiral, the principles of self-determination in the Helsinki Final Act and minority rights contained in the Paris Charter contravened the territorial integrity of the Turkish republic; because the provisions related to peoples under colonial domination, it could not apply to the republic by virtue of the Lausanne Treaty of 1923.

The submission reflected Turkish authorities' recognition of the need to provide a legal basis to the prosecution in order to give legitimacy to the proceedings. However, the nature of that submission betrayed the cavalier approach of the authorities toward international legal obligations. On the one hand, it prayed in aid of the specific application of the Final Act, and, on the other hand, it totally rejected the welter of other international obligations concerning the right to freedom of expression and to a fair trial.[72]

The disingenuous nature of the proceedings were confirmed by the events of the next few months. On 10 January 1994 six people were arrested at the DEP offices in Lice when it was shelled by the army, together with thirty-six other houses.[73] On 20 January 1994 DEP offices in Ankara and Mamak were also bombed. Ten days later the Derik office in Mardin province was hit. On 6 February, Murat Bozlak, the general secretary, was wounded by gunmen.[74] And on 18 February the main offices in Ankara were bombed, injuring sixteen people. As a result of these events, the DEP finally withdrew from the local elections on 25 February 1994.[75] This enabled the Islamic Refah Party to capture a number of mayoralties including that of the regional capital, Diyarbakır.

Then, in March 1994 the Turkish Grand National Assembly removed the immunity of Kurdish MPs, which led to the arrest of six DEP MPs: Hatip Dicle, Leyla Zana, Orhan Doğan, Sırrı Sakık, Ahmet Türk and Mahmut Alınak. Two further MPs, Sedat Yurtdaş and Selim Sadak, were arrested under Article 125 on 1 July 1994, following the Constitutional Court's decision to dissolve the DEP on 16 June 1994, when it upheld the submissions made by Mr. Demiral. On 8 December 1994, five of the DEP MPs were found guilty under Article 168, paragraph 2, of the penal code, for membership of the PKK, and each were sentenced to fifteen years imprisonment.

Another MP, Sedat Yurtdaş, was found guilty under Article 169 for aiding and abetting the PKK and given seven years and six months imprisonment. Mahmut Alınak and Sırrı Sakık were found guilty under Article 8 of the Anti-Terror Law and given three years and six months but released on bail pending appeal. The Supreme Court has recently confirmed the fifteen-year sentences.

Unlike other cases before it, the prosecution and eventual conviction of the DEP MPs was given widespread coverage in the international press. As a result, Western public opinion began to focus once more on Turkey's human rights record. On 12 April 1994 the Council of Europe's Parliamentary Assembly called for the immediate release of the DEP MPs, stating that, in its view, the MPs had not gone beyond the rights of free expression guaranteed under Article 10 of the European Convention. It went on to declare that the lifting of immunity and subsequent prosecutions were "a possible threat to the very existence of parliamentary democracy."

This view was subsequently adopted by the CSCE Parliamentary Assembly in its Vienna Declaration of 8 July 1994 and confirmed by the findings of the delegation of the Committee on the Human Rights of Parliamentarians of the Inter-Parliamentary Union (IPU), which reported on its visit to Turkey on 3 April 1995. Concern over Turkey's human rights record also found expression in the meetings of the EC-Turkey Association during December 1994 and March 1995, when the president of the European Union "informed Turkey that its record on democracy, human rights and the rule of law fell far short of the situation in Member States, and that Turkey should respect international standards, particularly given its obligations as a member of the Council of Europe and the OSCE."[76] These findings echoed the earlier public statement issued by the European Committee for the Prevention of Torture and Inhuman or Degrading Treatment or Punishment (CPT) on 15 December 1992, following its visits to Turkey in September 1990, October 1991 and December 1992. The CPT went public as a result of the "continuing failure of the Turkish authorities to improve the situation in the light of its recommendations concerning [i] the strengthening of legal safeguards against torture and other forms of ill-treatment in police establishments and [ii] the activities of the Anti-Terror Departments of the Ankara and Diyarbakır Police."[77] The conditions in Turkey were further confirmed by the report of the United Nations Committee against Torture (CAT) on 9 November 1993, when it concluded that there was systematic, habitual and widespread torture in Turkey.[78]

The increasing concern expressed by European institutions over Turkey's human rights record was met with alarm by officials in Ankara, who were endeavoring to seek support for Turkey's entry into the European Customs Union (ECU). As a result, the authorities' policy toward dissent shifted in focus once more. Particular attention was now paid to the Turkish Human Rights Association and associated lawyers who had been involved in the drafting of individual petitions to the European Commission of Human Rights.

The Turkish Human Rights Association (IHD) was founded on 17 July 1986. Its headquarters are in Ankara and it has a total of fifty-four branches spread over the width and breadth of Turkey. It has a membership of over fifteen thousand members, who elect nine hundred delegates, who in turn elect members of the head office. The IHD is a member of the International Human Rights Federation, whose head office is in Paris. The aims of the IHD are laid down in Article 2 of its constitution: "The single and clear aim of the Human Rights Association is to perform activities in the matter of Human Rights and Freedoms."

The scope of its activities are detailed in Article 3 and include research into human rights practices, publication of its findings, advice on citizens rights, and enforcement of such rights.

Throughout its existence, the IHD has been subjected to constant persecution by the Turkish authorities. Individual members and human rights activists have been subjected to threats, arrests, detention and ill treatment.[79] The 1990s saw members of various management committees murdered, including Verdat Aydın, chairman of the Diyarbakır IHD in 1991; Sıddık Tan, member of the Diyarbakır IHD Management Committee in 1992; Kemal Kılıç, member of the Urfa IHD Management Committee in 1993; and Mertin Can, chairman of the Elazığ IHD, also in February 1993.

As a result, most of the IHD branches in the Emergency Region have closed down from such harassment. In Istanbul the authorities have sought to close the IHD through legal measures for "separatist" offenses.[80] Diyarbakır IHD is now the only functioning branch operating in the southeast region and is the only organization actively involved in the protection and advancement of civil and political rights of ordinary citizens on a pro bono basis.

In doing so, the Diyarbakır IHD developed numerous contacts with European Non-Governmental Organizations (NGOs),[81] who sent missions and trial observations to the region throughout 1991-95. As the intensification of the Kurdish conflict continued into the 1990s, many Kurdish intellectuals found themselves exiled to Europe. Further contacts were established, which promoted a greater level of understanding of the system of redress provided for by the Council of Europe.

This led to the submission of over two hundred petitions to the European Commission during the latter part of 1994 and 1995. Much of this work has been undertaken by the Kurdistan Human Rights Project acting in tandem with the Turkish Human Rights Association and other defense lawyers within Turkey. The KHRP was founded in London in December 1992.[82] It is an independent, non-political charity committed to the protection of human rights of all persons within Kurdistan, irrespective of race, religion, sex, political persuasion or other belief or opinion.

To date over forty of its petitions have been declared admissible by the European Commission. These petitions detailed all sorts of alleged human rights abuses, including murder, extrajudicial killings, rape, torture, bombing, unlawful detention, and denial of the right to freedom of expression, association and movement.[83] They essentially corroborate the various findings of NGOs, such as Amnesty International, over the last five years.[84]

The increasing use of the Convention mechanism by the IHD is a direct result of the collapse of regular civil administration and the imposition of a state of emergency. The militarization of political and judicial structures within the region resulted in the loss of any practical redress for victims of human rights abuses in the domestic courts. The failure of the Çiller administration to respond to the PKK cease-fire of 1993 and establish a dialogue with those elements within the Kurdish intelligentsia still willing to promote a peace settlement through non-violent means, helped accentuate this development.

The subsequent repression of the Kurdish lawyers and members of parliament in 1994 also reduced the scope of political compromise and had the effect of moving the war of attrition into Europe. It was in response to these developments that the authorities shifted their focus toward the activities of the IHD and its filing of petitions. It is perhaps unsurprising then, that, in February 1995, seven members of the IHD Management Committee in Diyarbakır found themselves subject to prosecution.[85]

They were all charged with being members of an armed gang (PKK) and of making separatist propaganda under Articles 168(2), 31, 33 and 40 of the Turkish penal code and Articles 5, 8(1) and (2) of the Anti-Terror Law. The IHD Diyarbakır branch faces closure by virtue of Article 7(1) and 7(4) of the Anti-Terror Law. The prosecution is seeking sentences of up to fifteen years imprisonment. All seven lawyers face mandatory disbarment if they receive prison sentences of one year or more.

The basis of the charge relates to the IHD publication of its 1992 report, which the prosecution alleged was separatist in nature due to its documentation of extrajudicial killings by contraguerrillas controlled by the security forces. It is alleged that the publication of this report was part of a wider strategy to mobilize public opinion against the Turkish state and in favor of the PKK. On 13 February 1995, two of the three prosecution witnesses were called to give evidence about the defendants' involvement in this alleged conspiracy. Both witnesses retracted their statements, alleging that they had been obtained under torture. The case continues.[86]

What is interesting about the case is that the authorities waited some three years before launching this prosecution. The effect of this prosecution was to shut down the IHD offices and interrupt the filing and updating of petitions. At the same time as this prosecution, the authorities commenced proceedings against the Peoples' Democracy Party (HADEP), Diyarbakır branch.[87] Eleven defendants were arrested on 27 February 1995, including two lawyers, Fırat Anlı and Sinan Tanrıkulu, who were are also members of the Diyarbakır IHD. They were taken for interrogation to the Diyarbakır Gendarmerie HQ, where they were held incommunicado for ten days and allegedly tortured.[88] They too were subsequently charged under Article 168(2) of the Turkish Penal Code and article 5 of the Anti-Terror Law.

One of the express particulars of the indictment includes the act of sending unwarranted and unfounded applications to the European Commission on Human Rights. This clearly represents a radical attack on the authority and operation of the Convention itself. It challenges the very jurisdiction and power of this internationally binding agreement. Article 25 of the European Convention states that "the Commission may receive petitions addressed to the Secretary General of the Council of Europe from any person . . . claiming to be the victim of a violation by one of the High Contracting Parties of the rights set forth in this Convention, provided that the High Contracting Party against which the complaint has been lodged has declared that it recognizes the competence of the Commission to receive such petitions. Those of the High Contracting Parties who have made such a declaration undertake not to hinder in any way the effective exercise of this right.

Although the above provision is not a substantive right under the Convention, the Commission has previously held it to be illegitimate to discipline detainees who have entered into correspondence with either the Commission or the Court in respect of a complaint of violation of the Convention.[89]

These prosecutions highlight just how far the Turkish authorities are prepared to go to deny its Turkish-Kurdish citizens any effective representation in the domestic or international courts. This aspect has not gone unnoticed. One important finding of the European Commission is that Turkey has not established, as a matter of fact, that applicants have at their disposal adequate remedies under the state of emergency to deal effectively with their complaints. In the case of *Hüseyin Akduvar and others v. Turkey,* Application No. 21893/93, Decision on Admissibility, on 19 October 1994, which concerned the destruction of a villager's home, the Commission ruled as follows:

> It is a well-known fact that there has been significant destruction of villages in South-East Turkey with many people displaced as a result. . . . The Government has outlined a general scheme of remedies that would normally be available for complaints against the security forces. However, it is noteworthy that, although the destruction of houses and property has been a frequent occurrence in South-East Turkey, the numerous decisions by the administrative courts referred to by the Government all concern compensation for damage in different circumstances. The Government has not provided a single example of compensation being awarded to villagers for damage like that allegedly suffered by the present applicants.
>
> Nor have significant examples been given of successful prosecutions against members of the security forces for the destruction of villages and the expulsion of villagers. In this connection it would seem unlikely that such prosecutions could follow from acts committed pursuant to the orders of Regional Governor under the state of emergency to effect the permanent or temporary evacuation of villages, to impose residence prohibitions or to enforce the transfer of people to other areas.

Thus, the Commission effectively rejected the submission that judicial review was possible under Article 125 of the constitution or Article 1 of the Law on the State of Emergency[90] or that the Turkish penal code, which makes torture or ill treatment a criminal offence and lays down a procedure for the filing of complaints to the Public Prosecutor that the police are duty bound to investigate, has provided practical redress.[91] For example, of 109 cases submitted by the KHRP, only 68 applicants sought a remedy. Of those, thirty-eight investigations were opened with only ten concluded, with a decision not to prosecute in six cases. Five of those cases involved deaths in police custody. In four other cases legal proceedings were initiated but no convictions were reached.[92]

The cases before the European Commission are of immense significance, as they provide victims with a measure of redress, document the systematic nature of human rights abuses suffered over the last five years and call the Turkish government to account for its actions. Taken together, the cases provide a graphic illustration of the ways the Turkish government has consistently sought to silence all domestic criticism concerning its handling of the Kurdish issue.

The cases also confirm how the battle over Kurdish representation has moved from the press to the Parliament to the courts and now to Europe. A virtual silencing of the free press in Turkey on the Kurdish issue occurred during 1993. A virtual elimination of Kurdish representation within Parliament and the courts occurred in 1994. Now, 1995–96 is witnessing the destruction of the right of individual petition to the European Commission of Human Rights for Turkish Kurds.

THE IMPLICATIONS OF THE POLICIES OF ETHNIC-NATIONALISM FOR THE RULE OF LAW IN TURKEY

The effect of these policies on the rule of law within Turkey has been profound. In order to pursue these policies of repression, Ankara has undermined the whole republican basis of the constitution and the Turkish adherence to Western modes of government and law. Individual rights concerning freedom of expression, movement and association have been eroded by the introduction of a whole series of security measures, including the infamous Anti-Terror provisions. Traditional judicial structures have been undermined by the introduction of state security tribunals, whose jurisdiction and procedures have fundamentally compromised basic legal norms concerning fair trials. International obligations have been flagrantly breached. The separation of powers between the executive, judiciary and military has all but disintegrated, leading to the virtual destruction of civil society in the southeast region of Turkey. It can only be a matter of time before the collapse of law and order threatens the entire country, as the circle of violence and repression engulfs the European centers in western Turkey.

Turkey today is plagued by a nationalist ideology that is no longer relevant or capable of implementation. Its continued adherence to the Atatürk creed has stifled proper political debate and dialogue. For seventy years Turkish institutions have been straightjacketed by the principles of nationalism espoused by Atatürk.

The present constitution ensures that no state institution or citizen can legitimately question the nature or scope of these principles. They have become fixed and immutable tablets of stone that cannot be examined or refined.

This situation has led to a static political culture. The inability to question or refine Mustafa Kemal's political legacy has meant that no new thinking can be applied to age-old problems. Thus, while Turkish society changes rapidly with the onset of industrialization and urbanization, politics remain in a time warp. This ideology is now at odds with the social transformation that has already occurred in Turkey. It is increasingly unable to deal with the diverse and complex nature of the society it purports to characterize. Its continued existence requires the suppression of pluralism. It is a fight that it cannot hope to win.

The disenfranchisement of one-fourth of the population[93] has created an endemic source of instability within the political system, which leads to cultural and ethnic polarization in which minority groups hold no stake in the system and have every incentive to turn to less legitimate means of self-expression. Turkey must either redefine its idea of citizenship to encompass all sections of society or be prepared to eliminate those sections in the name of ideological clarity. It must either decide to change its ideology or reality. If Turkish policy-makers were to disconnect Atatürk's ethnic notions of the citizenship from the republican nature of the state, some real progress could be made. After all, what is wrong with a multicultural Turkish state?

The historical reasons that gave rise to the policies of oppression no longer exist. Turkey is an essential member of NATO and the Council of Europe. It enjoys vast trading links with Europe. It is seen as a bulwark against Islamic fundamentalism in an otherwise violent and unstable Middle East. The West can and will guarantee its territorial integrity.

The West should recognize that continued support for ethnic-nationalism will bring neither stability nor prosperity to the region. The Kurdish conflict continues unabated with no military solution in sight. The secular and republican nature of the state is on the brink of collapse. Islamic fundamentalism is on the increase as the disenfranchised turn to more extreme alternatives. In the general election held on 24 December 1995, the Islamic Refah Party recieved 21.6 percent of the share of the vote and became the leading political party of Turkey. Surely it is time for the West to recognize the link between stable government, social justice and strategic interests.

What is lacking, then, is the political will to confront and reform the outdated ideological basis of the state. Turkey's unconditional entry into the Customs Union on 14 December 1995, will not, by itself, create this political will. If anything, it will simple allay the fears of the political elite and allow them to delay fundamental reform.

The European Union can help engender this political will. It should resist simply calling for improvements in Turkey's human rights record. Instead, it should reiterate its geopolitical commitment to Turkey while insisting upon nothing less than the adoption of the basic norms of liberal democracy and a return to the rule of law. It should call for the slow dismantling of security provisions and demilitarization of political and judicial institutions. These demands should be coupled with a commitment to use its good offices to promote a just and peaceful reconciliation between all of Turkey's constituent parts. This can only be achieved if those that represent legitimate minority interests in the media, Parliament and the courts are allowed to express themselves freely and enter into meaningful dialogue with the authorities concerning legal and political reform. Only then will a measure of stability return to Turkey. In the words of Mustafa Kemal, "Changing the rules of life in accordance with the times is an absolute necessity. . . . Nations cannot maintain their existence by age-old mentalities. . . . Superstitions and nonsense have to be thrown out of our heads."[94]

NOTES

1. For a comprehensive analysis of Turkey's current domestic policies toward its Kurds, see Lord Avebury, "Turkey's Kurdish Policy in the Nineties," Parliamentary Human Rights Group, Dec. 1995.

2. The 1924 constitution vested legislative and executive authority in the Grand National Assemby, the representative of the people.

3. Niyasi Berkes, *The Development of Secularism in Turkey* (Montreal, 1964), 464.

4. In 1924 the office of *Sheikhülslam* and the *şeriat* courts were abolished.

5. The year 1924 saw the unification of public instruction and the creation of the Directorate of Religious Affairs, which were placed under the control of the ministry of education and the prime minister, respectively.

6. See Alec Lawrence Macfie, *Ataturk: Profiles in Power* (London, 1994), 136-52.

7. Mahmut Esat, Turkish minister of justice, 1926. See Berkes, *Development of Secularism in Turkey*, 471.

8. The Sykes Picot Pact of February 1916 envisaged direct French administration of Cilicia, Alexanretta (Hatay) and the coast of northern and central Syria, and a French Zone of influence in the Syrian interior, which would be nominally ruled by the Sharif of Mecca. The Vilayet of Mosul was also awarded to France, on the grounds that it would act as a buffer between Britain and Russia in the region. Britain would have Bagdad and Basra, while Palestine was to come under international control.

9. Berkes, *Development of Secularism in Turkey*, 470.

10. See Treaty Series no. 16, Cmd (London: HMSO, 1923).

11. The 1923 Treaty of Sèvres stated that "a scheme of local autonomy for the predominantly Kurdish areas lying east of the Euphrates" should be drafted "If within one year from the coming into force of the present Treaty the Kurdish people . . . show that a majority of the population of those areas desires independence from Turkey, and if the Council then considers that these people are capable of such independence and recommends that it should be granted to them, Turkey hereby agrees to execute such a recommendation, and to renounce all rights and title over these areas." (Section 3, Articles 62 and 64). See Treaty Series no. 2, Cmd 964 (London: HMSO, 1920).

12. See *Lausanne Conference on Near Eastern Affairs, 1922-23: Records of the Proceedings and Draft Terms of Peace,* Cmd 1814 (London: HMSO, 1923), 296; and Philip Robins, "The Overlord State: Turkish Policy and the Kurdish Issue," *International Affairs* 69, no.4 (1993): 657-76.

13. See Act of Publications of Non-Turkish Languages, passed in 1983, which effectively banned Kurdish and other minority languages.

14. See Christian Rumpf, "The Protection of Human Rights in Turkey and the Significance of International Human Rights Instruments," *Human Rights Law Journal* 14, no. 11-12 (1994): 394.

15. Mustafa Remzi Bucak, "Memorandum to Ismet İnönü, Prime Minister of Turkey" (New York, 1965), 6. Representative Bucak's memorandum was designed to advise İnönü on the creation of a federal republic of Turks and Kurds.

16. See Çağlar Keyder, "The Political Economy of the Turkish Democracy," *New Left Review* 42, no. 115 (1979): 3-44, especially page 4.

17. Ismet G. Imset, *The PKK: A Report on Separatist Violence in Turkey, 1973-1992* (Ankara, 1992): 1-49.

18. Article 12 of the 1982 Turkish constitution.

19. Article 27 of the 1982 Turkish constitution.

20. Article 13 of the 1982 Turkish constitution.

21. Article 19, *Freedom of Expression Manual 1993.*

22. Law 2935, adopted on 25 Oct. 1983, RG No. 18204 of 27 October 1983.

23. Law 1402, adopted 13 May 1971, RG No. 13837 of 15 May 1971.

24. Law 2941, adopted 4 Nov. 1983, RG No. 18215 of 8 Nov. 1983.

25. These provinces are Bingöl, Diyarbakır, Elazığ, Hakkari, Mardin, Siirt, Tunceli, Van, Batman and Şırnak.

26. RG No. 19517 of 14 July 1987.

27. See *Turkey Briefing,* vol. 4, no. 3 (June 1990).

28. See Robins, "Overlord State," 657-76.

29. See Christian Rumpf, "The Protection of Human Rights in Turkey and the Significance of International Human Rights Instruments," *Human Rights Law Journal* 14, no. 11-12 (1994): 400.

30. Judgment of 1 July 1963, Esas 207/1963.

31. See *Chrysotomos v. Turkey,* App. Nos. 15299, 15300 & 15318/89 4/3/91.

32. See *Council of Europe Parliamentary Assembly Report on Human Rights Situation in Turkey.*

33. In January, Turgut Özal's cabinet did decide to abolish the law restricting the use of languages other than Turkey, but it was shortlived. See *Turkey Confidential* 16 (Feb. 1991): 8-14.

34. *Broken Promises: Torture and Killings Continue in Turkey* (New York, Dec. 1992), 8.

35. See Amnesty International, "Turkey: Torture, Extrajudicial Executions, "Disappearances," May 1992, AI Index EUR 44/39/92; "Turkey: Walls of Glass," Nov. 1992, AI Index 44/75/92.

36. Hugh Pope, "Turks Make a Desert and Call it Peace," *Independent* 23 July 1995.

37. See Amnesty International, "Turkey; Escalation in Human Rights Abuses against Kurdish Villages," July 1993, AI Index: EUR 44/64/93.

38. On 22 January 1993 Stefan Waldberg, a German journalist, was arrested and subsequently convicted for being a courier for the PKK, *Info-Turk,* Jan. 1993, 4. On 29 April 1993 Andrew Penny was likewise arrested but later released, *Hürriyet,* 26 May 1993.

39. One such example includes the indictment of Mehdi Zana, the former mayor of Diyarbakır, for an alleged spearatist speech delivered at the European Parliament on 3 December 1992.

40. One such example occurred on 16 June 1993, when the Turkish Human Rights Association was banned from convening a symposium on the Kurdish problem involving a group of Turkish and Kurdish intellectuals.

41. Two such examples include the banning of Edip Polat's book, *Nevrozladık Safakları (We Made Each Dawn a Nevroz)*, in December 1992; and Ismail Beşikçi's books, *The Imperialist Repartition Struggle in Kurdistan, 1915-25* and *CHP Program-1931: Kurdish Problem* in May and June of 1993. Both writers were subsequently imprisoned.

42. For example, on 21 April 1993, *Sabah* newspaper reported that requests to reopen by ten private television and radio stations that had been closed upon the directives of the Wireless General Directorate of the Ministry of Transport were rejected by the State Council.

43. For a comprehensive account of media censorship during 1993, see Helsinki Watch: A Committe of Human Rights Watch, *Free Expression in Turkey* 1993; and Article 19, *Turkey: Censorship by the Bullet* 16, 9 September 1992.

44. Law 2911 of 6 Oct. 1983, RG no. 18185 of 8 Oct. 1983.

45. Law No. 2908 of 4 Oct. 1983, RG no. 18184 of 7 Oct. 1983.

46. Similar treatment was metered out to *Yeni Ülke*, *Azardı* and *Aydınlık*; see Helsinki Watch, *Free Expression in Turkey*.

47. See Mark Muller, *Censorship and the Rule of Law in Turkey*; Bar Human Rights Committee, Article 19, *Medico International*, Kurdistan Human Rights Project, March 1994.

48. Ibid., 6.

49. Ibid., 20-21.

50. See Muller, *Censorship and the Rule of Law in Turkey*; Bar Human Rights Committee, Article 19, *Medico International*, Kurdistan Human Rights Project (March 1994), 7-11.

51. See Gürbetelli Ersöz's defense, "An Impassioned Plea for Freedom of Expression" (London, 1994).

52. *Index on Censorship*, vol. 24 (2/1995), 188.

53. Paragraph 1 of Article 10 of the European Convention of Human Rights.

54. The *Observer and Guardian v. the UK* (Spycatcher case) at paragraph 59(a); *Sunday Times* (II).

55. See *Open Door Counselling and Dublin Well Woman Centre v. Ireland*, paragraphs 59-60.

56. See *Handyside v. UK*, paragraphs 48-50.

57. See *Marck v. Belgium* and *Dudgeon v. UK*.

58. In November 1995 the European Commission of Human Rights declared admissible an application brought on behalf of *Özgür Güdem* alleging various breaches of the Convention.

59. *Lingens v. Austria, Oberschlick and Schwabe*.

60. Castells case.

61. *Thorgeirson v. Iceland*, paragraph 63.

62. In *Castells v. Spain*, paragraph 43: "Freedom of the press affords the public one of the best means of discovering and forming an opinion of the ideas and attitudes of their political leaders. In particular, it gives politicians the opportunity to reflect and comment on preoccupations of public opinion; it thus enables everyone to participate in the free

political debate which is at the very core of the concept of a democratic society." Likewise, the European Court declared in *Sunday Times v. UK (II)*: "Whilst the press must not overstep the bounds set [for the protection of the interests set forth in Article 10(2) of the European Convention] . . . it is nevertheless incumbent on it to impart information and ideas on matters of public interest. Not only does it have the task of imparting such information and ideas: the public also has a right to receive them. Were it otherwise, the press would be unable to play its vital role of 'public watch-dog.'"

63. Muller, *Censorship and the Rule of Law in Turkey*; Bar Human Rights Committee, Article 19, *Medico International*, Kurdistan Human Rights Project (March 1994), 25-29.

64. See Mark Muller and Tim Otty, *Advocacy and the Rule of Law in Turkey: Advocates under Attack—A Case Report on the prosecution of defence lawyers involved in political cases in Diyarbakir, southeast Turkey*, Bar of England and Wales Human Rights Committe, Kurdistan Human Rights Project, *Medico International* (26 Jan. 1995).

65. The detentions were themselves unlawful in that they breached laws 2559 and 2803, which restrict the jurisdiction of the gendarmerie to arrest lawyers where an operative police force exists, articles 58 and 59 of the Law of Advocates (11036), which states that the interrogation and prosecuction of lawyers rests entirely with the public prosecutor, and Article 40 of the Law of Legal Representation, which requires no such investigation can take place without the prior consent of the ministry of justice.

66. Bekir Selçuk, chief state prosecutor, DGM, Diyarabakır.

67. Muller and Otty, *Advocacy and the Rule of Law in Turkey*.

68. Ibid., 17.

69. In particular, Article 3, which declares that the Turkish state, its territory and nation, is an indivisible entity, and its language is Turkish. See *Constitution of Turkey, in Constitutions of the Countries of the World*, ed. Albert P. Blaustein & Gisbert H Flanz, vol. 19 (Dobbs Ferry, N.Y., 1993-94).

70. *Kurdistan News*, Special Issue, 27 Sept. 1993.

71. "Bomb Attack on Murdered MP's House," *Hürriyet*, 12 Sept. 1993.

72. Articles 6 and 10 of the European Convention on Human Rights.

73. "DEP Building in Lice Shelled," *Özgür Gündem*, 12 Jan. 1994, 3.

74. "DEP General Secretary Shot," *Hürriyet*, 7 Feb. 1994.

75. "Democracy Party Boycotts Local Polls," Turkish Daily News, 26 Feb. 1994.

76. European Commission, Interim Report Concerning Turkey, B/08/95, July 1995.

77. Reported in *Human Rights Law Journal* 14 (1993): 49-54.

78. See *Human Rights Law Journal* 14 (1993): 426-432.

79. See Bar of England and Wales Human Rights Committee, Law Society, Kurdistan Human Rights Project: *The Law: Freedom of Expression and Human Rights Advocacy in Turkey*, March 1995; and *The European Convention under Attack: The Threat to Lawyers in Turkey and the Challenge to Strasbourg*, Sept. 1995, 4.

80. See Bar of England and Wales Human Rights Committee, *Report on Mission to Attend the Trial of the Istanbul Branch of the Turkish Human Rights Association*, Dec. 1993.

81. *KHRP*, Article 19, England and Wales Bar Human Rights Committee, Law Society, FIDH.

82. On the initiative of Professor Kevin Boyle and Françoise Hampson of the Human Rights Centre at Essex University.

83. See Kurdistan Human Rights Project, *KHRP Cases Declared Admissible by the European Commission of Human Rights*, vol. 1 (April 1995) and vol. 2 (June 1995).

84. See Amnesty International, *Turkey: Torture, Extrajudicial Executions, "Disappearances"*; *Turkey: Walls of Glass*, Nov. 1992, AI Index 44/75/92; *Turkey: Escalation in Human Rights Abuses against Kkurdish Villages*, July 1993, AI Index EUR 44/64/93; *Turkey: A Time for Action*, AI Index EUR 44/13/94.

85. Halit Temli, president; Mahmut Şakar, secretary; Abdullah Çağır, treasurer; Nemetüllah Gündüz, member; Melike Alp, member; Hayri Veznedaroğlu, member; Hüseyin Yıldız, member.

86. Bar of England and Wales Human Rights Committee et al., *The European Convention under Attack: The Threat to Lawyers in Turkey and the Challenge to Strasbourg* (Sept. 1995).

87. HADEP is a legal political party that supports the Kurdish cause in Turkey and is the successor to the DEP Party.

88. Bar of England and Wales Human Rights Committee et al., *The European Convention under Attack: The Threat to Lawyers in Turkey and the Challenge to Strasbourg* (Sept. 1995), 11.

89. Appl. 3702/68 X-v-Belgium 4 October 1968 (unreported) and Appls. 7126/75 and 7573/76 X and Y-v-United Kingdom (unreported).

90. Law 2395 of 25 Oct. 1983.

91. Articles 151 and 153.

92. See Bill Bowring, *Identity and Rights in the Middle East: Nationalism, Minorities and Rights to Defend the Rights of a Minority*, KHRP (1995), 20; and Aisling Reidy, *Seeking Remedies for Violations of Human Rights in Turkey: A Study on the Operation of the System of Domestic Remedies in Turkey*, KHRP (Sept. 1994), unpublished draft.

93. Kurdish Information Centre population statistics.

94. Berkes, *The Development of Secularism in Turkey*, 464.

CONTRIBUTORS

Gülistan Gürbey teaches political science and international relations at the Free University in Berlin, where she specializes in Turkish and Kurdish history and politics. Her recent publications include, "Kurden im Exil: A bis Z" (1993); "Auf der Suche nach einer Lösung der Kurdenfrage in der Türkei" (1995); and "Politishche und rechtliche Hindernisse auf dem Wege der Herausbildung einer Ziviligesellschaft in der Türkei" (1995).

Aram Nigogosian is completing his Ph.D. thesis at the University of Pennsylvania on "The Development of the Kurdish National Movement in Turkey since 1978."

Michael Gunter is Caplenor Research Professor at Tennessee Technological University. He is the author of *The Kurds in Turkey: A Political Dilemma* (1990); *The Kurds of Iraq: Tragedy and Hope* (1992); and *The Changing Kurdish Problem in Turkey* (1994). He is the author of over forty articles on Turkish and Kurdish history and politics. His most recent publications are "The Kurdish Question in Turkish Foreign Policy" (1994); "The Kurdish Factor in Middle Eastern Politics" (1995); and "The KDP-PUK Conflict in Iraqi Kurdistan" (1996).

Henri Barkey is professor of political science and international relations at Lehigh University. He has authored *The State and Industrialization in Turkey* (1990) and *The Politics of Economic Reform in the Middle East* (1992). Among his most recent articles concerning Turkish politics and Kurdish affairs are "The Silent Victor: Turkey's Role in the Gulf War" (1989); "Turkish-American Relations in the Postwar Era" (1992) and "Turkey's Kurdish Dilemma" (1994).

Robert Olson is professor of Middle East and Islamic history at the University of Kentucky. He is the author of *The Siege of Mosul and Ottoman-Persian Relations, 1718-1747; The Ba`th in Syria 1947-1979: An Interpretative Historical Essay* (1980); *The Ba`th in Syria, 1947-1982* (1983); and *The Emergence of Kurdish Natioalism: 1880-1925* (1989, 1991). Among his recent publications concerning the Kurdish question are "The Kurdish Question and the Kurdish Problem: Some Geopolitic and Geostrategic Comparisons" (1994); "The Kurdish Question and Turkey's Foreign Policy, 1991-1995: From the Gulf War to the Incursion into Iraq" (1995);

"The GAP Project, the Gulf War and Their Effects on the Kurdish Nationalist Movement in Turkey" (1996); and "The Kurdish Question and Chechnya: Turkish and Russian Foreign Policies Since the Gulf War" (1996).

Philip Robins is professor of politics and international affairs at the University of Oxford, England. He was formerly head of the Middle East Programme at the Royal Institute of International Affairs. He has published numerous studies and monographs on European and Middle Eastern affairs, including *Turkey and the Middle East* (1991). Among his recent articles are "Turkey's Policy and the Gulf Crisis: Adventurist or Dynamic?" (1992); "Between Sentiment and Self-Interest: Turkish Policy toward Azerbaijan and the Central Asian States" (1993); and "The Overlord State: Turkish Policy and the Kurdish Issue" (1993).

Hamit Bozarslan is the leading international scholar on Kurdish history and politics. He is Senior Researcher at the Centre Marc Bloch in the Free University of Berlin, where he teaches Middle East history and politics. He has published more than fifty monographs, articles and essays concerning Kurdish and Turkish history and politics. His recent publications include "The Kurdish Question in Turkish Political Life" (1990); "Turquie: un défi permenent au nationalism Kémalist" (1991); "Le Kemalisme et le problem kurde" (1992); "Einige Bermerkungen zur Entwicklung des Kurden problems in der Zwishchen Kriegszeit" (1992); "La régionalisation du problém kurde" (1993); "Marginalité, Securité et États: Le Cas Kurde (1994); États et modes de gestion du problém kurde" (1994); and "Kurdistan: économie de guerre, économie dans la guerre" (1996).

Yücel Bozdağlıoğlu is a graduate student studying political science and international relations at the University of Kentucky, where he studies with Robert Olson.

Mark Muller is barrister at law at Gray's Inn, England. He has been chair of the England and Wales Bar Human Rights Committee. He is a leading interpreter in Europe of Turkey's human rights policies, especially with regard to the Kurds, and is a leading international authority on issues of human rights and international law. Muller has accompanied several human rights committees' fact-finding trips to the Kurdish region of Turkey during the 1990s.

INDEX